Amy + T[...] [...]21

Happy

Selling!!

Rudy

ENDORSEMENTS

"A great handbook and my new go-to. It is a consolidation of tried-and-true sales best practices from the industry's best."

—*Shannon Seidl*
Sales Rep, Oracle

"Wish I'd had these sales tips when I started my career."

—*Sue Barsamian*
Board Member Five9, Auth0, Box,
NortonLifeLock, Gainsight, and Xactly

"Great practical insights from true sales professionals."

—*Tom Mendoza*
Previous President and Vice Chairman, Network Appliance
Board Member UiPath, Varonis, and VAST Data

"Your Go-To Sales Advisor is *the ultimate handbook for anyone in tech sales!*"

—*Troy K. Richardson*
EVP/COO at PTC

DO YOU WANT TO KNOW WHAT THE WORLD'S TOP SALES PROFESSIONALS DO AND SAY? HOW TO BUILD YOUR PIPELINE? HOW TO CLOSE MORE DEALS? HOW TO MAKE MORE MONEY? IF YOU'RE A TECHNOLOGY SALES PROFESSIONAL, THE ANSWER IS YES.

We are a community of active sales professionals from hundreds of leading technology companies. Randy Seidl started the Sales Community with the goal of providing a community and assets to help enterprise tech sales professionals (SDRs to CROs) exceed goals with ease and confidence.

Sales Community is an efficient, effective and motivating way to train yourself and have motivating content for your team. That's why we created the Sales Community, the Premiere Online Community for Tech Sales Professionals:

- An Advisory Board made up of 250+ of the best in the industry responsible for over $500 billion in annual revenue
- Our platform provides a unique opportunity to grow your skills and connect with likeminded sales professionals
- Features best-in-class content from world-class consultants, coaches and members
- Leverage best practices from Randy and other members to help you sell more and break into new accounts, and get exposure to top channel partners across the world
- Access to tools, tactics, and sales methodologies shared by Sales Community members who have been on the front lines with skill sets to close deals, build pipeline and generate revenue

Scan the code below to visit the Sales Community website:

YOUR GO-TO

Sales
Advisor

YOUR GO-TO

Sales
Advisor

Resources to Help You Be Your Best

RANDY SEIDL
FOUNDER: SALES COMMUNITY,
REVENUE ACCELERATION,
AND TOP TALENT RECRUITING

TONY JEARY
THE RESULTS GUY™

Clovercroft Publishing

PUBLISHING

Sales Advisor: Resources to Help You Be Your Best

©2021 by T & T Limited and Randy Seidl

Published by Results Faster Publishing in association with Clovercroft Publishing, Franklin, Tennessee

Edited by Nonie Jobe

Cover Design by Brooke Hawkins

Interior Design by Adept Content Solutions

Printed in the United States of America

ISBN: 978-1-950892-94-5

CONTENTS

ACKNOWLEDGMENTS

This book is a compilation of the works of many. Our sincere thanks to those on the Sales Community advisory board who submitted their best practices to share with those in the world of technology sales. We are also grateful to Nonie Jobe, Brooke Hawkins, Eloise Worden, Tawnya Austin, Lauren Yrigollen, and Misha Cherkashin from the TJI team and to Tucker Garfield and Jesse Ouellette from the Sales Community team for their hard work and dedication to making it happen.

DEDICATIONS
BY RANDY SEIDL

Thanks so much to my loving family—Janet, Philip, Shannon, Tommy, and Billy—who have always supported me along my journey. I love you all so much and am so very proud of you! Thanks and love you Mom and Dad.

Tom Grojean, for showing me how to be generous in all ways and how to be a great father, husband, friend, and grandparent.

Bill Burke, for being the closest person to God I know.

Bill Campbell (aka Coach), whom I was very fortunate to mentor under. He taught me the importance of authenticity; sales-centric CEOs, who are few and far between; giving back; hanging out with friends; and relationships.

Bob Reynolds, for his mentoring and showing me the importance of team development, that sales matter, getting great productivity from your leaders, being charitable, and having fun.

David Nour, a great executive coach who helped me take my relationships to the next level and is always challenging my status quo with inquisitive questions and ideas. Thanks for his immediate support and help with Sales Community.

Dick Egan, who cofounded EMC and was our long-term leader, and who was the amazing engineering and go-to-market brain with his hard-nosed focus, touch, and drive. He taught me how to be tough.

Frank Keaney, for leading the maturity and sales professionalism at a make-or-break point for EMC and for a laundry list of classic one-liners. We all learned a lot and grew up under Frank's leadership.

Greg Brown, for mentoring me and teaching me to use fact-based gut feel (if you know, you know; and if you don't know, then it is a likely no) and about framing up emails/discussion in three categories: FYI, need help, or asking a question (often people aren't clear).

Jack Connors, for his mentorship and showing me the importance of not just giving back, but also getting others to give, helping others when they are down, talking from the heart on stage, and being spiritual. He also taught me that a great gift you can give is attending wakes/funerals. I also want to thank him for being on the board of Workgroup Solutions when I was CEO.

Jack Egan (aka Legend), probably the biggest unsung hero of EMC, who truly gave of himself, running every function at one point or another, and who would answer all of my calls for help while in Australia and the UK. I worked directly for Jack more than anyone. I learned so much, including the importance of hiring well, beating your number, and being detailed always in all ways.

Fr. Jim Fleming, for his deep friendship, our weekly walks and get-togethers during COVID, his spiritual direction, and his love of God.

Jim Sullivan, I really appreciate all your help, feedback, and advice, personally and professionally. Lots of great times since we met playing rugby in 1984.

Mark Hurd, for asking tough questions while being very fair (and for teaching me not to BS if I don't know the answer), for conducting the most thorough QBR with an amazing command for detail in very complex businesses, and for his trust in and delegation of authority to me, for his flip-chart presentations, and for his maniacal focus on market-share growth.

Mike Ruettgers, who came in to EMC at a challenging time, first fixing manufacturing (operations, quality, and supply chain) and eventually running EMC during its hyper growth. Under Mike, I learned how to be a more well-rounded and polished business executive.

Paul O'Brien, thanks so much for mentoring me during a professionally challenging time in my life. Your availability, openness, and insights were much appreciated. Thanks for serving on my board when I was running Workgroup Solutions.

Peter Bell, thanks for always being there for me over the years and for your tremendous friendship. Thanks for serving on my board when I was running Permabit. You were inspirational in helping me start Sales Community so I can help those I know best, sales professionals.

Ratmir Timashev, for hiring me for my first big consulting job (twenty-two months), helping me understand all the areas where I can add value, bringing me under the tent, and showing me how to drink vodka, and for an amazing ski exec off site in Zermatt.

Roger Marino, who cofounded EMC, was the spiritual sales leader we all admired, and was famous for his "What is a Computer" class. He taught us Sales 101 and to never give up.

Scott McNealey, for reminding me that in spite of headquarters' crap, the customer and your sales teams are what count—so show up and do the right thing.

Tony Jeary (aka the RESULTS Guy), a great strategist for me in all areas of my life. Tony taught me how to add clarity to my team's execution and the importance of goal setting, improving my health, helping others, and continuously improving. Thanks for his help and support always, but especially with Sales Community. Also, in full disclosure, without his pushing me in a July 2020 meeting (at the RESULTS Center in Dallas) during COVID, I would never have considered authoring and publishing a book.

Walter Brown was a very special friend and taught me and so many of us our early sales skills that will stay with us forever. He was always available to help share his fantastic wisdom over the years. In the section that includes his two fantastic sales handbooks, you will see additional dedications from Brian Bell, Ken Dougherty, and me.

Introduction
YOUR GO-TO SALES ADVISOR

What does success look like? To us, it looks like adding value, giving back, and exceeding expectations, so you sell more.

That's what we hope to accomplish with this book. Providing value is an intrinsic desire that is deeply entrenched in both of us. "What if," we said, "we could create a veritable Wikipedia for sales professionals in the technology space that offered the best of the best sales practices, tools, and ideas from our over seventy years of combined experience *plus* one hundred or so best practices from top technology sales advisors across the world? And to meet our standard, it could contain proprietary tools and models that have given value to so many of our high-achieving clients, teammates, and friends over the years. We could even include selected current top sales methodologies on the market. To top it off, we could create note space after each segment where readers could record the best practices they want to take action on, which will leave them with a comprehensive plan for improvement." This book is the realization of that dream. We've intentionally packed it with value to help you, the technology sales professional, reach a higher level of mastery in your vocation.

The Authors

This book is an inevitable fallout from their meeting ten years ago. Tony was giving a keynote address for a thousand HP sales professionals in Las Vegas, and Randy—one of the top executives in the room—was in the front row. Their connection was immediate. Over the years, as Tony has coached Randy personally as well as his teams, they've developed a unique friendship and a mutual respect for each other that has led to where they are today—coauthoring this book together.

Randy has a second-to-none following and respect in the IT industry because of his unique personality, his utmost knowledge and expertise in the sales world, his impressive and loyal executive relationships, and his commitment to helping others win. With that same commitment, Tony has been blessed with the opportunity to personally coach many of the world's top CEOs, sales reps, and other high achievers to help them become their best. They challenged themselves to combine resources and construct a book that would be easy to read and present many perspectives; and, most importantly, it would deliver many *aha's* and *epiphanies* that would spike the thinking of sales team members in the technology space. What they've written is beneficial for entry level reps up to CROs, and anyone else wanting to learn more about sales. It's a must-have for entire sales teams.

Tony is a strategist, and for over thirty years he's built a firm that encourages thinking and enhances success for high achievers. He helps winners achieve even more extraordinary results, leveraging his experiences and accumulated best practices. Randy started his career as the thirty-third employee at EMC, and he has since risen to the top of many large technology organizations. In 2013, he launched Revenue Acceleration, a consultancy firm, along with Top Talent Recruiting, an organization that helps place sales professionals in the IT world.

Randy's COVID moment led to his launching *Sales Community* in October 2020 as a sales social network. Its mission is to be the best resource to add value to technology sales professionals (SDRs to CROs) by providing a community where they can all:

- Promote equity, diversity, and inclusion
- Learn more and grow
- Give and receive feedback
- Network
- Access a library of best-in-class resources
- Give back and have fun

Randy has amassed decades of notes, articles, and resources, and Tony (and his team at Tony Jeary International) have authored over sixty results-oriented books in the success genre. They have both dug deep to pull select experiences they can combine to hopefully make this book stand at the top of any technology sales tool that's on your desk or in your briefcase/duffle bag as your go-to sales advisor.

Together, they felt their unique backgrounds would position them to co-author a title that would deserve to be called a must-read. (See more about Tony and Randy in the "About the Authors" section at the back of the book.)

The Book

We start the book with a sales IQ assessment that will help you quickly self-discover a few of your strengths and opportunities to improve. Then the main part of the book is divided into five sections. The first section of the book is comprised of over one hundred ideas and best practices gathered from top global Sales Community Advisors. The second section is a special dedication to Walter Brown, sales advisor extraordinaire, and recaps of his two phenomenal books that are considered the best, *Chasing Quota* and *Chasing Quota 2*. The next piece is made up of twenty-three of Randy's tools and resources that he's used over the years to drive his success. Then in the next section you'll find the information we mentioned about the current top sales methodologies. And we wrap the book up with fifty of Tony's best practices, divided into the categories of prep, delivery, follow-up, and improvement.

We believe the format we've chosen will make the book a valuable and easy read, yet not necessarily a book you read through from cover to cover. You can do that, of course; or you can choose specific topics from the table of contents that may help you in an area where you've been struggling or you just want to know more about. In all of his signature books, Tony has put a list of the VIPs (very important points) at the end of each chapter. We've found that readers really enjoy having them for a review of the chapter or even a summary in the event they want to get right to the nuggets revealed in the chapter. We decided to use that same concept here and have provided a VIP after each of the topics presented in "Tony's Best Practices" and "Randy's Success Ideas." In fact, we've gone one step farther and pulled all the VIPs together into a list that appears in the back of the book to review at your convenience.

Over the years, one of the things that has caused Randy to rise to the top is his discipline of not just reading, but studying, highlighting, and summarizing what he's reading and committing it to both his mental and physical arsenal and sharing it with his teams. We recommend you do the same. Get ready to take notes, highlight, and even share select pages with others who are part of your world by sending them a quick snapshot from your phone.

Ready to get going?

SALES IQ ASSESSMENT

#	Topic	Rate 1–4
1.	How well do you strategically prepare?	
2.	How strong is your and your team's arsenal (toolbox), which includes such things as testimonials, case studies, presentations, models, etc.?	
3.	How well do you and your team research?	
4.	How purposefully are you leveraging your team members?	
5.	How well do you facilitate versus just presenting?	
6.	Do you focus on the right language (i.e., personality style)?	
7.	How committed are you to continually improving yourself and your team? Are you consistently looking for benchmarking and best ideas that could bring aha's and epiphanies to you and your team?	
8.	How spontaneous and flexible are you during a sales presentation?	
9.	How good is your follow-up?	
10.	How well do you lead?	
11.	Do you and your team have a culture of openly giving and getting feedback?	
12.	Do you lead by example and share best practices?	
13.	Do you use a 90-day fast-start plan for new roles?	
14.	How well do you leverage partners and indirect selling?	
15.	Do you know the critical objective and subjective metrics for how you are judged?	
16.	Do you prepare the best sales call meeting agendas?	
17.	Do you always have the next follow-up meeting scheduled by the end of the current meeting?	
18.	If you bump into the CFO in an elevator, can you quickly say your value (how you help generate revenue, save money, keep them out of jail)?	
19.	Do you cultivate and build your network?	
20.	Do you have CXO-level relationships?	
21.	Do you have a great territory plan?	
22.	Do you have a great brand?	
23.	Do you get value from your mentor?	
24.	Do your customers know you, like you, and trust you (i.e., are they relationships)?	
25.	Do you always ensure your customers agree with your close plan?	

I
SALES COMMUNITY ADVISORY BOARD MEMBERS' BEST IDEAS

The ideas are in alphabetical order and, to make it easier, each one is divided into what, why, and how. The Sales Community Advisory Board Members are among the top technology sales leaders in the world. We asked them to submit their best sales ideas and best practices to give you, the reader, an edge in your sales performance and help you reach a higher level of results.

1. Partnering in SMB
By Aaron Mills

What the Idea Is: I love SMB. No, really! Why? In my experience, no customer segment can match the breadth, depth, diversity, chaos, energy, and opportunity to be found in this vast sea of customers and people. Of course, those same attributes can make it vexing and maddening. How do you show up? Where do you show up? How do you make your presence meaningful, impactful, and mutually rewarding? It's much easier said than done. You start with a commitment to relationships. And, like all successful relationships, you freely contribute your strengths, acknowledge your weaknesses, and surround yourself with partners who make you better.

Why It Is Valuable: From the IT industry perspective, partnering in SMB is not easy. You've heard it all: "Channel partners are reactive in the segment." "Partners are too consumer-oriented." And/or "Partners only want to focus on larger accounts." For starters, all SMB accounts aren't equal. From an enterprise perspective, the vast majority of hospitals, regional banks, manufacturers, ad agencies, law firms, etc. in the United States are SMB. Not only are they the primary driving force behind economies and job markets, their data centers and need for innovation and sophistication are significant. They have money. And they can and will spend it. But you have to earn their trust and respect. You have to build the relationship.

How It Works: In 2008, our US Sales team was addressing the need for SMB growth in the wake of a severe global credit/financial crisis. After evaluating the market landscape, we elected to proactively focus our limited field sales resources on three verticals: credit unions, hospitals, and electronics manufacturers. Each had critical mass, was represented in

every geography, had money to spend, and was under pressure to inno-
vate their approach to IT. Strategically, it made sense. But how would we
execute?

Again, it boiled down to relationships—many of which did not exist. We
knew we could count on the support of our dedicated inside sales team. But
we recognized our limitations in terms of vertical know-how and the highly
regional nature of our channel relationships when it came to proactive enterprise SMB solution selling. With this in mind, we took the following steps:

1. We developed industry "personas" to educate ourselves on key
   industry drivers, pain points, and ISV solution footprints, and we
   developed value propositions that addressed areas of critical customer need.

2. We identified and engaged leading industry ISVs with an offer to
   build infrastructure solution stacks and reference architectures that
   directly complemented their need to deliver innovation and value.
   Not all were interested, but many were. It turned out that they were
   generally not comfortable addressing their clients' concerns about
   infrastructure related to evolving VM, cloud, and security technology platforms, and they welcomed our help in that regard.

3. We developed an RFP process to identify and select regional VARs
   who would commit to developing an industry "practice" in a defined
   multi-state geography. The RFPs were geared to encourage the channel partner investment and commitment of resources to build the
   practice.

4. In return, we aligned our marketing development, inside sales support, field sales team, lead generation, and ISV alliance expertise to
   the selected channel partners.

Once in place, we felt we had the makings of a strong go-to-market program. Several important challenges remained as we moved toward launch.
These included, but were not limited to:

1. Industry education across all internal sales (field and inside) assets,
   ISVs, and selected channel partners

2. Goal setting

3. Measurement, reporting, and reward systems

4. Management of channel conflict policy

5. Realignment of marketing resources and dollars

6. Creation of an ISV/vertical team

Once in play, we quickly saw the benefits of the value and relationships we had created. As one example, we identified credit unions as an exciting growth market. The credit crisis had resulted in billions of dollars moving from banks to credit unions as customers sought safer havens. However, the credit unions often lacked the internet banking, online bill pay, and client services their new members (customers) had come to expect in the world of big banking. As the credit unions scrambled to respond, we worked with the credit union ISV community to build formulaic, repeatable, and scalable approaches to these challenges, which were well received. As opposed to hundreds or thousands of individual sales calls, we went to credit union trade shows and ISV user conferences, where we experienced nonstop customer interaction and developed a wealth of high-quality opportunities.

This same approach was repeated in other select vertical and horizontal solution areas. Our progress was rarely linear or easy. The relationships took time, commitment, and work. The results were well worth the effort. We saw outstanding and sustained growth and performance across the entire team, led by the "designed-solution" selling effort. It was widely recognized as a "best in practice" program and growth engine by the channel and ISV partners we collaborated with.

2. Selling in the Latin American Market
By Alfredo Yepez

What the Idea Is: Selling in the Latin American market by capitalizing on people diversity and employee development.

In my thirty-plus years of leading sales organizations within Latin America, I have learned that you need to leverage this geography's diverse culture rather than making the mistake of placing people in group leadership roles based on your own race or ethnicity. It's human nature for leaders and organizations in the LATAM region to make the common mistake of surrounding themselves with employees or teams who share their same nationality, because they feel more secure. Additionally, leaders tend to be more comfortable with having a more comprehensive understanding of the way people from their same culture conduct themselves within the accepted norms of a communal society group. For instance, it's expected to think that Colombians work well with other Colombians, or that Brazilians with Brazilians, and so on. However, you must remember that LATAM is a geography composed of more than thirty countries, each with its own language, and each country has a wide-range of indigenous dialects. English, Spanish, Portuguese, French, Dutch, are just a few of the languages spoken here. We are a region rich with an assortment of people and various cultures. Every year, businesses in these countries are becoming more global. So let's not assume that a multicultural organization may present difficulties from its inception or from a management standpoint. In my view, its diversity is what makes the geography so fascinating, besides being so alluring. By combining all the different areas of expertise from the various LATAM countries, you can achieve faster and more proficient results, while simultaneously becoming a more well-rounded and global executive.

Why It Is Valuable: There are several factors that play into and make this a critical issue, and even more so now, with the precarious and challenging times we are going through due to Covid-19. Because of the many travel restrictions, all companies are scrambling to work in this new virtual environment and adapting to new work tools such as Zoom, Skype, etc. What is most important among these new platforms is the cultural diversity and expertise you can bring to the table by having such a diversified and talented leadership team. Diversity and inclusion must be at the forefront of each executive's priorities. Inclusive teams encourage creativity and "out-of-the-box" thinking. Diversity is not a metric defined around male versus female percentage; it's more about creating multicultural groups where everyone is respected and his/her opinions are heard and taken into consideration. It's about sharing and promoting new sales ideas among all the members. It's amazing right now to see how many large IT American corporations are being led by a non-American person; that is a testament to the fact that the focus should be on talent, expertise, and skill for performing the role, rather than on the country of origin of the leader.

How It Works: The most important component in the process is to start recruiting and/or creating your team based on the talent and expertise required for the role rather than being surrounded by people "close" to you (mainly people from your same country of origin). The more you organize your group to have common similarities, the more they will be rejected by the leaders of other countries. I believe that's because one of the main advantages of operating a business in this geography is the ability to combine the expertise of the different market environments from some of the largest countries and economies of the region.

Allow your country's sales leaders to "tropicalize" your sales plan; create the framework, but be flexible with the local implementation, because every country has its own culture. I normally explain to the members of my team that a "mariachi plan" (typical music from Mexico) doesn't work in a country that prefers "samba" (the most popular music in Brazil). Local content needs to be allowed, as long as the main objective of the sales strategy and the core of the initiative are respected or maintained.

Develop and rotate your leaders. Never disconnect from the geography and/or business. For example, while I was leading the Latin American geography, I served a dual role in Brazil as a country manager for almost a year, and then a few years later I did the same thing in Mexico. This allowed me to get a more in-depth and first-hand expertise of the business and culture in those two countries, which currently represent the largest markets in the region. I'm very familiar with all the other countries. After that experience I decided to have some of my leaders do the same; so as part of their development plan, I have rotated some of them to different countries and put them in regional roles. Consequently, this practice is allowing me to create a prolific group of quality employees for new roles, as well as creating a bench of executives to replace any who may decide to leave the company unexpectedly.

In summary, concentrate on talent, not on ethnic race or nationality. Surround yourself with those who have the same mission as you do. Become a hands-on leader, do not get disconnected from the day-to-day activities, and get involved in the most relevant topics of the business operation. Empower and trust your team members and delegate tasks to them so you may free up your time for more vital tasks. These best practices will unconsciously begin to develop the employee. Care for and nurture your team members; it's a shared responsibility— a teamwork effort— and high-performance teams are more conducive to work better when all members feel respected and integrated.

3. Playing for the Consolation Prize
By Andy O'Brien

What the Idea Is: You want to win every deal you are engaged in, but how you lose and position yourself after that is very important. Human nature, personal possessiveness, and follow-up from your boss shape this. Remember your brand—be self-aware when you are losing, and position yourself for the consolation prize with that client. Focus on how to find the next deal where you can get a commitment on the spot, thus getting a contract in place and finding revenue for the company.

Here's an example: If you lose your deal in a production environment for $5M, how do you lose gracefully and ask for a smaller deal in a development environment? Have the self-awareness to know when to flip gears; don't get off the big deal too fast; but once it is apparent, look for other specific asks. Be very specific—ask, "Will you give me a deal here, now?" If you can get the development deal as consolation prize, you can get a contract in place and perhaps build a go-forward revenue annuity.

Why It Is Valuable: It's about your brand; build it as a mature person who is looking to have a productive, mature, and trusting relationship. Get something in place that gets the heavy work out of the way and creates more access than you had in the past. Once you have one signed deal, it's easier to go back again and ask for something else.

How It Works: Sales planning is critically important. If you have built a sales campaign, this strategy should be a part of the plan. (Building a reverse timeline is a great practice; see the next idea for the details.) If you get bad news, know what your plan will be to handle that situation. Remember, existing customers are a lot easier to sell to than new ones.

4. Reverse Timeline
By Andy O'Brien

What the Idea Is: This practice is very effective! Once you win the deal, look at it from the closing date backwards and outline what needs to happen, step by step, along the way.

Here's an example: If you have a deal that will close on 9/30, build a reverse timeline for everything that needs to happen to make it happen by the committed date.

- Start with identifying the decision maker who will sign the contract and allow you to book the revenue (the one who issues the purchase order).
- Ask, *What does this person need in order to do that? Who do they need to have final recommendations from in order to get specific details?* Typically:
  - The business unit needs budget approval
  - Engineering needs to certify the functionality
  - Operations needs to certify the reliability
  - Procurement needs to confirm the commercials
  - The executive needs to sign off on it all

You will be building the funnel from the tip upward.

You must be very detailed in developing the timeline; it must include dates and the person responsible for each action in order to create accountability for each component. The salesperson becomes the overall project manager for the process.

This process works remarkably well when it is put into writing, reviewed regularly with the extended sales team, and rigorously managed well with all the needed constituents in place.

Following each step in the process is critical to ensure the deal gets done within the committed time frame.

Why It Is Valuable: It provides clarity, focus, and execution, which builds predictability into the deal; using this process, you should never be surprised by an outcome.

This process also creates stronger buy-in and builds the relationship with the client, because you ask the client to review to ensure it matches up with:

- What the client has agreed to
- What the client needs
- What the client will provide

You are acting as a strategic partner, not just a vendor.

How It Works: The salesperson owns the process as the "project manager," and the process is rigorously followed, meaning that it is regularly inspected at all internal levels.

When you share your timeline with the client, ask him/her to inspect it to see if you are missing anything and confirm that it is a reasonable timeline. When presented the right way, clients love being a part of setting the expectations. It strengthens your relationship and establishes your brand with them, and it builds trust. If you see the deal is not going to happen, let the team know as soon as you can, and tell them why.

Using this process actually increases closing rates, and it provides a great predictability of the timing of the project. Culturally, it creates a better team environment. It eliminates stressors because everyone knows what is happening, and they all want to hold up their end of the deal and not let their team members down because of a failure to execute.

5. Making a Business Case/ROI Presentation
By Ben Solari

What the idea is: I've developed a methodology to use in today's day and age when selling disruptive technology that is not budgeted or is a new category that requires a significant unbudgeted investment. This methodology helps you determine how you can work with customers/prospects on measuring and quantifying the business metrics.

1. **Enablement Pieces:** Hiring and fostering people who are suitable for the role
   a. Screen candidates thoroughly for this type of methodology. Think through the hiring prospects. One important trait they should have or develop would be business fluency, meaning

the candidates should have a finance or business-center background that enables them to think more holistically about how the technology they are selling fits into the broader business. Being analytical with an innovative approach to looking at alternative solutions to solve a business's issues gives them a definite edge in the process.

b. This requires a macro-level analysis. The team developing the business case will come in, look at how the business makes money, and determine the best way to implement the technology into the business.

c. There are questions you can ask in the interview process to help you gauge the critical thinking skills of your candidates. Ask them to describe:

i. How they are making their customers money

ii. How they impact their bottom line today

iii. How they think our technology impacts the bottom line for our customers

The candidate's answers to these questions will help you determine whether this individual can think about the bigger picture, is able to think critically, and understands how your technology fits into the business.

2. **Training:** How do you create collateral or training to instill in your team a level of comfort in dealing with executives (C-Suite) who need to level up beyond feature functionality? Think about your customer. He/she is going to need to justify spending money that doesn't exist to bring in a piece of technology. Brainstorm with your team to come up with cost/revenue levers that your technology relates to, or break down their business (i.e., if you are selling to an engineering dept with $XX budget that has XX fixed number of engineers, and the department will spend $XX per engineer per year, that creates a target for you for that year that your technology can potentially impact). What are some levers the customer can pull that would allow him/her to feel confident that the money he/she spends will pay for itself?

Why It Is Valuable: The customers want to know whether the technology works. Is this technology valuable and/or does it present an opportunity for a return on investment?

The business case shows your work/math behind justifying the answer that this is a positive return on investment.

How it works: It is asset/collateral that comes about after the proof of the concept, using an executive readout deck that has two pieces:

1. A business impact slide that shows assumptions on impacting the levers you have identified and says, "Here's what it can mean for you." This slide generally answers the question, "Does the technology work?" It includes screenshots of software with the customer's data in it, which allows you to tell a customized story that shows how the technology will benefit the customer. It also contains an analysis of how it relates to the data, indicates areas for improvement, and so on.

   In your business case, outline levers around cost/revenue that innovates faster, reduces costs, and improves the yield of the current team. Include assumptions that are supported by the customized data presented initially, and allow the customer to have a conversation around how the data is presented.

2. An investment slide that outlines what the total cost of the investment would be. This should generate a conversation around how the technology would pay for itself.

How do you measure its success?

1. If you are able to improve the business fluency and invest in a business-case template that the reps can successfully deploy, one quantitative measure you should see over quarters is an increase in your average deal size as your sales force becomes more confident in the business value they are creating. This gives your customer a clearer understanding of that impact, which justifies a higher spend.

2. The win rate from the POC should start to improve as you increase your success rate in unlocking any spend in general and are able to better equip your buyers by showing your work on why this investment would be valuable.

Supporting templates, forms:

You should develop your own PowerPoint or Google slides to use for your purposes.

Here's something to think about: If you have a champion who wants the software, the hard part is helping equip him/her to sell it internally to the final decision maker (finance/executive team) by having a well-polished, thorough business case. When you have reached that point, this person has already bought into the idea (the purchase), and this extra help supports him/her when having to sell internally for a net new spend.

6. Five Ways to Create a Wow! Customer Experience
By Bill Hogan

What the Idea Is: The five most important things a founder or CEO should know in order to create a Wow! Customer Experience.

Why It Is Valuable: A lot of times, people talk about what scales, and the number one thing is happy customers. On day one, you have to place customer experience as a top priority for your organization. A company is the sum of its people, processes, and systems and it's imperative to create a team and product that your customers need and enable them to be successful. Never lose touch with the fact that happy customers become evangelizers on your behalf.

How It Works:

1. Your customers should live at the center of your universe. Their success should be your priority; it should be what drives you and helps shape how you develop your people and your product. By putting their needs first, you are showing them why you are an indispensable partner. In other words, you have to be willing to do the things your competition won't.

2. **Personal Accountability:** This is a value I consistently bring up, because we can train people as much as we want, but if you don't enable them to have personal accountability or ownership, they won't feel empowered to help solve problems as they arise. Founders and CEOs should lead by example and show that each and every person at their company is empowered to do what it takes to solve problems and showcase value.

3. **Be Authentic:** So much of customer experience is being able to empathize with your customer, understand what their needs are, and put yourself in their shoes. By being authentic and honest with your communications, you're helping to develop a deeper relationship than simply being client and customer. Trust is gained through authenticity, and customers understand and appreciate a company that takes the time to develop a real relationship.

4. **Solutions/Results-Focused:** Another one of our company's core values is being solution-focused. It's very easy to point out problems, but the challenge is to find a solution to that problem. Making this a core part of the customer experience is essential. Customers want to know that you not only understand their problem but will use every resource at your disposal to solve it.

5. **Integrity:** Some companies may not care how they win as long as they win. This may result in short term gains, but it always comes back to haunt you. It is essential to care about how you get results, and that means maintaining integrity—being honest and respectful and having a long view of a relationship. Remember that your reputation is always on the line, and customers want to work with companies that they respect.

Here are a few things that can be done to encourage happy customers to open up and become a part of your family and inspire others to reach out to you:

- Companies can share the experience (as long as it's publicly facing) on social media, share stories in an anecdote, and generally be willing to publicly speak about the experience.
- They can participate in community-building groups where CXOs and other executives get together to exchange tips and strategies.
- They can bring us to their board and C-suite to share the value we can bring.

7. Intelligent Mapping Framework
By Bill Hogan

What the Idea Is: Partnering effectively by getting into a room and pairing up.

Why It Is valuable: You would be leveraging your strengths and going as far as you can with them. By partnering effectively, your ability to sell something additional to an existing customer has a much higher degree of success.

How It Works: Leaning in and partnering effectively, looking at short-, medium-, and long-term outcomes, is what works best. Partners have obvious strengths in their install base as well as their strong ability to upsell to an existing customer. Bringing partners leads at places where they already have paper (i.e., good relationships, order history, etc.) makes good sense.

Too often salespeople pick five joint white-space accounts and try to sell to them together. Partnering with someone with whom you have never sold anything jointly has never seemed like a smart play. Leveraging your respective strengths makes sense. Organically, programs and campaigns in joint white space can help you both, but that is a long-tail play.

Successful partnering is when you see each other as a true extension of your respective sales teams, and your behavior shows it. When your team efforts begin to blur lines, where your customer can't see where you and your partner begin and end, that's a good measure of a strong partnership.

Intelligent Mapping Framework

Partner + SSC Joint Customer	Partner Customer SSC Dormant	Partner Customer SSC Whitespace	Partner Whitespace SSC Whitespace
Goal: Expand Footprint in Joint Accounts	**Goal:** Leverage partner relationships & re-activate SSC brand awareness	**Goal:** Leverage partner relationships to acquire new SSC accounts	**Goal:** SSC & partner new account acquisition

Methods

- Facilitate rep to rep intro, communication, & engagement
- Share account intelligence, TAM analysis, & reference accounts
- Continuous rep education and enablement about our solutions

- Joint Sales Calls
- Incremental opportunity identification & planning
- Specific subject matter enablement between AEs & SEs

• Technical Refreshes • User Groups & Workshops • Advisory Services to uplevel programs	• Partner to provide install base info: what was sold, where, dates & key contacts • Business Outcome focused proposals and approaches • Opportunity registrations	• SSC to lead brand awareness w/ customer • Leverage SSC's & Partner's arsenal of marketing activities & events: *Webinars, Partner-branded Content, Video Series, Comedy Hour, Social po* • Include key customer contacts in SSC & co-branded marketing activitie • Develop white-label Partner marketing collateral & Digital content • Joint sharing of potential target lists • SSC inside sales telemarketing or co-branded cold-call blitz days • SSC/Partner lunch & learns; chug & hugs, & enablement sessions

SecurityScorecard

8. The Critical Impact of Focusing on Key Relationships
By Bill Hogan

What the Idea Is: Focusing on key relationships, both internal and external, who are critical to your success is essential.

Why It Is Valuable: People get too self-absorbed, and they often don't realize that strong relationships are key to their success. It's important to nurture your critical relationships and ensure they know how important they are to your success.

How it Works: **Step one** in the process is to identify who these people are. Take some time for introspection and reflection, and identify six people within your organization (your "Super Six") and twelve people outside your organization (your "Dirty Dozen") who are important to your success.

Your Super Six will consist of the six company resources (internal) whose alignment, support, and execution are most critical to your success right now. This group could be comprised of a manager, SE, support person, rep, channel person, leadership, etc.

Your Dirty Dozen will be twelve people external to your organization who will play the biggest roles in enabling your success in the next fourteen months. They could be your customers, your partners, a couple of channel owners, people in your networking groups, a coach or mentor, someone from your alliance communities, or anyone else who will have demonstrable material impact on your success. They should be people who know you and are willing to go on this journey with you. These are the people who are or should be as vested in your success as you are.

Step two is to write a brief summary telling why each of these people in your two groups holds this place for you and what you are doing to make sure they know how important their role is to your success. Also tell why it should be important for them to want to play a role in your success (explaining how your success can also help them).

After you've done these first two steps, look over your list and make sure they are the best people to be on them. Make changes if necessary.

Step three is to communicate to these people how important they are to you.

Step four is to determine what you can do to continue to nourish and cultivate each relationship, and then focus on doing just that.

9. What I Wish I Had Known
By Bill Power

What the Idea Is: What I wish I had known earlier in my career

Why It Is Valuable: These are great words of wisdom to consider living by.

How It Works:

1. The most successful people listen more and talk less. The more someone tells you how much they know, the less sure they really are.

2. The smartest people don't have the best answers; they ask the best questions and know what to do when they hear the right answer.

3. Don't be afraid to ask the question that might seem obvious. It's usually the question everyone wants to ask but doesn't have the confidence to do so. It usually means the speaker hasn't articulated his/her idea well enough.

4. The best way to show someone you care about him/her personally or professionally is to be inquisitive.

5. What are you doing outside of work to be better at your job? Are you taking research home on the weekend? Are you reading *Barron's* or *The Economist*? Who do you admire and why? Are you emulating them, reading their biographies, etc.?

6. The little things matter. What can you pick up from clients that your competitors don't? People form opinions based on what they see people do, not what people say. When was the last time you sent a hand-written thank you note?

7. Spend time thinking about what makes you great! What is your "value add"? Lead with your strength, but understand your weaknesses and work with others who can complement them!

8. Work to improve your weaknesses, but even harder on your strengths. That is what will make you great!

9. Don't waste your time with people who don't care.

10. A-quality people hire A-quality people—because they want to work with the best.

11. B-quality people hire B- and C-quality people because they want to feel better about themselves and are threatened by A-quality people. That is what kills a corporate culture.

12. What you decide to read will influence how you think. Try to read articles that are in opposition to what your view might be. Read articles and books that will help you think for the long term. Short-term data points will only help you in the short term. Think long term!

13. Relationships are what will make you successful at work and at home! You need to invest in them if you want to receive the benefits they can provide. Don't sacrifice one at the expense of the other.

10. Set Clear Expectations on Day One
By Bill Swales

What the Idea Is: Set clear expectations on day one. I began my career leading small sales teams; however, that quickly evolved as my career progressed and I had the opportunity to lead some very large sales organizations. In the first face-to-face meeting with every sales leadership team, it is critical to set clear and prescript expectations, while simultaneously finding the appropriate balance to demonstrate who you are and how you operate at your core. For the past twenty-five-plus years, I have been using the same content to kick off every new sales leadership team meeting I inherit. This single PowerPoint slide (reproduced below) is the most sought-after content from my past sales leadership teams, and it has been wonderful to see so many of my direct reports and peers personalize this content and use it with their respective teams.

Why It Is Valuable: In one discussion, I set clear expectations on day one. From that moment on, there will be no excuses for not meeting these expectations. This content presents a sales leader with the opportunity to have very direct and clear conversations with those who are not meeting expectations and to celebrate those who are.

How It Works: When I join a new organization or obtain a new assignment, I kick off each new sales leadership team meeting with the following. Each bullet obviously has a story or experience behind it.

Professional Manifesto: In a 24/7, always-on world:

1. Be **consistent** and **predictable**.
2. Be **number one**, but give the credit to others.
3. **Develop talent**, embrace diversity and inclusion, and lead by example.
4. Surround yourself with people you **like, know, trust, respect,** and can **learn** from.
5. Be **challenged** every day.
6. Have a **zero tolerance** for any ethical compromise.
7. Set your **goals**, write them down, and share them with those who can help you achieve them.
8. Bring **humor** into everything you do.
9. Have **fun**.
10. Make **money**.
11. To **believe** you cannot do a thing is a way to make it impossible.
12. Understand the psychology of winning and **visualize success**.
13. Build your **brand**.
14. Give **second chances**.
15. When you meet someone for the first time, look them in the eye, **smile**, and offer your hand for a handshake.
16. Quickly **disengage** from people of compromise.
17. Find **balance**.
18. **Explain** the business on one piece of paper.
19. Become a **destination point** for others.
20. **Win** constantly. Make excellence a habit.

I have also found it important to lead by example, and the following content helps my new sales leaders better understand who I am at my core.

Personal Manifesto: In a 24/7, always-on world:

1. The best things in life are **free**.
2. **Two** is too many.
3. We all have a **social responsibility**.
4. **Exercise**, eat good **food**, get plenty of **sleep**, and drink lots of **water**.
5. Be the millionaire **next door**.
6. Spend what you can **afford**.

7. Insure and **protect** your family assets.

8. There are **525,600 minutes** in a year.

9. Take amazing **family vacations.**

10. In order to **participate** in the lives of your children, you must be physically and mentally present.

11. Buy your significant other flowers, take him/her on a date, and express your **love** to him/her constantly.

12. Have your **financial affairs** in order.

13. Make a house a **home.**

14. **Celebrate** life.

15. Always **help** family and friends through difficult times.

16. **Never** go to bed angry.

17. It's better to **give** than to receive.

18. Drop everything when there is a **family** emergency or crisis.

19. Find a way to **stay connected** with your most loyal friends.

20. **Volunteer** and give back to your community.

11. Aha Sales Practice: Managing TEAM Productivity
By Billy Bob Brigmon

What the Idea Is: Aha Sales Practice: Managing TEAM Productivity

Why It Is Valuable: Resilient and adaptive sales leaders create the conditions for their teams to learn fast. You have a lot of autonomy to orchestrate how your team works, and the salespeople learn from each other. If you want consistent and sustainable success, start managing team productivity rather than individual rep productivity.

How It Works: Most sales organizations have a standardized sales process, a standardized sales methodology, and standardized metrics that come from standardized CRM fields. With all this emphasis on standardization, it's surprising how little attention is paid to the ways *sales teams* work.

In my experience, the "ways of working" vary a lot from team to team within any sales organization. By "ways of working," I'm specifically referring to how the sales leader chooses to use team meetings, recurring one-on-ones, and collaboration tools (whether that's email, Slack, Chatter, or even group texts). On some teams, the leader uses all those interactions for inspection. On the best teams, the leaders are constantly refining the *ways of working* so their team learns and adapts quickly. Sales teams that learn faster earn faster.

12. Sales Leader U Value Prop/Differentiation
By Billy Bob Brigmon

What the Idea Is: Sales Leader U Value Prop/Differentiation

Why It Is Valuable: Now that buyers have unprecedented choices and access to information, the companies that sustain high growth are those that continuously make buying easier and customer success more likely.

How It Works: This requires healthy collaboration and trust between sales leaders and the leaders in marketing, customer success, human resources, finance, product, and operations. Sales Leader U helps you find sales productivity leverage in these intersections between sales leaders and the leaders of the functions that support sales.

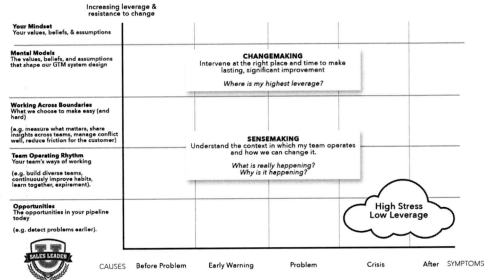

13. Getting in Front of Your Prospect
By Blake Galvin

What the Idea Is: Sometimes you just have to make a commitment to be willing to do whatever it takes to get in front of a potential new client.

I'm not a big fan of "the process" or any true "sales methodologies," etc. I just try to keep it simple and sell based on relationships. In other words, my number one goal and top priority as a sales guy, and more specifically as a successful sales guy, is to think outside the box when needed in order to get in front of decision makers and be "likeable."

Why It Is Valuable: I tell you this story in the hopes that you will start thinking of more "out-of-the-box" solutions to getting past the gatekeeper and win the sale.

How It Works: Here's my story: In 1994 I was working in the Chicago sales office for EMC, selling the Harmonix storage platform. One of my target accounts was a hedge fund headquartered in downtown Chicago, which was a large AS/400 shop. Erik F. was the head of IT there.

I tried numerous times to get in front of Erik to tell him how great EMC's storage was, with little to no luck, until one day when his admin innocently mentioned that he was out of the office and was in Las Vegas.

The following week I showed up in his office, which I had done several times before with no luck, and I handed a sealed envelope with his name on it to his admin and asked that she hand deliver it to him; nothing more was said. In the envelope was a single playing card—the 10 of spades.

I proceeded to do that three more times, sporadically, over the next couple of weeks, each time leaving a similar envelope and progressing through the deck with each delivery—the jack of spades, the queen of spades, and the king of spades. By my fourth appearance, the admin at the front desk was laughing and asking "What's in the envelope?" I just smiled as I left the office and told her she'd know soon enough.

By the fifth time I showed up, two or three days later, I entered the office and asked the admin to finally call Erik and let him know I was waiting in the lobby. "And who shall I say is here?" she asked. I responded, "Tell him the ace is here!"

Well, Erik literally sprinted to the lobby to meet me; and on top of becoming an EMC Harmonix client, he has become one of my dearest friends in life! True story.

14. Experiential Selling
By Bob Horn

What the Idea Is: Creating unique, engaging, and memorable experiences throughout the customer journey, starting with the first touch throughout each stage of the sales cycle, implementation, value realization, and adoption phases.

Experiential Selling creates an emotional attachment from the customer to the product itself and the sales team. Here's an example: Instead of delivering a typical show-and-tell demo, turn the tables and have the customer do the demo. Find the biggest skeptic in the room, give that person the laptop, provide some hand holding, and walk him/her through the demonstration. It's a great way to engage the audience, show your product and its ease of use, and have some fun with the audience. They will remember the first time they saw a demo of your product.

These amazing experiences can become a part of the culture of the company and can help create a price/value premium for your product. If you give your clients a great experience, it will lead to a better, more trusting relationship and greater acceptance of your ideas. If the customers trust you, realize value from your products, and have a great experience, they will become your best salespeople.

Why It Is Valuable: Customers buy based on three things:

1. Trust
2. Value
3. Experience

Most sales professionals spend time on product capabilities, features, and their benefits, alongside value. Many times we neglect the importance of building trust and customer experience to complete this triad. Customers want to spend time with people they trust and those who deliver an engaging or unique experience.

I'll never forget receiving a call from one of my most important customers. I asked her how the meeting had gone the previous day, and I could hear the disappointment in her voice. We had earned her trust so much that she had circled our meetings on her calendar; she looked forward to them because the team had always delivered something interesting with a unique experience.

I was flattered to know my team had done such great work over time and had set the bar so high; but in this case we had not spent the time to properly prepare for this engagement. We needed to make sure we not only had done our homework and prepared for the meeting, but also that we delivered the message in a way that could be enjoyable, emotional, personal, and memorable. Experiential Selling is where preparation meets creativity.

There's a line in the movie *Hidden Figures* when Mary Jackson, who later became a NASA mathematician, was addressing the court where she was petitioning to break the college color barrier. She said to the judge, "Of all the cases you are going to hear today, which one is going to matter 100 years from now?" The judge was sold because she appealed to his interests while also making the narrative personal, memorable, and emotional. How could he say no? This is what Experiential Selling is all about.

How It Works: This concept begins with setting the stage early and establishing the necessary hiring, onboarding, and enablement program, while fostering an environment where preparation meets creativity and opportunity. Look for people who can analyze and create the assets you will need to provide this kind of experience—everything from design to video creation combined with research and data analytics, as well as other resources. If you are able to get the right people on the team, you will be able to develop your Experiential Selling concept much quicker.

I suggest you begin with setting up the initial customer call in an engaging manner, potentially using some form of multimedia, video, and storytelling versus the typical boring presentation customers endure every day. Include something customized to fit that person and his/her organization. Do something to generate an understanding with the customer so you can talk about his/her experience and problem and look for solutions.

In the follow-up call, have the customer actually do the demo; if you have done your homework, it will create a much stronger buy-in experience. Theme it as well, analyze the annual reports and any other information you can obtain, include a creative aspect to it, and walk the customer through the process to develop a hands-on feel for the outcomes.

After the sale, follow up by having a really great customer success team continue creating a cadence of weekly, monthly, and quarterly info and dialogue on how to use the product more effectively and drive increased value, leading to wider adoption. Experiential Selling will change the game for both you and your customer.

In summary:

1. Do your homework and have a clear perspective of the customer's vision and associated problems.

2. Create a story that will serve as the personal and emotional hook.

3. Deliver your story in an engaging way beyond the norm, such as customizing a video or having the customer drive the demo.

4. Be memorable.

5. Continue to deliver experiences throughout the customer journey.

15. Six Pillars to Scaling Your Organization
By Bob Horn

What the Idea Is: There are six fundamental pieces to having your organization set to scale for growth. Here are the components, some of which you may already have in place at various times in the life of the company.

1. **Talent.** Getting the right people for the right stage of the company at the right time in their career (with a number of different skills needed for the various positions)

2. **Experience.** Give your new hires an amazing experience. If they have a great onboarding experience, they are 69 percent more likely to stay onboard for at least three years.

3. **Value.** Lock in on your value drivers—have a clear understanding of them, message appropriately, and create consistency in the messaging so all are giving the same answers.

4. **Great Outcomes.** The real results your customers are getting from your products/services. This is where great customer service comes in for the win. Defining the outcomes also allows you to course-correct when needed. Once you define what you are actually delivering, you may need to refine your messaging.

5. **Process.** Make sure you have established a methodology that is repeatable to make sure everyone is rowing in the same direction. Your methodology must also be flexible to enable you to make changes when needed to make sure you are doing it the right way at the right time.

6. **Data.** Analytics feed the rest; use the data wisely and make sure you are capturing the right data, as it can create unintentional decisions if you are using incorrect or incomplete data. Determine the criteria down to the type of analytical tools to use, and make sure they are pulling the right data for your decisions. After you ensure it is good, use it to make the necessary adjustments as you chart your course.

Why It Is Valuable: These pillars clarify your priorities and show you where you need to focus (everybody wants to boil the ocean). Choosing the specific six things you need allows people to focus on the best priorities for that point in time.

How It Works: Deployment actions for each of the pillars may vary, depending on where you are in the business cycle of the company. Do not deploy all six at once; focus on specifics, one at a time. Figure out where the gaps are, then understand the process, data value, experience, and outcomes.

16. Getting 5+ Percent More
By Brian Bell

What the Idea Is: When you're running a sales team and other organizations, top performance seems to be getting that last 5 percent. It seems getting the first 80 percent is pretty much in the bag, but getting to 90 or 95 percent takes another level. And consistently getting to 102+ percent takes excellence.

Why It Is Valuable: Where do you as a leader find this 5+ percent? More activity metrics? More pipeline calls? More demands? I think the answer is elsewhere. I think the 5+ percent comes from:

1. You as a transformational leader
2. The makeup of your team
3. The GTM approach—the wind in your reps' sails

How It Works:

Transformational Leaders: Who is your team "fighting for" every day? Just for themselves? This will always create challenges. Are they fighting for their regional teams? That's a step in the right direction. Does your team care enough about the overall team to want to fight for them? Will they drive out on a Sunday night for a P.O. on a deal that does not get them to their quota, but that helps the overall sales team get to its team goal? Does your team care about you? Do they want you to be successful? This only comes about if you care about them. Are they just a part of the machine? Do you know their career desires? Have you done something to help them out?

I remember one story early in my leadership career when a brand new rep just out of college had a tough situation at home (she was from out of state). She had no money and no vacation time, since she had just started out. Of course I said, "Go home and help your mother out," and I handed her a few hundred bucks. Well, that rep turned out to be one of my superstars, and it's been reinforced over and over. Before you ask people to do something for you, do something for them. It's simple, really. People want to work for people who care about them and who see them as more than just a "producer."

Makeup of Your Team: There is a lot written about organizations, and specifically about sales organizations and talents. I think it comes down to contributors versus consumers. You need a team full of contributors. Contributors may not always be at 100 percent, but they are working the plan, are great teammates, are coachable, and you can point to positive interactions almost every time you meet with them. Consumers are the opposite; they use excuses versus seeing challenges as opportunities to turn things around. They complain about the comp plans, the territory, and/or how "easy it is for John to get to quota" because of his mature patch. Turning consumers to contributors—or removing them—is hard to do. But it is necessary if you want to build a sales machine. If you don't have the fortitude to do this actively, you will not find that last 5+ percent—or you will kill yourself trying to get there on the backs of the contributors you do have.

Wind in Your Reps' Sails: How are you helping your reps build bridges with new customers? New-customer acquisition is challenging because there are so many unknowns for the target customer. It involves a new relationship with a company, a new relationship with a product, and a potential new relationship with the sales executive. You need to find a system that will remove some of this "newness." Here is one example, in enterprise sales, of leveraging the channel to create some of these tailwinds: One of your target enterprise prospects whom you have never sold to has previously bought from a veteran channel company sales executive and has a great relationship with this reseller/system integrator; and now the channel sales executive is selling a new product from a new vendor (you!). However, your prospect knows the sales rep and trusts her, so you just created some wind in your team's sales! You can also get the same effect by finding ways for prospect companies to engage with your product in a freemium-to-premium path—think enterprise SaaS companies like Slack or Twilio. You remove the "newness" and the fear and hesitation that come along with it. There is much more I could write on this, but just know that you as the GTM owner are responsible for finding this "wind" and getting it into your team's "sails." In transformational leadership, a team full of contributors is essential; but you also need to wrap this machine with a GTM approach that maximizes at-bats, and minimizes friction in the customers' buying process.

17. It's a Long Life in a Small World
By Chris Lynch

What the Idea Is: It's a long life in a small world. It's important early in your career to understand the value of relationships.

I have been selling/doing business with the same 100 people for thirty years. When I was in my twenties, I didn't realize how unique and important that was. It sounds like such a simple thing. I meet young people today who are very transactional; they need to understand that relationships matter and that they make a huge difference.

Why It Is Valuable: Consider that this is a small world. If you want a long career, treat everyone with respect and understand that every relationship is built on reciprocity. Ensure that you are satisfied with the relationship, but make sure the other person is satisfied as well. Don't leave the success of the relationship to fate or chance.

Everything is built on relationships, and they are a force multiplier. You must earn the right to ask. It's not just a matter of being bold or aggressive; your right is based on reciprocity.

How It Works: Contacts are only as good as the frequency in which you nourish them. Relationships get stale. Rather than always calling them to ask for something, be proactive in calling to offer something.

Frequency builds relationships. Figure out ways to stay on the person's radar, and offer something to the person that has value.

18. The Power of Saying No
By Chris Lynch

What the Idea Is: When you learn the power of no, that's when you start selling and uncovering the real objectives of the client. You need to learn when and how to say no to an opportunity.

Why It Is Valuable: The most important skill a salesperson has is not closing. Qualifying is hard; but if you qualify right, your deals close themselves. If you get a customer who is not qualified, time is your enemy. You're in a numbers game, and you have a finite window in which to touch customers. You can't afford to waste time with someone who shouldn't be your customer and doesn't value your service.

How It Works: The truth works. When you were young, you probably liked to take the scenic route. However, as you have gained more experience, you likely tend to take the direct route. If your customer isn't a good fit, thank the person for his or her time, offer a solution with another company that may be a better fit, and move on. You will build your network and build your credibility with that person.

19. Leadership Qualities
By Chris Riley

What the Idea Is: Unforgettable bosses possess qualities that may not show up on paper but always show up where it matters most—in the minds and even the hearts of the people they lead.

Why It Is Valuable: Memorable bosses inspire others to achieve their dreams—by their words, their actions, and most importantly, their example.

How It Works: Here are some of the qualities of truly unforgettable bosses:

1. **They believe the unbelievable.**
   Most people try to achieve the achievable; that's why most goals and targets are incremental rather than *inconceivable*.

   Memorable bosses expect more—from themselves and from others. Then they show you how to get there, and they bring you along for what turns out to be an unbelievable ride.

2. **They see opportunity in instability and uncertainty.**
   When facing unexpected problems, unforeseen roadblocks, and major crises, most bosses take down the sails, batten the hatches, and hope to wait out the storm.

A few see a crisis as an opportunity. They know it's extremely difficult to make major changes, even necessary ones, when things are going relatively smoothly.

They know reorganizing an entire sales team is accepted more easily when a major customer goes under. They know creating new sales channels is a lot easier when a major competitor enters the market. They know reorganizing manufacturing operations is a lot easier when the flow of supplies and components gets disrupted.

Memorable bosses see instability and uncertainty not as a barrier, but as an enabler. They reorganize, reshape, and re-engineer to *reassure, motivate, and inspire*—and in the process they make the organization much stronger.

3. They wear their emotions on their sleeves.

Good bosses are professional.

Memorable bosses are highly professional and yet also openly human. They show sincere excitement when things go well. They show *sincere appreciation for hard work* and extra effort. They show sincere disappointment—not in others, but in themselves. They celebrate, they empathize, they worry. Sometimes *they even get frustrated or angry.*

In short, they're human. And, unlike many bosses, they act as if they know it.

Professionalism is admirable. Professionalism with a healthy blend of humanity is inspiring.

4. They protect others from the bus.

Terrible bosses throw their employees under the bus.

Good bosses *never* throw their employees under the bus.

Memorable bosses see the bus coming and pull their employees out of the way, often without the employee even knowing it until much, much later—if ever, because memorable bosses *never try to take credit.*

And if they can't, *they* take the hit (and later speak privately to the employee in question).

5. They've been there, done that—and *still* do that.

Dues aren't *paid* (past tense). Dues *get* paid each and every day. The true measure of value is the tangible contribution we make on a daily basis.

That's why no matter what they may have accomplished in the past, memorable bosses are *never too good to roll up their sleeves*, get dirty, and do the "grunt" work. No job is ever too menial; no task is ever too unskilled or boring.

Memorable bosses never feel entitled, which means no one feels entitled to anything but the fruits of their labor.

6. **They lead by permission, not authority.**

All bosses have a title. That title gives them the right to direct others, to make decisions, to organize and instruct and discipline.

Memorable bosses lead because *their employees want them to lead*. Their employees are motivated and inspired by the person, not the title.

Through their words and actions they cause employees to feel they work *with*, not *for*, a boss. Many bosses don't even recognize there's a difference—but memorable bosses do.

7. **They embrace a larger purpose.**

A good boss works to achieve company goals.

Memorable bosses also work to achieve company goals—and achieve more than other bosses—but also work to serve a larger purpose: to advance the careers of employees, to rescue struggling employees, and to instill a sense of pride and self-worth in others. They aren't just remembered for nuts and bolts achievements, but for helping others on a personal and individual level.

Memorable bosses *embrace a larger purpose*, because they know business is always personal.

8. **They take real, not fake risks.**

Many bosses, like many people, try to stand out in some superficial way—maybe through their clothes, their interests, or a public display of support for a popular initiative. They do stand out, but they stand out for reasons of sizzle, not steak.

Memorable bosses stand out because they are willing to take an unpopular stand, take an unpopular step, accept the discomfort of ignoring the status quo, and risk sailing uncharted waters.

They *take real risks, not for the sake of risk but for the sake of the reward* they believe possible. And by their example they inspire others to take risks in order to achieve what *they* believe is possible.

20. Don't Forget What You Are Selling
By Chuck Smith

What the Idea Is: Don't forget *what* you are selling:

1. Yourself

2. Your company and its product or services

3. Ultimately the *outcome* for the customer

Focus on being best in class in all three areas, and you will have long-term sales success.

Success selling across these three areas doesn't always come naturally, and it doesn't always come at the same time in your career; yet you have to deliver on all three of these elements in order to achieve long-term success. You could be very good at understanding the details of the product and service but may be too fixated on that and not on the outcome for the customer. Or you may be very focused on selling yourself and creating the relationship and forget about "what's in it for the customer." Being too focused on selling yourself versus what is being sold and the outcome can also be a problem. Finally, concentrating only on the outcome but not on how you get there can also be an issue. Broadening your attention to each of these three dimensions can not only make you successful on your near-term goals; it can also help you as you develop your career and work as a sales executive with broader and more material responsibilities.

Why It Is Valuable: As a salesperson, you have a reputation you are building with a customer; if you have a valued relationship because of the way you present yourself, and if you are knowledgeable about the offering and how you benefit customers, you will create a lasting value for yourself as a sales person.

As tantalizing as closing a deal is, if you haven't thought through the right product or service, you may not ultimately create a **model of sustained success** in your selling career. And that's what it's really about. You want to create sustained success by using this lifetime behavior set. It's simple, but not easy. It takes a ton of effort to work on all the dimensions in front of every customer to keep that approach going.

Ask yourself:

• Are you a leader in what is being sold?

• Are you a subject-matter expert?

• Do you understand the results the customer is looking for?

How will you continue to create/improve yourself as you're continuing to sell your products or services? All the concepts we've talked about are beneficial—not just for your current role, but also for your career success.

How It Works:

Selling Yourself: There are a variety of approaches, habits, and techniques to help you improve and grow in this area. I believe some of the key attributes you need are persistence, humility, and integrity. You must be attentive and focused on listening, not talking. Continuously show with your behavior, your attitude, and your presence that you are there to help the customers with their issues or projects, and be able to show that your own approach, style, and presence will be beneficial for them. Have you built your relationship map within the customers you're calling on? Do you have details on the people you will need to help you "day to day," such as gatekeepers like administrative or executive assistants? Do you know the decision-making map, and have you established your own relationships and position within that map? These are only a few of the key questions you need to answer.

Company Products and/or Services: To be successful in this domain, you must really know what you are selling. Create a great elevator pitch, practice it to perfection, and make sure you can deliver a quick but compelling synopsis on how your product or services can benefit the customer. Its critical to work within your company and within those teams to have a network of individuals who can assist you in having effective conversations positioning your product and services. You shouldn't be the "lone wolf," especially in large value transactions; you need to have a full extended team behind you, and you need to lead that team. It is critical to bring people along in the process, leveraging those relationships, selling yourself and the company on what they deliver and what the customer requires. In the end, building this network and building your knowledge of the offering, the company, and the people who deliver its value are critical to your long-term success. When you have the opportunity, go to the internal training sessions, not only to make sure you are well informed and that you understand the offerings, but mostly to establish and build your network of leaders who can help you deliver on your goals. Before going to the training, look at your funnel to see what your customer needs or is asking for. Then align your calendar to get trained in those areas; but more importantly, establish relationships with the subject-matter experts who can help you and your customer be successful.

Outcome for the customer: You must know the benefit and ultimate results that the customer will experience by buying your products or services. You need to be constantly mindful about the outcome a customer will experience. In some cases you need to essentially walk a mile in their shoes. What does success for this individual or this team mean? What is their ultimate motivation for successfully executing this project or activity? A great way to help them understand for themselves is to investigate similar examples and bring in other customers or internal resources who had good outcomes for others in this situation. You need to educate yourself on the outcome, as well as help the customer understand and realize it. Have you read the company's financial statements as well as investor and public presentations? Are you aware of the broader business implications of the project? With this knowledge, you can typically change the approach to the deal or the relationship to sway it even more to your advantage.

21. Does Culture Impact Productivity?
By Coley Burke

What the Idea Is: Does culture have an impact on productivity? Yes! I am a firm believer that a healthy, thriving company culture can fuel productivity gains and success across all departments.

Why It Is Valuable: There is a significant focus on tangible efforts to improve productivity, but what about the intangible elements that buoy morale and drive the entire organization to go the extra mile every day, no matter the function? I see culture as one of those intangibles that can lead to improvements in productivity on all fronts.

How It Works: The best cultures happen organically, shaped by leadership, company values, and mission. In selling organizations, the spotlight is often put on sales teams and their efforts. However, if the kudos and celebrations are not balanced across the other supporting functions, it can lead to resentment and the stall of innovation, effort, and focus.

Sales leaders must recognize their role in creating, nurturing, and living "culture." I use a simple concept to help show that sales growth doesn't happen without every person's collective efforts in the company: ONE (Ownership Needs Everyone). Telling people and their functional groups how they matter to the sales outcome instills ownership, pride, and willingness to go the extra mile. These people are critical to the company's success and significance. By taking the time to recognize the efforts and celebrating the success of the people outside the sales organization who make the operation work, a sales leader can bolster morale, nurture the culture, and add a powerful intangible that drives success. Culture matters!

22. Two Winners in Every Deal
By Colin P. Mahony

What the Idea Is: Even though we tend to think about winning every sales opportunity in the absolute sense, there can actually be two vendor "winners" in every deal. Of course, the actual vendor who wins the customer's business is the true winner, but the vendor who qualifies out of it earliest and moves on to the next opportunity will also win. I was taught this very early in my career, and it has helped me create the right focus and deal qualifications. It sounds simple, but it seldom happens as early as it should.

Why It Is Valuable: I learned this the hard way, and I continue to see it happen often in the tech industry. Companies and selling teams will pursue opportunities all the way through, be excited about making the "short list," and then not be chosen. Usually, there are three vendors on the short lists, and two of them will end up spending invaluable time and money going the distance, only to lose. Had they qualified themselves out early and moved on to greener pastures, they likely would have already closed an alternative deal. These days, opportunity cost is everything.

How It Works:

- Qualifying out of an opportunity as early as possible requires confidence, discipline, and frankly a mindset that often creates friction against typical pipeline and opportunity progression models. When done properly, it can enhance focus and win rates dramatically. Companies will quickly find their true market fit.

- Never be the sucker. The suckers are the vendors who go the entire distance, expend all their resources and time, and ultimately lose the business.

- With proper post-mortem analysis, it usually becomes very evident very early in the sales process that the deal wasn't actually winnable. The earlier in the cycle you can figure this out, the more valuable your decision is.

- The decision sounds easy, right? Wrong. When you think about sellers, most of us believe that at some level we can influence the customer and that our skills will change the odds every step of the way. We may have managers who keep telling us to "do our job" and sell. This is especially true when a seller joins a company because they are working with a limited pipeline of opportunities. While there is certainly some validity to our "self-confidence," it is often never enough to overcome most of the customer decision hurdles. If you agree to be on the shortlist, make sure you have a greater than 80 percent chance of winning at every stage.

- Data, data, data. The key to truly doing this well, of course, is data and history. Take the emotion and ego out of it. In the early days of a start-up, just about anything looks like a qualified opportunity. As you gain experience with the product and market, you start building a corpus of feedback in your mind, your CRM system, and probably lots of emails and notes. Analyzing this information to determine the early warning signals will be immensely valuable. After every win and loss, make sure you spend time truly understanding whether the odds were greater than 80 percent at every phase and why.

- Share your qualifying-out logic with the customer. One of the best ways to leverage this is to call the customer early on once you have determined that you are qualifying out. Thank them for the opportunity and share your logic. They will likely be impressed by your confidence and transparency. They will also be able to quickly validate this for you, or they may actually tell you your calculus is wrong. This feedback is invaluable. I've actually had situations where I thought for sure we had no chance and consequently we politely pulled out, only for the customer to practically beg us to stay in—and we ultimately won. During this call, customers will often open up much more about your competitors as well.

23. Building a Repeatable, Predictable and Scalable Revenue Engine
By Craig Hinkley

What the Idea Is: Summary points:

- In today's digital world, how successful your company is at extracting value from your clients in the form of revenue is more a function of how multiple parts of the organization work together versus the performance of the sales organization as a stand-alone component.

- The revenue function in today's modern organization is more analogous to an engine, where all of the functions that are part of delivering high-quality revenue are cylinders that need to be connected, synchronized and aligned to perform at their collective best.

- The planning and discussion on revenue is no longer merely a discussion on the quality of the sales organization, but rather a broader discussion on the quality of all the functions that make up the revenue engine.

- By revenue functions I am referring to:
  - Sales, including sales development reps and sales reps
  - Marketing, which includes demand generation, sales enablement, product marketing management, analyst and press relations, etc.
  - Customer success/customer renewals
  - Customer onboarding
  - Business operations which includes sales and marketing operations
- In the revenue engine model, the stages of the sales process form a revenue "butterfly," starting with demand/lead generation and working its way through the sale process, ultimately resulting in the won deal, which is the center of the butterfly. At this point, the process expands again as you renew and expand business with the client.
- All the way through the "butterfly" the various revenue functions play a specific role at that point in the sales process. The purpose and intended outcome of each function may be different, depending on what stage of the "butterfly" the sales process is in.
- A major factor in building a repeatable and predictable revenue engine lies in the ruthless application of a sales methodology (e.g., MEDDIC, Sandler, etc.). Select whatever sales process is best for your team, market, or industry and adopt it. The true power of a sales process is not the process itself, but the rigor, discipline, and commitment to the sales methodology you have chosen to use. The power and effect of a sales process is in the passion and commitment to the methodology—not in merely the methodology itself.
- Whether your company has a CRO or these functions report to different executives, I believe they have to be considered, discussed, and planned as one connected system—as part of one connected revenue engine that is being applied to the sale process of "butterfly."

Why It Is Valuable:

- It builds alignment between the leaders of the revenue functions and common goals and metrics. It also creates a stronger sense of trust, teamwork, and collaboration because each function has a greater understanding of the relevance they play in the larger revenue engine.
- It ensures there is clarity on expected outcomes of each function as well as how the functions' efforts and outputs become the critical inputs to the next phase of the butterfly.
- It creates end-to-end playbooks for each ideal customer profile (ICP) spanning: where and how to identify opportunities, nurturing and dispositioning leads, winning deals, and renewing and expanding business.

- The revenue engine and sales process "butterfly" provides the framework for applying and reinforcing the rigor, discipline, and commitment to a particular sales methodology.

- Metrics and measures at each stage of the "butterfly" can be defined and then operationalized and measured through the sales process as it executes, thereby enabling the much needed ruthless, objective, and continuous inspection of the revenue engine, of the core metrics, and of the deals themselves.

How It Works: Let's look at how the core revenue functions work together in a virtuous cycle.

Revenue Functional Alignment

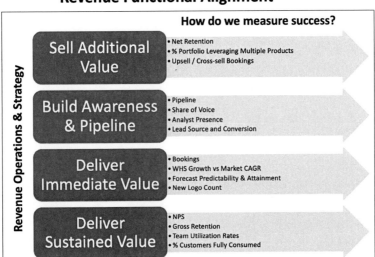

- As the diagram illustrates, all elements of a revenue engine work as part of one connected machine.

- The effectiveness (power and output) of the engine is governed by how well all the components are synchronized and working together.

- You can pick any part of the circle or any function to begin and move your way around the cycle in the order indicated by the arrows.

- The intent of the arrow is to indicate the relationship between the two functions in the cycle. The boxes off to the side of the cycle indicate some of the KPIs and metrics that are typically used to measure the success of the functions and the cycle in its connected execution.

- At the center of the functions is the strategy driving the overall goal of the revenue engine, supported by the revenue operations function that provides the critical, ruthless inspection of all elements/cylinders of the engine.

- The revenue operations function is critical in building and operating a highly efficient and effective revenue engine and revenue "butterfly" (which will be explained later in greater detail). The reason is that the revenue operations function provides the necessary transparency and visibility into how the functions are performing. Without this objective evidence, as a revenue leader, you are unable to understand and determine the areas of under-performance, the levels of friction in or between functions, or the drive of accountability into the functional leaders and teams.
- When it comes to sales methodology, which for some companies is treated almost like a religion, I have the following belief:
  - It is not the religion that is powerful; it is the follower's commitment to adhere to the doctrine that makes a religion powerful.
  - The same can be said about the sales process being adopted by a company. The specific sales methodology (e.g., MEDDIC, Sandler, Challenger, etc.) is less important. The key is the consistency, rigor, and discipline that is applied by the entire sales organization to the agreed-to sales methodology.

Let's walk through the revenue "butterfly" and see how the sales process of a revenue engine makes the revenue "butterfly" come to life:

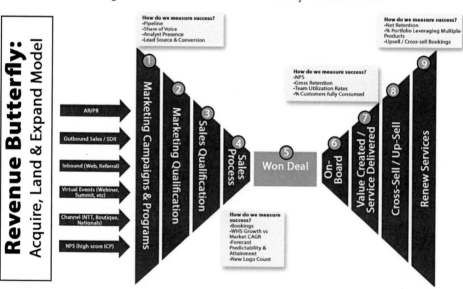

- The key to how these parts of the revenue engine work together is how they are connected through the revenue "butterfly."
- Today's revenue motion has a distinct pattern, which I like to call the revenue "butterfly."
- The nine phases of the revenue process are depicted in the Butterfly diagram above.

- o At a high-level or level of abstraction, the nine-phase, end-to-end revenue process looks like a butterfly.
- o It is shaped like a butterfly; think of each phase of the sales process as representing the potential size of the pipeline, the number of deals, bookings, and revenue.
- o E.g., marketing demand gen activities produce a large raw pipeline; as you work the deals/pipeline through the revenue process, it naturally becomes smaller until it is its "smallest" in terms of the actual deals you win, which are bookings and revenue.
- o Post winning deals, the goal is that the install base then grows and expands as you renew the business and upsell/cross-sell into the install base.
- o This expanding-contracting-expanding motion, when depicted as a diagram, creates the visual of a butterfly.

I use the analogy of a butterfly because of the "butterfly effect" in chaos theory. The butterfly effect, an underlying principle of chaos, describes how a small change in one state of a deterministic nonlinear system can result in large differences in a later state (meaning that there is sensitive dependence on initial conditions).[1] A metaphor for this behavior is that a butterfly flapping its wings in Texas can cause a hurricane in China.

I liken the butterfly effect as a parallel analogy to the revenue engine of a company, whereby the changes in the functions of this connected revenue system can have a great effect on its output.

Said simply, if you don't line up all parts of the revenue engine, you will not get the highest level of output, nor will you get a revenue engine that is repeatable, predictable, and scalable.

The nine phases of the revenue butterfly:

- The phases of the revenue "butterfly," as depicted in the above diagram, are:
  - o Marketing campaigns and programs
  - o Marketing qualification
  - o Sales qualification
  - o Sales process
  - o Won deal
  - o On-board
  - o Value created/service delivered
  - o Cross-sell/up-sell
  - o Renew services

- This is the way I have chosen to map out the sales process in creating the revenue "butterfly." This is not the only way. If you start using the revenue "butterfly" model in your business, I would encourage you to map your sales process and revenue objectives to create a version of the model that works for your business and your team.

- The exercise itself to create your revenue "butterfly" may provide great insights into the leaders of each function of the revenue engine and how strategic or tactical they are in their own leadership development and also assess their awareness of the need to work as one revenue engine moving forward.

- Similarly, the version of the revenue "butterfly" shown above includes some of the key metrics that we have used inside our business and therefore are relevant to what we deem as success. Similarly, in creating your own version of the "butterfly" I also encourage you to discuss, debate, and define the metrics you and your leaders think are best for measuring the success of your revenue "butterfly" and revenue engine.

- As you know there are metrics that exist at each stage of the sales process. There are also industry standard and accepted "best-in-class" rates for pipeline conversion between stages, etc. So the exercise to define your metrics is not a creative exercise, but more one of selecting the right metrics that measure the right outcomes from the teams and process doing the right things.

- As you go through the exercise, I would encourage you to define some broader and more far-reaching metrics that provide deeper insights into the end-to-end effectives of the sales process, the revenue "butterfly," and the output of your revenue engine.

- One of the metrics I like to use to measure the connectedness and effectiveness between the sales and marketing team in understanding the product-market fit and the associated collateral needed to communicate the value proposition, competitive positioning, etc., is to measure the usage by the sales team of the collateral created by the marketing organization. This may not be right for you or your business; however, what I have found is that a sales and marketing team that is connected and working well together creates a set of material and collateral that is so clear and compelling that it is used frequently by the sales team. Also, the collateral is updated or new collateral created as the customer and market evolves because there is a level of information flow between the sales and marketing teams that drives such updates and new material being created.

- How can you measure this effectiveness? One approach is to ask for a report on the sales collateral created by your marketing (product marketing) team and the number of times that material has been downloaded and accessed by the sales team. This level of utilization should give you insights into how well the teams are connected.

- o If the collateral is being used frequently by the sales team, they find the material beneficial and supportive of the sales motion with customers, prospects, etc.
- o If underutilized or not utilized at all, it shows there is a problem. There could be many reasons for the problem, but it indicates there is work to do to understand the gap and close it.
- o Lastly, one of the reasons I look at this utilization metric is to determine the amount of lost cycles in the sales and marketing teams. Underutilized collateral means lost productivity. That is, the effort, energy, time, and resources dedicated to creating the assets were a waste. It also means that the sales team is off creating its own assets and/or telling the customer what they believe the message is.

Now that we understand how the revenue "butterfly" is constructed from the sales process, let's walk through the revenue "butterfly" to understand how the cylinders of the revenue engine work together to make it come to life.

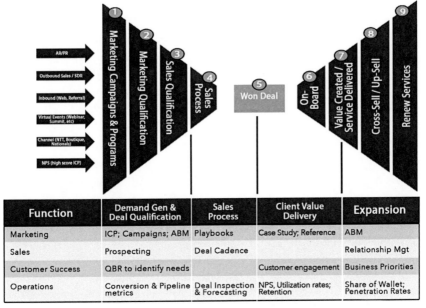

Function	Demand Gen & Deal Qualification	Sales Process	Client Value Delivery	Expansion
Marketing	ICP; Campaigns; ABM	Playbooks	Case Study; Reference	ABM
Sales	Prospecting	Deal Cadence		Relationship Mgt
Customer Success	QBR to identify needs		Customer engagement	Business Priorities
Operations	Conversion & Pipeline metrics	Deal Inspection & Forecasting	NPS, Utilization rates; Retention	Share of Wallet; Penetration Rates

- In building upon the butterfly effect from the chaos theory, it is important to note that the different cylinders of the connected revenue engine play a different role, or they exhibit different characteristics/behaviors, depending upon what stage of the revenue Butterfly they are being applied to.

- Undertake the exercise to build your own revenue "butterfly." To maximize the horse-power of your revenue engine, engage your leaders to work collaboratively to define the set of activities, expected outcomes, and metrics to align each cylinder in the sales process and maximize the overall output of your revenue "butterfly" journey.
- The revenue "butterfly" allows you to examine what a specific function enables and delivers across each step of the sales process by taking a horizontal view across the "butterfly." Let's look at marketing, for example.
  - In phases 1, 2, and 3 of the "butterfly" the marketing team is driving a set of campaigns with multiple programs to build a pipeline, using the ICP and ABM techniques to target specific personas and buyers. There are also a number of activities the marketing team is doing to nurture and qualify leads to hand over to the sales team.
  - In Phases 4 and 5, the marketing team has playbooks, battlecards, value calculators, etc. that help the sales team demonstrate the value of your company's solution over your competitor's.
  - In Phases 5, 6, and 7, the marketing team is looking to build case studies based upon the clients use-case for the solution and working with the customer to become a reference.
  - In Phases 7, 8, and 9, the marketing team is using ABM to continue to nurture the existing client and target them with specific offers that are relevant to their needs as a way of building opportunities to expand share-of-wallet in the account.

- The revenue "butterfly" also allows you to examine and align activities across functions for each stage of the revenue by taking a vertical "phase-specific" view of the "butterfly." Let's look at Phases 4 and 5, sales process, for example.
  - In these phases, as we mentioned above, the marketing team has playbooks, battlecards, value calculators, etc. that help the sales team demonstrate the value of your company's solution over your competitors'.
  - The sales team is using the marketing collateral and executing the sales process in terms of quoting, building close plans, etc.
  - The operations team is using the CRM system to perform forecasting and deal inspection, and they are providing delivery forecasts to the service delivery team. If the reps are not following the sales process and putting deal details in the CRM system, then the operations team can flag the sales representatives and their deals for deeper inspection with sales leadership.

- While a completed revenue "butterfly" may be similar across companies, I believe in the benefits that come from each organization's performing their own exercise. These benefits include:
  - Identifying gaps in certain functions to support a certain sales process stage of the revenue "butterfly" that otherwise would have gone undetected gaps or misalignment on what the functions are doing to be connected and drive the best overall outcome for the revenue engine.
  - Team and leadership development opportunities. The exercise will help the team to build trust, teamwork, collaboration, and empathy by a collective understanding of the strengths and weaknesses of the revenue engine; and it will build commitment because everyone can see the opportunities to make the revenue engine perform better.

Conclusion:

- In today's digital world, how successful your company is at extracting value from your clients in the form of revenue is more a function of how multiple parts of the organization work together versus the performance of the sales organization as a stand-alone component.
- I believe the concepts of a revenue engine, revenue "butterfly" and a zealous approach to sales process and discipline are the foundations to building a repeatable, predictable, and scalable revenue engine.

Definitions/Terms:

- Share of Wallet (SoW) – Represents how much of the overall spend of the client's budget you have for all the services you have that the client could purchase (e.g., if you have five different solutions or offerings that meet five different needs the client has, or that a client is using a competitor's offering to deliver that value, and you have sold them two of your services to deliver that value, then you have 40 percent Share of Wallet.)
- Penetration Rate (Pen Rate) – If a client is using you for a discreet service, how much of the total available spend on that service is being spent with your service/solution? This could mean that the remaining dollars are being spent on a competitor's offering or that the client has not expanded your offering to cover the other assets your service is applicable for. This could be for a variety of reasons, such as a lack of budget or those assets do not have the same business priority or importance as the assets under service with you.

ICP — Ideal Customer Profile. (See *https://blog.hubspot.com/customers/ideal-customer-profiles-and-buyer-personas-are-they-different*.)
ABM — Account Based Marketing. (See *https://6sense.com/*.)

24. Determining What is Truly Important
to You as a Sales Representative
By Dave Casillo

What the Idea is: Many sales representatives become frustrated with their current sales position and/or company and begin searching for an alternative where the "grass is greener." Securing a new job within your existing organization or accepting a sales role in a different company will introduce a substantial change and disruption into your everyday life. As it pertains to your career, do **you** really understand what are the most critically important elements in your life?

Why It Is Valuable: The biggest issue I have witnessed in my thirty-five years of selling is that individuals typically do not take the time to determine what is *truly important* to them at that exact point in their career/life. They *think* they know, but the reality is that they have not undertaken the necessary steps to truly validate their high-level beliefs.

How It Works: I would like to introduce you to an extremely worthwhile and eye-opening exercise to ensure you know what you really want in a new role. The exercise consumes forty-five minutes on day one and then takes five minutes every day after until conclusion. The exercise usually lasts two to four weeks. Typical overall time investment is less than two hours. This is a minor and invaluable investment for such a significant event in your career. If you are like most individuals, you will be surprised by your "Top Five."

1. In no particular order, list every item that has importance to you as it relates to employment (typically twenty to twenty-five items).

   - Examples: overall on-target earnings (OTE), salary, bonus, commissions, equity, no compensation caps, title, global responsibility, regional coverage, company car, a specific territory, management of people, select industries, travel (more/less), size of corporation (small/medium/large), public company, private company (family owned, private equity, or start-up), friend or acquaintances at new company, no relocation required, trust, stability of company, free weekends, employee benefits, defined career path, strong management, minimal corporate politics, position located at corporate headquarters, ability to work remote, work/life balance, reputation of company, Glassdoor rating, etc.

2. Pare that list down to your top twelve, and then initially place them in priority order. Disregard all others and never consider them again. They should never become a part of the evaluation process once eliminated.

3. Each and every day, review and reorder the top twelve from a priority perspective.

4. If your top seven all remained constant **for three consecutive days**, eliminate the remaining five items. Note: It is fine that the sequential order of the seven elements changed. The key is that all seven elements remained in the top seven, even if the order differed over those three days.

   - Example: Salary could have been number three of seven on Monday, number four of seven on Tuesday, and number one of seven on Wednesday. It still remained as a top-seven element for those three successive days.

5. Each and every day, review and reorder the top seven from a priority perspective.

6. When three consecutive days have passed and there have been *no changes to both the top five elements, as well as the exact priority order of the top five—the exercise is complete!* In essence, numbers one through five remained identical for three straight days. At this point, you truly have identified what is important to you.

Final Action:

Compare the new sales role to your Top Five list. If the position you are considering meets at least four of your top five priorities, then there is a natural match. If it only meets three of the top five, then it must align and perfectly match your top three. Accept the new role if it meets either of those two parameters and don't look back. Pass on the position if it fails to meet these, as it does not satisfy your most vital requirements.

25. "1, 2, 3" Rule: The Key to Partnering
By Dave Casillo

What the Idea Is: One of the largest obstacles that sales representatives face is the ability to scale themselves. Natural constraints such as available selling time, limited expertise, and a semi-fixed number of customer relationships place boundaries on a salesperson's ability to maximize sales bookings. One of the best ways to scale your sales efforts is to take advantage of the breadth and depth of your partner community.

Why It Is Valuable: Partners will expand your customer reach, enhance your brand, and augment your delivery capabilities. Unless your sales organization is operating under a 100 percent direct-sales model, you can exponentially grow your sales bookings if you adhere to the following basics of partnering.

How It Works: Scaling your territory is incredibly vital and will ultimately determine success or failure for a significant majority of the sales representatives in the world. Partnering can be a no-lose proposition that will allow you to reach heights that you could have never reached alone. You should always be cognizant that members of a channel partner community (reseller, distributor, consultant, integrator, dealer, services company, etc.) operate independently from your company. They have their own unique corporate goals and objectives, as well as key focus areas. These partners also have dramatically different selling models, margin expectations and expense ratios. At the end of the day, partners always act in their own self-interest and will be extremely cognizant if your partnership provides incremental value (1+1>2). The ultimate question is how do you gain mindshare and engagement from your partner community?

- To ensure success in a new or existing partnership, you should live by the "1, 2, 3" rule:
  - The "1" intangible you **always must provide** is *value*
  - The "2" sentiments you **need to both foster and grow** are *trustworthiness and likeability.*
  - The "3" principles you should **never deviate from** are *simplicity, consistency and clarity.*

- While you will experience many distinct differences between your partners and your company, there are common themes that are shared in nearly every one of these positive relationships. Your partners will strongly engage and drive sales with:
  - People they respect and have confidence in
  - Companies that provide the path of least resistance to sales
  - Companies that make it easy to understand and communicate the value proposition for both the customer and partner
  - Companies that maintain their direction and processes
  - Companies that are transparent and easy to understand

Corporate partnerships are no different than personal relationships. You will be more likely to put more effort into a friend or colleague who is consistent, likeable, clear, uncomplicated, straightforward, and honest. Implementation of the "1, 2, 3" rule will form an incredibly strong basis for a great partnership. If you construct a strong foundation, you will be on your way to accelerated sales growth!

26. Meet Your Commitments to Your Customers
By Dave Donatelli

What the Idea Is: While it's exciting to talk about the great presentation or the fancy dinner that helped close the deal, the simple act of always meeting your commitments to your customer is probably one of the most important elements in having a successful long-term career in sales.

Why It Is Valuable: The world gets smaller every day. Your reputation, either good or bad, will follow you wherever you go. As you progress in your career, you will be surprised how many times you run into past customers in new selling situations or resume business with companies you have dealt with in previous jobs. Your ability to succeed in these situations will largely be dependent on how you have served and treated these people and organizations in the past. I was struck by this thought during a recent encounter I had with a major US Airline. I was accompanying our rep on a call for a very competitive deal. There were two customers present, and I vaguely recognized one. After we got through the introductions, the customer I recognized turned to his boss and said "You remember Dave. He was the person who fixed that problem for us while he was at XYZ (my prior company)." That problem fix was something I had done many years before this meeting. Based on the trust that had been built in that situation, we won the competitive deal.

How It Works: It's simple—meet your commitments before and after the sale. If you promise a proposal by Friday, get it there by Friday (or sooner). Honor any commitments made during the selling process. Most importantly, if there are post-sale issues, work diligently to resolve them. The products I have sold can unfortunately result in customer downtime if something goes wrong. If this happens, call the customer! Work to understand and resolve the issue. Do not hide! Believe me, I have had plenty of customers yell at me during the heat of a downtime incident. Invariably, problems get resolved and temperatures calm down. Customers respect the fact that you were there for them during their time of need. In fact, I have found that customers I have resolved a problem for are more loyal than customers who have never had a problem, because they know they can trust me when the chips are down. That security with your customers is invaluable to them and to your long-term career success.

27. Customer Success Framework
By Dave Frederickson

What the Idea Is: Establishing territory plans, account plans, and client business reviews in a far more structured way than what was previously done.

Why It Is Valuable: This process can be used for various purposes:

1. It establishes a foundation for account managers to be able to understand their targets and the business they expect to close, and from what accounts. The complexity of today's business gives a wide portfolio to the manager—from services and software licensing to traditional procurement. Services are the key thing they are honing in on today, and they pay less attention to tactical business. They must establish a keen understanding of the key target accounts and make sure account plans are centered around what they are trying to achieve in terms of business outcomes. That is the foundation for building a plan with key stakeholders who are internal to the organization (client service managers, digital architects, etc.), along with having relationship maps based on business outcomes of the key client stakeholders and how they translate into key IT priorities for these stakeholders.

2. It can define what we are really good at and how we can map those things back, giving real business value orientation to the client. It can also identify who within the organization is best equipped to be part of that solution for the customer.

The account plan rolls into a **territory plan**. (For example, account managers may have one account within their territory, or they may have multiple accounts.)

How It Works: Account managers can use it to develop an understanding of what their customers are trying to achieve, tying it back to their core capabilities and how they can execute on value to the customer. They can also use it as a **communication tool** to get inputs on a regular basis. Service delivery people may have better insights on what is going on and can provide that information to the sales people, which helps them tap into that source.

A key step is that this process moves account managers toward a regularly scheduled **business review with the client that includes key stakeholders and an executive sponsor**; they can hire a facilitator to come in and build out a roadmap for their client (an envisioning workshop).

They could literally do a one-to-two-day session, when all the key people within the account would come in to build out this plan. (These are more of an exception.) The value that pops out from that, for both the customer and the organization, is incredible.

You can have many components, with:

- Some being more internally appropriate
- Another with a version you would use with your clients (internal could include sales by LOB, margin or profitability by LOB, SWOT, share of wallet, potential threats, where your competitors are positioned, etc.)
- Another version where the plan is more suited to make this into more of a client-facing event—a workshop that builds a bond and provides value.

At the end of the day, it helps you review operationally how you may have been doing against a current set of services a client is receiving from you. It also gives you an important opportunity to ensure all key stakeholders understand what you are doing and capable of. Additionally, it offers up the opportunity to introduce innovation, based on what you see of other clients that could have similarities in size/verticals, that can translate over to this client. It also allows you get way more aligned. Challenge your mindset!

If you are coming up to a renewal period, this process clearly illustrates the value the client received throughout the previous time. It also helps bring a new person onboard quickly when he/she assumes a role in the client's organization, and it helps build the foundation with the new person. Or, if you lose an account manager, there is a back-up plan for someone to pick up and transition into the role without having to pull all the information out of many people to have it available. IP is easily captured through this method. It's a journey, not a destination; it is never done.

The main thing you should try to get out of this is that traditional sales people think account planning is typically one-sided, where they have to draft a framework for an account. In truth, data doesn't differ too much from place to place, but it gets done and then put on the shelf; it does not stay a living document that can continue to bring value to the team and to the client. With this method, though, it becomes more of a process/procedure than just a document. It becomes a communication tool with inputs from multiple key stakeholders. The business is complex, and this not only helps clarify the whole situation; it can also help track the process as it moves forward and ensure the necessary support and accountabilities both of and for the sales person are achieved.

For many, I am sure this isn't new or a revelation; but often ensuring that it doesn't end up being a done-once annual check box is what is really important. I have prepared templates of a very brief PowerPoint territory summary slide, an outline of a full account plan in Word and a short version of an account plan in Word. These can be found on the salescommunity.com website. I hope you find them useful.

28. It's Not Who You Know...
By Dave Vellante

What the Idea Is: We all know that having a network of connections is of paramount value in sales. The question is, what's the best way to build a network that can help you reach your goals and dreams?

My philosophy flips the old saying, "It's not what you know; it's who you know." Rather, I approach networking as "It's not who you know, but who knows you."

In other words, it's nice to identify people who can be helpful; but it's a far more powerful concept if: a) the person knows you, and b) you've actually created value for that individual without necessarily expecting anything in return. Deliver value, make a friend, and very often good things happen.

Why It Is Valuable: If you apply this practice consistently, you can reach many more people. You end up helping many folks who, in turn, may be willing to help you someday. And it cascades into a network effect that allows you to reach people you may not even know, but who know who you are. This is important because it can build your personal brand, and it certainly beats cold-calling.

How It Works: You have to be willing to work hard in order to make this concept effective. You have to ask yourself, *What am I willing to do to become the most valuable and trusted sales person I can possibly be?* My answer is to build expertise and create content—in the form of blogs, videos, and social media. And you must do this on a regular basis; it can't be a one-off.

We live in an age with incredibly powerful tools that didn't exist twenty years ago, yet most people don't take advantage of them because it's too much work. But if you really put in the time and effort, the payback will change your sales life.

Here's how it works:

1. Become an expert in a topic that is relevant to your sales objectives.

2. Publish content on a weekly cadence, using your network of contacts to formulate your content agenda.

3. Research and read to advance your thinking on topics, and create independent, thoughtful content.

4. Publish videos, then summarize those videos in written form on your own blog or another platform. (My business partners and I created our own: theCUBE, SiliconANGLE, and Wikibon.)

5. Distribute that content on LinkedIn, Twitter, and other social platforms to create network effects.

6. Engage, build a following, and keep doing it.

It's hard; but if you work at it and form habits, you will create a competitive advantage that 90 percent of sales people don't have.

Here's one of many examples: *https://wikibon.com/breaking-analysis -with-dave-vellante/.*

29. Situational Leadership
By David Boyle

What the Idea Is: Solicit feedback on challenging leadership issues from frontline leadership teams. I generally get feedback from over fifty leaders (it could be any number) of the most pressing challenges they have in their businesses.

I frame up the feedback I want around: (1) people, (2) partners, (3) customers, and (4) go-to-market. What I want is actual, live, current issues that generally land in one of these four topics.

Why It Is Valuable: It is real and live, and the issues are fairly consistent across leadership. The challenge is that many leaders operate in a silo environment and don't realize others are going through or have been led through many of the issues that are front and center.

How It Works: I use this Situational Leadership format two times a year, generally around a leadership-development program/session. I send out a document showing the above four topics as a guide, with a specific example of a situation that relates to each topic. I ask that each leader share one of their most pressing issues. From the fifty situational challenges I generally receive, I select the ten most challenging or most common.

The forum becomes live when I am hosting a leadership meeting. The session lasts for one to one and a half hours.

I present the top ten responses on a one-page format for all to read. (I know who each of the responses are from.) I then go around the room and solicit feedback, asking "What would you do in this scenario?" I usually get three or so leaders to provide feedback and weigh in with what they would do or have done.

After we have had some good dialogue, I will then turn to the leader who wrote this particular issue and ask what they learned and whether they have what they need to resolve this issue.

Then I go on to questions 2 through 10 with the same approach. Ten questions, along with some very good feedback about situational leadership, generally fill up the one to one and a half hours.

30. Relationship Economics®
By David Nour

What the Idea Is: Relationships are important; very few people really internalize and understand their significance. Most perceive relationship building to be a soft skill. I have spent the last two decades studying and proving out that when you are intentional—when you become strategic and thus quantifiable—about the relationships you choose to invest in, they definitively accelerate your ability to get things done.

Most sales professionals agree that building relationships is an investment of time, effort, and resources. Any astute investor will tell you that you cannot invest blindly. Sociologists tell us that an average individual can proactively manage about 100 to 150 relationships. The million-dollar questions become: Which ones do you invest in and how do you know? If you cannot invest in everyone equally, how will you prioritize which relationships you choose to invest in?

Why It Is Valuable: Not all relationships are created equal. There are some universal laws in building business relationships:

- Gratitude – When you do something for someone, at a minimum they should say, "Thank you!"
- Reciprocity – Maybe not today, tomorrow, or next week, but at some point they should reciprocate your kindness.
- Pay it Forward –If you do something for someone, ideally you should observe them passing on that generosity to someone else. After all, none of us are an island!

Investing your time wisely and meaningfully into the right people can pay off greatly in the long run. By combining black-and-white quantifiable economics with the soft skill of building relationships, you can exponentially accelerate successes, increase loyalties, and garner access to countless new opportunities.

How It Works: If you throw enough time, effort, and resources at any challenge for an opportunity—selling a new product, expanding to a new market, etc.—you will eventually get there. When faced with the opportunity, most people will ask what we should do and how we should do it. We need to do a much better job asking who questions:

- Who do we need? Who can make that one phone call, send that one email, or make that one introduction to dramatically accelerate your journey?
- Who do we know? You know a lot more people than you think you do; we're just all really bad at keeping up with them and maintaining and nurturing them.
- How do we connect the dots with value add between the relationships we already have and ones we need to accelerate our path to results? Investments in your relationships and capitalizing on those investments are the lubricant that move ideas forward.

If you believe the supposition that relationships are an investment and can, in fact, accelerate your traction, your milestones, and your results, you must understand that you cannot effectively, efficiently, and successfully ask for a favor when you haven't earned the right to do so. It's a lot easier to have your hand out if you begin by giving a hand. In twenty years of working with hundreds of global clients, that is exactly what we have done.

By creating a Relationship Currency Roadmap™, you can take various pockets of relationship successes and institutionalize them, thereby seeing reduced acquisition costs, increased loyalty, and access to new opportunities.

The key components of a rewarding Relationship Currency Roadmap™ are:

1. Exchange Relationship Currency®
2. Accumulate Reputation Capital®
3. Ultimately enhance and elevate your Professional Net Worth®: your relationship assets minus your relationship liabilities

While charting out your roadmap, be sure to keep the following in mind:

1. Think through the process backwards and execute it forward.
2. Relationship-Centered Goals: What are you trying to accomplish? What are the outcomes you are after, and what do they require from you?
3. Pivotal Contacts: Who do you need? Who is that one person you can make a phone call or send an email to who can remove roadblocks and accelerate your access and success? Who can dramatically get you to the end result, accelerating your ability to reach your goals?

4. Current Relationship Bank: Who do you know? Most of us know more people than we think we do; we are just not good at keeping up with them, nurturing them, and sustaining them, and we are apprehensive about requesting their help without feeling weird about it. Take the time to nurture your existing bank sufficiently.

5. Relationship Currency Deposits: This is your "favor" stash. What investments can I make? What am I willing to make? What do I already have in my arsenal?

Executing this process consistently is what we call *Strategic Relationship Planning*™. To further assess and maximize your relationships, visit the link below:

https://www.nourgroup.com/relationship-economics-quiz

31. Balance of Trade, a Win-Win
By Eric Koach

What the Idea Is: HPE bought hundreds of millions of dollars' worth of hard drives, but SEAGATE didn't buy any servers, storage, network, etc., so they would negotiate at the highest level. It gave them the ability to leverage product into a customer who was not buying or was underbuying.

Why It Is Valuable: It generates revenue. It takes an under-performing or non-performing customer to the next level in sixty days when there is an inverse balance of trade you are positioning to fix.

How It Works: Meg Whitman pushed this at HPE, and it became a sales play that they would run. Every quarter, go through revenue numbers and check for underperforming customers; then work back to leverage that out. Push/negotiate a much deeper sales play to leverage multiple platforms there—servers, storage, network, professional services, software, etc. Executives get it. They will have their team expedite orders for you in a quarter to create a quick leverage play, which can be a multi-business-unit play. It has to be done at the executive level, where there are kingdoms/ fiefdoms/ protectionism in place.

When done properly, it isn't adversarial; it's a statement of business facts, and it's a fast revenue.

32. Employee Purchase Program
By Eric Koach

What the Idea Is: Add the EPP to every corporate purchase agreement; this makes it easy for the customer to get discounted products for its employees.

Why It Is Valuable: It's a procurement play; they love being able to go to the employee pool and say they have "negotiated" superior pricing on products for them. Make it super easy for them to buy at a better price than they would elsewhere. This plan makes procurement a hero—when you do have a sticky situation, they are on your side (it's a get-out-of-jail-free card). It also creates long-term brand loyalty from the customer and you become a champion when moving to a new employer.

How It Works: Add the EPP agreement to every corporate sales agreement. Sometimes the customer can declare a time limit, subsidize the employee, and/or do payroll deductions to cover the purchases. Using the words "urgent" and "scarcity" make it more of a significant benefit. Put it all online so it's easy for the employees to do.

This idea should be implemented in every corporate account! You can measure its success by how many units you sold and how many of the employees made purchases (the penetration rate with employees).

These are the benefits you will gain when you launch an employee purchase program:

- Increased incremental top-line revenue
- Increased incremental margin dollars
- Increased overall corporate spend
- Increased business-product sales (hardware, software, printers, monitors, and other various products)

33. Leveraged Spend
By Eric Koach

What the Idea Is: If you are at a company that has multiple divisions or sales teams covering different business units, try to leverage spend across all groups to help sell everything you have. When I was at Dell and HP, we would try to do this for the various business units (servers, storage, networking, services, cloud, laptops, printers, etc.). And if your company spends more with your customer than the customer spends with your company, politely/nicely point that out and try to get your fair share (especially by leveraging the decision-maker at your company that your customer sells to).

Why It Is Valuable: Increase revenue and profit in the same account; create incremental margin dollars. Actually, this creates a lot of good things for the customers when they get the products from one provider—it gives them everything they want.

How It Works: It is a sales play. Focus on the chief procurement officer/ CIO. Leverage someone whose role it is to save money; spend more with him, and eliminate other vendors, thereby lowering the costs associated with multiple vendors. Here's an example: HPE purchased $2.5 billion in processors from Intel annually, and the Intel spend was significantly lower with HPE. When the sales play was executed, the senior executive funneled more business to the sales team. Dell's business model of direct to consumer lined up very well for this. A compelling event can help this even more.

34. Accelerating your Sales Career by Embracing the Channel
By Frank Rauch

What the Idea Is: Most companies do business through an indirect channel (i.e., a group of resellers and distributors who represent and sell your product). This definition has expanded through the years, but we will stick to this definition for this discussion. These resources can prove invaluable to help either new or seasoned sales professionals crush their numbers.

Why It Is Valuable: The first half of my career was more or less in direct sales. As a very junior sales rep right out of college pounding the pavement in my blue and grey suits for IBM, I realized sales was not going to be a cakewalk. I had the number one brand in the industry behind me, but I just did not have the contacts to be as successful as I wanted to be. So I found the channel. It was an amazing revelation and a point of acceleration in my sales career. All of a sudden, I had channel partners, many of whom have become lifelong friends, introducing me to top CIOs. This took months, maybe years, off sales campaigns, which eventually led to promotions, President's Clubs, and of course more commissions.

How It Works: The question is how you find reliable partners who can not only execute sales campaigns but can also represent your corporate and personal brand. This is a task any sales professional has to take very seriously. There is no five-star guide to partner capabilities. The selection process requires research. The key attributes you should be looking for are peer and customer references, competitive positioning, resources, demand-creation capabilities, extensive customer base, and overall integrity. That sounds great; now all you have to do is find them. It may not be as hard as you think. Your channel team, peers, customers, and digital resources can help accelerate your success in this search

Congratulations! Now you have found a group of partners. The next step is to create mutual alignment. The easiest, most direct route comes from a quote from the movie *Jerry Maguire*: "Show me the money." The fundamental hurdle is that your money is a different currency than your channel partners. Most producers of goods or services pay their sales reps on revenue, bookings, and now ACV (annual contract value). Your channel counterparts are usually paid on a percentage of gross profit, often referred to as gross margin. Your ability to understand, align with, and influence this concept is critical to your success.

GROSS PROFIT FORMULA **=** **SALES PRICE - COST**

The gross margin calculation is a simple one, yet it is misunderstood by many. Gross margin is calculated by subtracting the price (usually from a distributor) from the sell price by the partner to the customer, divided by the sell price to the customer. For example, you are selling a product to the customer for $100 and your cost from the distributor is $80. Your gross profit is $20, and your gross margin is 20%. It is not always as simple as this basic equation, but it is a good starting point for the conversation. The next point is how you, as a direct sales rep, can influence this outcome. You can increase the margin by allowing the partner to provide services, which typically is more profitable than product sales, or you can offer the partner deal registration (an exclusive discount increase to incent partner value). If you learn and practice this skill, you will thrive with a community of loyal and aligned partners.

The next question is how many partners you need. Your first instinct is probably to say, "As many as I can get." This may not be the best answer, since an infinite model is usually a dilutive model, which will not produce the loyalty and results required. An easy way to think about this is by looking at the rules of five and thirty-three.

This is a basic guideline to determine channel coverage. If you are an individual contributor/territory sales rep, you need 5x the channel reps and you need the channel to contribute at least 33 percent of your pipeline. This is also an easy way to create a dashboard and key performance indicator to manage your territory.

I have spent the second half of my career leading channels for HPE, VMware and Check Point. I have been humbled to have received a lifetime achievement award, have been recognized in the top twenty-five channel sales executives, have mentored over twenty people who are now leading channels, and have led teams to more than seventy channel awards. As I look back through both the direct and indirect sales lens, I realize it is not one or the other but both that contribute to success. Wishing you the best on an incredible sales journey. Don't forget to celebrate with your channel partners, become a lifetime learner, and never lose sight of the people you met on your road to success.

35. Build a Sales Execution Approach
That's Focused on Your Buyers
By Grant Wilson

What the Idea Is: Build a sales execution approach that's focused on your buyers

Why It Is Valuable: Great sales execution requires sales organizations to balance an external focus on the customer with an internal focus on sales management best practices. It takes alignment, consistency, and the right framework to enable sellers to successfully execute at the buyer level.

How It Works: Top-performing companies focus on these key areas to drive sales execution success:

Cross-Functional Alignment

Without alignment, it's difficult to scale and keep a buyer focus throughout your organization. For sales teams to execute consistently at the buyer level, your leadership team needs to be aligned cross-functionally around the buyer. If leaders can't agree on where to focus with your buyers, how can you expect your sales teams to effectively execute on a buyer-focused sales message? Don't underestimate the importance of leadership alignment as a critical first step in defining a buyer-focused sales execution approach.

Leadership Agreement on Four Essential Questions

Four essential questions help companies lay the groundwork for buyer-focused sales execution.

The Four Essential Questions:

- What problems do you solve for customers?
- How do you solve those problems?
- How do you solve them differently and/or better than the competition?
- Where have you done it before?

Agreement on the answers to these questions enables sales reps, BDRs, marketers and customer-success teams to focus on the buyers' greatest needs in their critical roles. When you have internal alignment on the answers, you'll provide consistency and ensure your salespeople understand how to articulate your value and differentiation in a way that has meaning to the buyer.

Clearly-Defined Value Drivers

Strong sales execution supports great buying decisions. Sales teams need to understand what's important to your buyers, then demonstrate your value in a way that aligns with the positive business outcomes your buyers are trying to achieve. Establish well-defined value drivers that are based on the pain points and business objectives your buyers face every day. The right value drivers set the stage for successful buyer conversations that are focused on your customers' problems and outcomes instead of the features and functions of your product.

The Ability to Differentiate from the Competition:

Buyers want to know that their needs are understood and that you can provide them with the best possible solution. Having a solid grasp on how your products, services, and company are different and better than the competition creates an opportunity for your sales team to execute in a way that proves your value to the buyer. Make sure your sellers are "audible ready" to address what makes your company different.

Define your company's differentiators:

- **Unique Differentiators**: What attributes does your company offer that are not available from any other competitor? (Leading technologies, patents, innovative service guarantees, etc.)
- **Comparative Differentiators**: What attributes does your company offer that are superior in some specific way to competitive alternatives? (Usually a feature or function comparison)
- **Holistic Differentiators**: What company-level attributes establish your credibility and reduce the risk of choosing you? (Financial backing, longevity, etc.)

A Tool To Enable Consistency

Buyers need to hear a consistent message throughout each stage of their buying journey. Sales organizations need to enable their teams to deliver those messages consistently. Once your organization has aligned around the problems you solve and why your solutions are different from others in the marketplace, you'll need an easy-to-use tool that enables that execution, repeatedly. The Value Framework is a tool that can provide that consistency. The Value Framework isn't a script. It's a repeatable framework that guides the customer conversation face-to-face, over the phone, and digitally, throughout the customer engagement process. It can be used not only by reps, but also by managers, customer success, marketing, product, and all other customer-facing departments. *https://www.forcemanagement.com/blog/what-is-a-value-framework*

To build a buyer-focused sales execution approach, you'll need alignment, consistency, and a messaging framework that enables your customer-facing teams to successfully execute at the buyer level. Work back from what's most important to the customer, and you'll deliver a sales execution approach that supports great customer buying decisions.

36. Selling Products Vs. Selling Value
By Greg Calhoun

What the Idea Is: One "aha" moment occurred early in my selling career when I experienced the difference between selling products and selling value. I selected a short list of high potential accounts and invested the time to understand each business and how its CEO measures success.

Why It Is Valuable: The business goals or metrics for success trickle down into every business unit, whether you are working with the president of a business unit, the CIO, the CFO, the CMO, or typically anyone at a VP or director level. Business leaders are held accountable to accomplish these goals and are compensated accordingly. Understanding the goals and providing solutions to help your customer achieve their goals elevates you among your competitors by making you relevant, unique, and valuable to your customer.

How It Works: The first step is to learn everything you can about the company, identify a logical entry point, and set up a meeting. You can learn about the company via its corporate web site, 10-K, press releases, and news stories. Use the data to identify an entry point and map your business solution to the customer's objective.

Examples of where I helped different customers achieve their business goals by utilizing technology solutions:

1. Reduced the number of redundant applications via rationalization and consolidation post acquisition for a CIO

2. Accelerated data analysis for a chief marketing officer to provide a competitive advantage and accelerate time to market

3. Consolidated infrastructure to minimize data-center expansion for VP of IT operations.

4. Enhanced application performance and availability of critical business workflow software for the president of a business unit by moving onsite poorly managed applications and infrastructure to a software as a service model.

Finally, through this process establish a relationship with the customer and become a part of their team. Be accountable along with your customer for the success of the project, and measure your progress via a dashboard with your customer. Set quarterly reviews with project leaders and annual reviews with the CXO or business unit leader.

37. Focus on the "Why" Versus the "What"
By Greg DiFraia

What the Idea Is: Often with sales/marketing we like to focus on what the product or solution does versus why we developed it in the first place. Many of the products on the market were developed to help solve a pain or a need; and instead of focusing on this, which relates better to potential customers and prospects, we tend to talk about *us* and what the product does, its features, speeds/feeds, etc.

Why It Is Valuable: Getting your customers and prospects to agree with you on your methodology and why you do what you do is the most important accomplishment in the engagement. When customers buy into the "why," they are confident that your product/solution will meet their needs. However, it is vital that customers feel you clearly understand them and their pain/challenge, and that you have taken this into account for the solution deliverable. It's not about you; it's about the customers.

How it Works: Ensure your teams focus on the components of the message, especially the "why"—why we do what we do, with defensible proof points and metrics. Articulate where you have done this before and how you were able to solve their pain, and ensure the customer buys into the methodology. Once they do, then you can review the product (the "what") and solution particulars. It's common for salespeople to want to talk about the "what" first, which is something that you as a leader need to constantly coach and reinforce.

38. Product Features Don't Win Deals—They Lose Deals
By Greg DiFraia

What the Idea Is: Product features don't win deals; they lose deals. Many times customers ask sales if they support a feature or function. You must be careful how you answer this question, as the wrong answer can exclude you rather than include you in the deal.

Why It Is Valuable: The key is to first understand what the customer is looking to solve with the feature before responding. Just understanding the feature itself does not tell the whole story about why they need it, what pain the organization is looking to solve, and the negative effect the feature can bring if it can't solve their problem. You must clearly understand the business and technical requirements that are aligned. Your ability to change the decision criteria is key to winning the opportunity. You could be fighting the feature battle if you don't understand the root problem and you're not providing a comprehensive approach to solving this uniquely differentiated situation.

How It Works: As leaders of sales teams, we spend time reviewing opportunities and where we need to strengthen our stance, using the MEDDIC methodology as our qualification guideline. Two of the key components are decision criteria and ensuring the team understands. It's crucial that we dig in to understand the requirement that is driving our customers to ask for a specific feature. In our space, there are typically three to five ways to solve the problem technically, but we will need more insight in order to guide the customers down the right path for them, rather than just stating, "Yes, we have this feature." If we can execute this process, our win percentage is drastically improved.

39. The Three Ps Are Your Friend: Purpose, Process, and Payoff
By Greg DiFraia

What the Idea Is: The three Ps are your friend: purpose, process, and payoff.

Why It Is Valuable: Leveraging this simple model to help structure your meetings and engagements with both customers and partners helps everyone understand the goals, how you will achieve success, and what the benefit is at the end of the meeting. Managing your meetings in this fashion will help streamline your communication and make each meeting more impactful, thus improving your time management. You will be able to achieve more, in less time, with improved outcomes, just by applying the three Ps to every meeting and every call you make in your business.

How It Works: Simply define the purpose, the process, and the payoff in the body of your invites to partners and customers for every meeting or call; make it a best practice. You will also want to restate and reframe at the start of each meeting or call to ensure alignment by all, and update if needed based on the responses from everyone involved.

40. Advice I Would Give Myself Starting Out Twenty to Thirty Years Ago
By Greg Scorziello

What the Idea Is: Advice I would give myself starting out twenty to thirty years ago.

Why It Is Valuable: Starting the sales process at the senior executive level will significantly reduce the amount of time wasted on campaigns that are not aligned to business outcomes and therefore will either never come to fruition and or will get bogged down in lower-level politics. What is surprising to new sales reps is that the senior client executives are really nice people and much less objectionable than the lower-level line managers. In short, don't be afraid to pick up the phone and call them, provided you understand how what you do can have a strategic impact on the business.

How It Works:

1. Start at the top whenever possible, provided you can articulate the material benefits you can deliver around profit, time to market, and risk mitigation. Senior executives are easy to speak with. They are willing to try something new if it can move the needle; and most importantly, they are not religious about technology. For example, if you were to try to sell an Apple fanatic a Microsoft computer that was half the price and had twice the processing capability, better graphics, and a superior service plan, it would be next to impossible. However, if you were to go to the CEO with the same proposition for 1,000 laptops, he or she—who is measured on cost, speed to market, and quality of service—would be much more inclined to listen and take you up on your offer.

2. Underpromise and overdeliver. Always meet your commitments; and if you are struggling, don't be afraid to ask for advice and help. This is not a show of weakness, but maturity.

3. Use all the resources available to the company internally and externally to help you deliver on your objectives and promises.

4. Focus on the problem, not the product. The more problems/objectives you can impact for the client using your technology or services, the larger the size deal you will be able to secure. Once you have quantified your impact in hard-currency terms and operational impact, you are in a better position to discuss and justify your commercial proposition.

5. All CIOs are measured on the same metrics, which are to reduce cost, improve quality of service, accelerate application time to market, and reduce security exposure. The more of these metrics you can understand and address, the more likely the customer will be asking you for the order.

And finally, people need to lighten up and have some fun. There is nothing wrong with being a joker occasionally.

41. Fundamentals of Building a High-Performance Sales Team
Greg Scorziello

What the Idea Is: The fundamentals of building a high-performance sales team.

Why It Is Valuable: There is a rule of thumb that 20 percent of the salespeople generate 80 percent of the revenue in start-up and/or growth companies. A lot of time and money can be burned hiring mediocre to average sales executives. Paying over the market for the best people will actually save the company time and money, as they will be able to build smaller high performance teams with more dedicated support, which will ultimately lead to higher revenues and profits.

How It Works:

1. Hire the best people in the industry.

2. Pay them 20 percent or more than the competitors; however, expect 50 percent or more in return. And most importantly, never cap the amount of commission they can make, because the company will always make five to ten times in profit for every dollar it pays a sales rep in commission. Most companies who fail to do this are usually heavily influenced by their accountants, who are focused on saving money versus generating revenue. As a result, they not only cap commissions; they also make their commission plans very complicated in order to erect multiple hurdles created to limit commission payment.

3. In addition to hiring the best people and paying them market-competitive or better compensation, rotate your best sales performers into marketing to develop and provide the sales team with the success formula and resources they need to win. This includes providing near real-time updates on new competitive offerings and how to position against them, even if your product is not as advanced.

4. Focusing on customer value versus product features will also be core to your success.

5. And finally, be faster and more agile and creative than your competitors when it comes to structuring deals aligned to clients' budgets and needs, and doing whatever it takes to win.

42. Fundamentals to Winning Large Deals as a Technology Start-Up Company
By Greg Scorziello

What the Idea Is: The fundamentals of winning large deals as a technology start-up company.

Why It Is Valuable: Most companies develop their solution/product pricing based on what their competitors are charging, and not necessarily what value their solution delivers to their client in terms of increased revenue, profit, and operational efficiency. Sales reps who take the time to quantify the above benefits in many cases will secure contracts that are at or significantly above list pricing and in return will achieve materially greater commissions.

How It Works:

1. *Repositioning the company to a customer- versus technology-focused business.*

   Many technology start-ups have developed great new products; however, all their messaging is focused on the products' features and not on the business outcome they can deliver. When I start working with a new company, what I want to understand is how the company's products will deliver material improvements in operational efficiency and business competitiveness, as well as reduce their clients' business and operational risk profile. The next step is to help them quantify these benefits in hard currency impact, which then enables us to build a pricing that reflects the value we deliver to the client. My mantra has always been to focus on the problem, not the product.

2. *If you do the above right, the company and sales teams are well positioned to increase* the *company's average deal size by five to ten times.*

   The more compelling the value proposition is in terms of strategic impact, the easier it will be to gain access to the C suite. This will set your proposition apart from your competitor's, as your solution will be viewed as a strategic component of the client's business strategy. This does not negate the fact that you still need to get buy-in from the technical team, as they can easily delay or even kill the deal if the CIO is less technical and therefore highly dependent on their support.

3. *Success breeds success.*

   Securing large and high-profile wins is then extremely helpful in convincing resellers and integrators to invest in building a practice to promote and drive incremental revenue and profit based on the company's solution.

43. The Most Consistent Traits/Attributes of the Top Tech Sales Professionals
By Greg Scorziello

What the Idea Is: The most consistent traits/attributes of the top tech sales professionals.

Why It Is Valuable: My mantra to sales executives is "Focus on the problem, not the product." The sales executives who understand their client's operational, financial, and business issues/objectives better than their competitors do will secure more and larger orders.

How It Works:

1. Business case focused; able to quantify material value their solution can deliver in hard currency

2. Committed to delivering on their promises to their clients and their company (under promise, over deliver)

3. Not afraid to ask for help and/or advice if they are struggling to meet their objectives (and doing so early on in the quarter)

4. Always looking outside the immediate opportunity in order to grow the deal opportunity and/or make their solution be more strategic

5. Leverage partners, industry leaders, and company resources

44. Building a Network
By Gregg Ambulos

What the Idea Is: Building a strong individual network

Why It Is Valuable: Everyone needs a strong network; it is imperative to their success. Individuals are known within their fiefdom (the area they work in/sell into); and as people progress outside that area and take on new challenges, they often don't know how to network in that space.

How It Works: Many people have not utilized this process before, and it holds them back from succeeding in their career. Knowing the influencers is crucial to being able to take the next steps. Get executives involved and let them see you in front of your customers as you have career conversations with them and continue to build your network.

Here is an example where someone may have an aspiration to have a different job: There are a number of steps to prepare for this move. First, find out who will approve the position and ask yourself if you have made it known that you have an interest in this job. The approvers are influenced by the people who surround them, and they need to look at this like a sales campaign. If you want to be able to capture this role within a certain time, you need the approver to understand your goals and capabilities, and you should make contact with this team to make your presence known. Share your qualifications and ask what the approver is looking for to fill the role. Make it clear with the person who is moving on that you are interested in assuming that role and get pointers from him or her. Think strategically and long term. Understand the playing field and who the influencers are who will help you achieve your goals.

Many people are fortunate to have influencers who are outside their domain. You need to spend time with these people to make sure they understand your role and what you want to accomplish so they can help spot opportunities for you. If you are solid inside, you will have opportunities.

If you are looking outside, you need to build your presence and your network there so you can execute a strategy with people of influence to get them to support you.

It's a great help if you can get a sponsor/champion to mentor you about your career and your blind spots and help get you in touch with other leaders and external influencers who can set you up for success.

You must do the hard work yourself and follow through and take action. When you see an open door and put your campaign in place, you must stay in contact. Come up with reasons to stay in front of people and build a system for making this happen so you don't have to reestablish contact at the last minute.

When your time comes and you have achieved success, pay it forward and hire those who can succeed so you can have a very positive impact; then mentor them and watch them move forward in their career. Go after top talent and bring in those who can potentially be stronger than you. Do what you can to give back.

45. Servient Leadership: What Do You Need to Master?
By Jack Schwartz

What the Idea Is: For the purpose of this discourse, let's start by agreeing to the basic definition of servient leadership: As leaders, we are here to help our employees be as successful as possible. We work to support their efforts that, as leaders, we need to align to our own corporate goals.

In order to help our team members drive their success, it is important to work with them individually and as a team. We need to build a culture of teamwork and shared vision.

From their perspective, we sales leaders burden our teams with sales plans, opportunity reviews, and QBRs. The typical internal agenda is for us to understand their business so we can report up the trends and forecasts. As servient leaders, we must ensure that these exercises are also valuable to the sales teams.

The intent is always good balance, where we get the information we require but also help sales teams build their executive relationships as well as identify and close opportunities. We need active engagement to support our teams with their clients.

Do you know your top ten to twenty clients' executives?

As an example, most reps fail to include the customer when they conduct an account planning session. Smart sales teams schedule time with the client in their own QBR. They cover what was accomplished for the client this quarter, what roadblocks or issues we ran into, other successes and issues or asks, etc. They also define the next steps we will be taking on their behalf for the next quarter or two. Eventually, as trust builds, the client collaborates by sharing their plans, initiatives, etc., as well as other areas where we can work with them. As sales leaders, we need to participate to help support the sales teams with the executive relationships.

This sets the stage for an internal opportunity review, which builds to a meaningful account QBR. QBRs drive success. When you collaborate on account plans and make conducting opportunity reviews a common practice, it drives standards into the culture. The key here is teamwork; it is about having a set of goals built around standards and around how you work together to achieve those goals.

Why It Is Valuable: It contributes to the success of the team by ensuring all angles have been looked at and all opportunities are being recognized. It invokes a higher level of confidence in where they are in a specific deal and what it takes to close (funnel management). It also contributes to a good culture of teamwork—one in which everyone feels his/her opinion is valued.

How It Works: Create supporting templates and forms to keep your team aligned on key metrics. The collaboration of identifying the opportunities together is the most important component.

- Templates should be about 90 percent the same for everyone.
- Once standards in documentation and document flow are in place, adhere to those standards.
- Commit to making this practice a standard operating procedure and follow through with it.

46. Keep a Good Network Going
By Jas Sood

What the Idea Is: Treat every relationship with importance, whether it's a formal one or just someone you have met along the way. Having a diverse network is crucial because, as we know, it takes a village to support each other with a variety of voices, expertise, and viewpoints to use as sounding boards for bouncing around different ideas.

Why It Is Valuable: A good network gives you a full 180-degree picture of something you want to implement, because you have access to different viewpoints that you may not have previously considered. For instance, speaking with a customer could yield unexpected viewpoints if you've only been considering the perspective of the salesperson.

How It Works: To begin creating a good network, you must:

- Find people in your ecosystem; learn from leaders in your organization or others who are in the know about the key touch points you need to make a strong connection with.
- Reach out and be open, honest, and collaborative in your efforts; then your actions will be well-received. You want to make sure it is more of a team environment than a competitive one.
- Nurture your network. You must continue doing this, even through job changes, relocations, and other events. It's good to reach out every so often to keep your touchpoints warm. Remember their special days, like birthdays, which is easy to do when you keep those dates in your contact data. Even a text is a special gift to many people. Share fond memories you have on special holidays like Thanksgiving and Christmas or during special sporting events, etc., or use any excuse just to say hello. Get to know the people in your network and know what is special to them, and always be sure to keep them in the forefront.
- Recognize them on social media when appropriate. Offer encouragement and share accomplishments. Support those who need it.

You can measure the strength and success of your network by the response you receive when you find yourself in a bind or a sticky situation. Are those you reach out to quick to respond and lend a hand? Your network should know the value of helping you; and if you've nurtured these relationships, they should be ready and willing to help out however they can.

By keeping a strong network, you build your own community. That community grows over time as you change jobs, locations, etc. because you are connected via other trusted sources. People you know in your network will willingly make new connections for you with people they know. The transfer of trust is key in making this happen.

47. Common-Sense Practices
By Jay Snyder

What the Idea Is: "Common-sense" practices to implement when coming into a leadership role within a national or global sales organization.

Why It Is Valuable: These practices give you some solid footing to move forward with a new team and establish standards so expectations are clearly understood by everyone, and they put systems and processes in place to create duplicatable actions. They also help win over the hearts of your new team members by involving them in the process.

How It Works:

- Have quarterly all-hands meetings. Make these a standard every quarter, and make them fun and informative, and take this opportunity to recognize individual and team success. Create an annual set of strategic priorities and update folks against them each quarter.

- Set up weekly one-on-ones with all your direct and matrix reports, and **don't talk forecast**; talk anything but—talk about people, career, company, or strategy; seek input, get feedback/give feedback; and, most importantly, ask what you can do to help them.

- Set up every other week one-on-ones with key support folks, including teams such as alliances and channels, marketing, finance, HR, etc. (This is the same concept as above.)

- Ask every one of your VPs and/or regional sales leaders for their top high-potential sales folks (managers and reps), and then set up a one-on-one time with each one individually to get to know them, ask how you can help, ask what has made them successful, and ensure they have a good mentor in the company. (Show you are invested in them.)

- Ask each of your VPs and/or regional sales leaders for one to two accounts that are must-win, must-grow, or critically strategic, and get personally engaged. Attend all sorts of meetings, even if they are with the janitor. Take an active role to personally understand the key customers in the geography you're responsible for.

- Write an email (bi-weekly) that is "from the field" that contains your personal stories about the accounts you are engaged in, have met with, etc.; how your company is delivering value and driving its business; and why your company is critical to their success. (Inspire with your own touch.)

- Think about starting newsletter. I often do something such as "Impact of the Week," which gives you a chance to highlight wins and best practices and an opportunity to recognize people.

These common-sense practices really worked well for me and won over the hearts and minds of the crew.

48. IC Fridays
By Jay Snyder

What The Idea Is: I call it "IC Fridays." Each Friday on my drive to and from the office, I call two to four individual contributors in the organization. They could be sales reps, presales, alliances, or support in my direct hierarchy or matrix, or they may even support the business in my region but report to someone else. Often I may not even know the folks. (One of my organizations had over 5,000 people.) I spend about twenty to thirty minutes getting to know them—what they do, what they enjoy, and what ideas they have for making things better—and I ask how I can help them be more successful in their current role or career.

Why It Is Valuable: I always say, "The best ideas come from the field," and every conversation I have validates that. If I take any actions or "to do's" to follow up on during the call, I make it a point to close the call out with what's been done. With these calls, I accomplish several things: 1) I get great feedback on things to do (usually if one person is feeling something, it's likely that many others are too), 2) I stay connected to the organization, 3) I create a culture of a "servant leader," where my teams know I'm interested in their best interest and go the extra mile to help them succeed, 4) I build loyalty, and 5) I inspire the teams. In every organization I've done this in, after a few weeks or a month of practice, the phone calls go from, "Jay Snyder! Uh-oh, am I getting fired?" to "Jay Snyder! Is this my one-on-one call? I'm so excited! I've heard about these and was hoping I might get a call."

How It Works: I partner with human resources to help generate a rotating list of individuals to ensure I go across function and across geography and get a diverse set of inputs and actions.

Special Tribute: Anne Jaggars was my HR business partner when we came up with and implemented the IC Friday idea. I remember it like it was yesterday. Shortly thereafter, she was diagnosed with leukemia, and it was a horrible battle that eventually took her life much too young. The last thing we (a group of sales leaders) were able to do for Anne was hire a private plane and fly her to her daughter's wedding (she was too ill to travel commercially). She died shortly after that.

49. Driving Continuous Sales Transformation
By Jeff Casale

What the Idea Is: Driving continuous sales transformation

Why It Is Valuable: A key characteristic of any high-performing sales organization is consistent execution—the ability to drive predictable results quarter after quarter. These organizations are maniacal about tracking metrics, creating playbooks, and following disciplined sales methodologies such as MEDDIC.

The challenge is that the same process that creates such predictable results can also produce a resistance to warning signs that the landscape is shifting. It can create blind spots as the customer priorities evolve and competitors gain traction with compelling but new-use cases.

Ultimately, sales teams begin missing their numbers, which results in stress and confusion mixed with finger pointing between product and sales teams. An inevitable "reset" happens as the strategy is evaluated and ultimately modified based on the new reality.

The alternative is to create a culture of "continuous sales transformation" as an additional characteristic of the GTM function. This can be easily implemented and will provide a mechanism to capture the "leading indicators" that there is a potential shift taking place. There are additional benefits as the process becomes a development opportunity, allowing key players to become part of the future GTM strategy.

How It Works: Start with a small working group made up of a cross section of your GTM team. This can work regardless of whether it's a 100-person start-up or a multi-billion-dollar company. Ideally, you want to have a representative from both sales and presales and to the extent possible add other functions, such as customer success, consulting, alliances, etc.

Reiterate to the team the existing GTM strategy as well as the current state and expected future state. Keep it simple. If you can't easily explain it with one slide, then ask for one from your CEO that was created for a board deck or other analyst/fundraising meeting. (If no one has one, then you may have your first leading indicator of an issue!) Share the slide with the team and then share the existing quarterly goals and metrics. Then ask three questions:

1. What are the challenges to achieving the future state?
2. What could we be doing differently to increase our ability to be successful?
3. What are we doing today that we should stop doing?

The questions are both simple and purposely broad. The intent for the first two questions is to identify early signs of challenge and opportunity and create metrics to track those. Think of this as a more agile versus a waterfall approach. They don't have to be perfect, but they should be easily implemented and easily discarded after a few months if they are not useful.

The third question is intended to help you understand what part of your execution machine is already off track and pushing you in the wrong direction. It is equally important to understand where you don't want to spend your time and energy.

50. Adding Value to the Role of Partnership in the One-to-One Category
By Jeff McCullough

What the Idea Is: Partnering gives you extension and reach beyond what you could normally afford for your own workforce. Partners bring the bodies to accomplish the work, along with the relationships those bodies bring, the logistical processes, and the financial services to expand your organization's opportunities.

A company's DNA might not support the act of partnering, and this can be a struggle for some. Learning the value and logistics of partnering gives you an important skill set regardless of the industry. Partnership selling is a critical way to consistently reach a broader set of customers with more wide-ranging capability than you could on your own.

Simply put, many companies that started direct plateaued at a point where the cost exceeded the value of the process. EMC started as direct, but they had to quickly engage and work with partners. Dell started as a direct-to-consumer company and resisted the partner selling model for years until market demands forced them to adopt a partner strategy.

Partnering helps companies move past this plateau. Amazon Web Services is a great modern model of that. To gain access to the customers they want, AWS has adopted partner programs as partners bring those critical relationships to the table. As the company sees that plateau and a need to gain access to larger customers, they need to break through to another set of partners to take them further.

Why It Is Valuable: Partnering extends your sales organization. When it's working well, you will see growth year over year. More insightfully, you will see pipeline development; you can see how much business is coming from your channel and how much business is coming from your own sales team. It gives you better insight on your ROI in total. The real value you are looking at is what do partners bring to the table? What is your margin rate, compared to others? Are they discounting until they get to "yes"? Close rate would be another metric, as well as speed to close. Reps and training status add other factors that are good indicators.

How It Works: Define what your channel **value proposition** is. Why should a partner care about working with you, when there are so many other opportunities out there? Partnering brings choices to the table. Customers go to partners for choice. They represent many products; and they can do competitive comparison with their products, so you need to define your value proposition that would let you rise to the top and be "product of choice." Think about how you differentiate yourself, and therefore your partner. How can you help them increase their sales velocity with your offering? Can you help them close their pipeline faster? Increase their pipeline? Develop new business that they would not have otherwise have access to? How much revenue can they make? What is their return? A great channel value proposition answers these questions.

There is also the question of distribution partners. These partners can help you on your channel journey by increasing access to more partners.

What is the advantage of going direct to find your partners vs. distribution partners? Most companies will start with their direct-to-partner model. They get the partner on board, train their sales reps, train technical experts who can talk more specifically to the product, and help the customer by understanding their problem and offering solutions.

At a certain point, adding a distributor network will help take some of the work off your plate while giving you access to more partners. The distributor can also take on financial benefits to provide for your partners, which can be a big help. From a growth standpoint, if you can demonstrate a set percentage of growth year over year, some would say keep doing what you are doing (until you slow down). Others would say that this is a great time to get more distributors onboard, while things are going well. It takes the pressure off when this partner is already in place.

You would need to create a single-tier or multi-tier financial model, as well as a channel P&L so you can illustrate the benefits to the partner. Margin is the main factor, and rebates are another incentive. You can influence the value chain by balancing the front end (margin) and the backend (rebates) to dial in the right incentives and rewards to touch the different key players (reps vs. owners) in your partners.

There are channel leaders and consultancies that can help you execute this type of relationship. They can help you:

- Define your value prop
- Develop your business model
- Create the program you need to become a partner
- Identify the benefits for the partner
- Define how you can provide support for the partner
- Determine how you will be differentiated from the rank and file that are not delivering the value you can

51. Virtualization of the Selling Process
By Jeff McCullough

What the Idea Is: The tech industry has been built on a model where the manufacturer builds the product, which is then shipped to a warehouse and kept there until the distributor has a customer to sell it to. Now, the product is sold possibly even before production, and it goes directly to the client. As virtual marketplaces (Amazon for physical items and AWS for applications and computer services) take hold, the cloud vendor holds the key to accessing these transactions. Adopting your business to work in the virtual world, whether you make a physical item, a software product, or a service, is critical to your success. For businesses that rely on partner selling models, your partners are at risk of being replaced by a website and a credit card.

Why It Is Valuable: Remember the saying made famous by Wayne Gretzky, "Skate to where the puck is going, not to where it has been"? Changes are coming rapidly! The cloud has been a major market disruptor, starting with wide-spread adoption of AWS in 2010 and the launch of Microsoft Azure in 2012. The reality is that things that people once held most important—like having big offices in big buildings—are not what is needed today to keep a business moving.

There will always be things to sell; but in the technology space, consumables are now on the periphery and customers are more in the virtual bucket. It has become increasingly important to modernize the proposition for the cloud era. Ask, *Where is the best value to invest my dollar? Is my traditional route to market effective and getting a good margin? What is the sales cycle? Can I reduce a sixty-day cycle to thirty days, a thirty-day cycle to fifteen, ten, or five days? One hour? Virtualized solutions can be sold instantly. How does my sales network compete in this space?*

How It Works: The partnering model will be shifting over the next couple of years, where a partner's value will be less about getting access to a product to getting access to people and services that *know* about the product and help you use it. The risk does not stop there, though. IT services are becoming virtual, and your partners face the risk of being replaced by AI and different technology advances.

You must make sure you are aligning with partners that can collaborate and sell in a virtualized space (i.e., sell the services/outcomes, not a "product"). They must offer services that can provide great outcomes, like reducing costs or looking at different application platforms that will lower the cost of some portion(s) for the provider. Are your partners investing in people? Are they standing up service offerings that complement your products? Are you creating service opportunities with your product for partners to sell?

The big challenge is how do you attach your own IP to this outcome? How do you ignite your partners' ability to deliver their own value in the services you want them to sell? It's a matter of being great at helping your partners sell their own products/services around what you are trying to sell to a customer who has a lot of options.

52. Building a Territory Revenue Plan (TRP)
By Jeff Miller

What the Idea Is: Building a Territory Revenue Plan (TRP)

Why It Is Valuable: It effectively drives productivity across the whole field.

How It Works: This is the foundational key to how you as a rep should run your franchise. It is the territory management, daily driving, and stack ranking of your accounts that will help guide you in qualifying a prospect and developing your business plan for each potential sale.

Say you have 100 accounts. Research those accounts, reference them against like-minded customers to verticalize and understand the buyer in the market, and then sell into that market. Next, get an understanding of the customers that have a propensity to spend, figure out what their IT budgets are, determine what their CIO objectives will be and whether they are public, review and understand their 10Ks, and review their board mandates and other factors.

Using a Google Doc, a spreadsheet, or a system software that allows for continual adjustment by people accessing the document, stack rank the accounts into three levels, categorizing them either numerically or alphabetically. Adding a color for each rank helps you achieve a quick glance snapshot without having to look at a lot of detail. Determine what makes an "A" an "A" and so on—size of account, type of revenue, impact to your bottom line, and/or any other criteria that define your company's success.

Now build out how the prospect fits into the key factors for your business. Here are some typical success factors that will help you determine what rank they would fall into on your system:

1. Fortune ranking

2. Vertical they serve

3. Whether they have engaged/penetrated the account

4. The requirements for your particular business (i.e. database)

5. Differentiators

6. Your key business drivers (to ensure they are looking at the right factors)

7. Whether they have the right propensity to buy

8. Who their cloud provider is

9. The incumbent technology base

10. Their sphere of influence—the partner ecosystem that surrounds that customer

11. Who you would likely sell with that allows the customer to deploy more—hardware provider, access to power, access to spending, etc.

12. Their internal account champion

13. The person who has the authority to sign off on a deal

14. Their success criteria

    a. Roll four quarters of potential revenue. It may begin with zero if it's a new account. Where do you forecast that revenue to be in renewals, etc? You should have this for every account.

There will probably be somewhere around twenty A's, thirty B's and fifty C's.

Next Steps:

It may take you three to six months to completely fill out all the information in this process. It will continue to evolve with each contact and interaction. A "C" may turn into an "A" as you get more information, or they may go from an "A" to a "C," based on new information that comes in during the qualifying processes.

A sales leader would want to have a tab for everyone in the region (area) to track all progress under his/her lead. This is helpful when you want to identify accounts, drive quarterly business reviews, and for your meetings.

This is an internal document for capacity planning, and building bones for a start-up. Look at your color framework. Do you need to go higher, add heads where they can be productive, or move accounts as needed to get the most productivity? See what has had activity and what needs to be moved or adjusted to meet your objectives.

You can then build your success plan with the client as a result of the information gathered.

53. Life on the High Wire: Questions to Ask When Thinking of Joining a Start-Up
By Jennifer Haas

What the Idea Is: Questions to ask and things to consider when thinking of joining a start-up.

Why It Is Valuable: Joining a start-up is very different from joining a large company. Start-ups move quicker, provide hands-on opportunities to build skills rapidly, and often involve equity ownership. They can also involve more risk than a larger, established company. When choosing a start-up to join, it is important to ask the right questions and do your due diligence to make sure your risk is calculated. Make sure you get everything in writing.

How It Works:

1. How much experience does the founder (or founders) have? Make sure you are comfortable with his/her experience level. Look into the founder's background and talk to any contacts you may have in common.

2. Ask to see the board packet, financials, and statement of operations.

3. Would you be the first executive hired?

4. How is it funded? By whom is it funded?

5. What was the company's last funding round?

6. How much money have they raised?

7. Are they past the MVP (minimum viable product) stage? How mature is the product?

8. Do they have any customers? How many?

9. Do they have revenue? How much?

10. How many employees do they have? Contractors?

11. What is the average tenure of their employees? What is their employee turnover rate?

12. What is their burn rate? How many months of cash do they have in the bank?

13. Talk to a few other people at the company—board members, executives, etc.

14. Why is the position vacant? Expansion? Replacement?

15. What are the goals for the role? What does success look like? Define the KPIs.

16. What is the career path? Make sure this role will allow you to meet your career goals.

17. Will you be running a P&L? This experience is important if you want to hold a C-Suite role in the future.

18. What is the company's exit plan?

19. What is the executive compensation package? Ask about:
   a. Base
   b. OTE
   c. 401K
   d. Benefits
   e. Vacation
   f. Exit package/golden parachute (change of control, involuntary, voluntary)
   g. Forward acceleration clause for stock on change of ownership
   h. Guarantee for ramp period (three to four months)

54. The Three Ships: Mentorship/Sponsorship/Leadership
By Jennifer Haas

What the Idea Is: The three ships: Mentorship, Sponsorship, and Leadership

Why It Is Valuable: Throughout various stages in your career, you will require various types of support. Sometimes coaching or guidance is most beneficial, and other times you may just need an opportunity to develop, practice, or showcase a skillset. These kinds of support are all valuable. It is also important to give back, pull others up, and help build the next generation of leaders when you have the opportunity.

How It Works:

Mentorship
Keep your network strong. As you connect with people in your career, keep in touch with them. Reach out to leaders outside of your team who are a few steps ahead of you in their careers. Ask for advice. Return the favor by mentoring others. Be good to people and think of ways to give to others. If you have a recruiter call you with a good job opportunity that you are going to pass on, refer him or her to someone in your network who is looking. Pay it forward.

Sponsorship
Find leaders you trust and ask them to keep you in mind for projects and opportunities to grow and diversify your skillset. Make sure your work and your results are exemplary. Let people know when you have achieved notable results.

Leadership
As you are looking to grow your career, it is very important to look for opportunities to lead—whether it's projects, people, or strategy. This allows you to showcase and grow your skill set as well as get noticed by people who can further your career and may need your talents. Always be growing your skill set—read, take classes, ask questions, and be curious. All

colleges have executive education courses in leadership, finance, technology, etc. Take advantage of them. Never stop learning, and make sure you apply your new skillset in your current role or find a volunteer opportunity to practice and cement your new skills. Look for ways to help develop the next generation of leaders.

55. Top Tips for Sales Professionals
By Jesse Ouellette

Tip No. 1:
What the Idea Is: Sell your products and services as a low-to-mid 4 rating online out of 5.

Why It Is Valuable: By selling your products and services like they are perfect, you drive your buyers to go find the flaws.

How It Works: Lead with authenticity and transparency in all aspects of the sale, and your buyers will come to you. People love to buy but hate to be sold.

Tip No. 2:
What the Idea Is: Too many sales professionals focus on only a rational impact, such as an ROI, value metric, or cost justification.

Why It Is Valuable: If there is no emotional impact, the person will not push to make the purchase.

How It Works: Focus your attention on finding your buyers' emotional impact.

Tip No. 3:
What the Idea Is: Technology can amplify success or failure in sales professionals.

Why It Is Valuable: Focus on the process before you invest in technology and doing more of something.

How It Works: A great process is amplified by technology; a bad one amplifies failure. Many reps use technology to amplify a bad process.

Tip No. 4:
What the Idea Is: Don't focus just on sales; marketing is just as important.

Why It Is Valuable: Having a single point of failure brings a system down if it falls.

How It Works: Measure on performance and conversion versus more results and effort.

56. Identifying Buyers Looking for Sellers
By Jim Ball

What the Idea Is: Today's market is increasingly becoming "buyers looking for sellers," and if companies and individuals don't adjust their approach, they will miss out on many opportunities to compete for and win business. We are a small- to medium-size company, and roughly 80 percent of our sales opportunities come from clients looking for solutions who are finding us. Clients now want to purchase complex enterprise solutions in a similar manner to how they purchase consumer goods—by initially evaluating the technology and business proposition without the face-to-face interaction that many good sales professionals have become accustomed to over the years. Once identified and "screened" by the client, we typically see clients wanting to have WebEx presentations and product demonstrations delivered electronically.

You meet this challenge by developing your company/product website to be user friendly. It should have an easily accessible means of bidirectional communications (chat link, email contacts for questions, etc.) so clients can reach you to ask questions to further qualify the technical and business value of your company/solution.

Why It Is Valuable: This approach allows you to identify clients who are unseen, waiting to be discovered. Again, we see about 80 percent of our sales opportunities derived from buyers looking for sellers, including the very largest government agencies, commercial entities (healthcare, financial, technology, service providers, etc.), and national and international entities.

These methods have made us much more efficient and offer us the opportunity to appeal to a much wider audience (geographically) and have greater attendance from clients at our meetings. It has also improved our time to closure for opportunities. We close multimillion dollar deals without ever physically seeing the clients.

Company websites are just one method of electronic communications. Salespeople have to be engaged with prospective clients through social media (LinkedIn, Sales Community, Instagram, Facebook, etc.) to maximize their productivity and to reach clients.

How It Works: You must keep your website tuned with the latest information regarding your company, products, and sales contacts. There must be a method to measure the effectiveness of the site. You can usually do this by using tools like Google Analytics to determine if the site is gaining viewership or by looking at the trends for the number of qualified leads coming through initial contact from the website. If your leads are not growing, you need to tweak your site visually or with new, updated content that attracts the key words buyers are using to find sellers.

It cannot be overstated how critical the use of our website to locate buyers is for the success of our company. We have literally received $10,000,000 + size opportunities from qualified buyers who find us; our direct sales efforts pale in comparison. Our sales people become much more important after we turn over a lead.

57. Brand Identity/Brand Leadership
By Jim Hart

What the Idea Is: Brand identity is a salesperson's trademark. You can create your brand identity by asking yourself:

- What are you best known for?
- What is your management style?
- How are you perceived by your customers? Your peers?
- Most importantly, what makes you stand out from a crowded talent pool?

Why It Is Valuable: We all have a brand identity in both our personal and professional lives. It's how others view us, perceive us, and draw opinions about us as individuals. It's what we've developed as our own style, skill set, and talent from within. We live in a world where people buy from people they like and trust. Creating a trademark or brand identity allows for you as a successful sales person to be memorable. It helps create awareness of your strengths. It also enables you to create a legacy to be remembered by after your career is over (i.e., he/she was known as a storyteller … a great networker … a valued leader … a problem solver … a person who really cared … someone who understood the financials well, etc.).

How It Works: The important thing to remember as you're creating your brand identity is to be *yourself* and start with an à-la-carte menu—meaning, you are who you are. Your style and brand have been developed over the years, most likely with influence from others you've dealt with in business—a peer, a partner, a customer, someone you valued as a good leader, etc. We tend to morph into who we are plus who we desire to be more like. For example, the brand I've developed over my career includes much of who I am, both professionally and personally; but, I've also picked up a few things along the way from others I've admired or whose characteristics I wanted to develop into my own style. Copy the homework. Your brand should be a cumulation of great experiences, great people, and great talent you've encountered along the way. In return, your brand and legacy will be an inspiration and influence to others.

58. Reverse Timeline
By Jim Murphy

What the Idea Is: A big idea that has helped my business is the concept of an agreed-upon project *reverse timeline*. If you can get the customer to agree to the date they want to start recognizing value from your solution, you can build out all the necessary steps that have to happen in order to achieve the stated goal.

Why It Is Valuable: It is valuable because you find out pretty quickly if the prospect is really interested in relieving their pain or if they are just shopping around. Is there enough pain for them to pick a date to get started? Do they agree to these five to ten steps that need to happen in order to achieve the shared deadline?

How It Works: You work with the prospect to identify the date by which they want to be deployed and start realizing value. Together, you identify the necessary steps to get there—NDAs, legal docs, POVs, procurement paperwork, reference calls, request for budget, executive presentations, orders, shipping, installation, etc. If a prospect isn't willing to agree to a detailed timeline like this, then they are unlikely to buy (or at least buy within the fiscal quarter/year).

59. Use MEDDICC to Sell More
By Jim Sullivan

What the Idea Is: Use MEDDICC to sell more.

Why It Is Valuable: If you have a good product and/or service, relationships are extremely important. You must have a repeatable, value-based, proven sales process that is not overly cumbersome to help a client be successful.

How It Works: Over the years, I have partnered with Force Management, whose repeatable, thorough, and simple-to-use MEDDICC sales methodology helps you improve your win rate.

These slides explain the Force Management process:

Slide 1: MEDDICC: Go through these items as a checklist when working a relationship with a client.

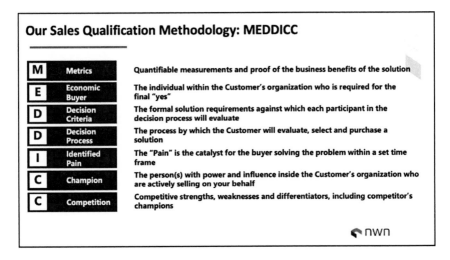

Slide 2: Qualify the customer with a value-based conversation. Ask these questions:

- What are your goals?
- What are your ideal business outcomes?
- What are the required capabilities to make this work?
- How will you measure your successes?

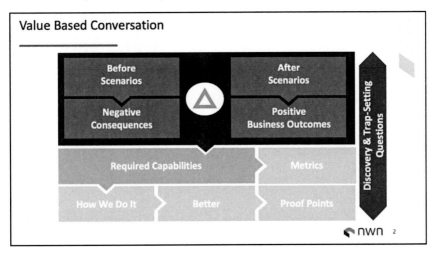

Slide 3: Go back and share what you heard the customer say to you, along with your feedback with what he or she can expect to experience in the future by using your product/services, and share the differentiators between your company and other organizations.

The Mantra – The Ultimate Summation

- "What I hear you saying Mr./Ms. Customer is that these are the *Positive Business Outcomes* you're trying to achieve…
- In order to achieve these positive business outcomes, we agreed that these are the *Required Capabilities* you're going to need…
- And you'll probably want to measure these required capabilities using these *Metrics*…
- Let me tell you *How We Do It*…
- Let me tell you *How We Do It Better/Differently*…
- But don't take my word for it.. *(Proof Points)*"

nwn

Slide 4: This is a simple illustration of your key points to all the relevant parts of the equation. You can add the appropriate bullets for each of the boxes to easily outline your key statements.

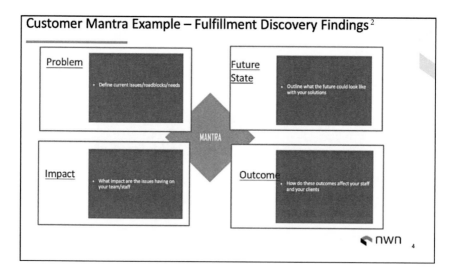

Customer Mantra Example – Fulfillment Discovery Findings[2]

Problem
- Define current issues/roadblocks/needs

Future State
- Outline what the future could look like with your solutions

MANTRA

Impact
- What impact are the issues having on your team/staff

Outcome
- How do these outcomes affect your staff and your clients

nwn 4

60. The Five Pillars for Building Your Best Salesperson Avatar
By Joe Flanagan

What the Idea Is: There are five basic characteristics that make up the best salesperson avatar in this industry.

Why It Is Valuable: Finding these five characteristics in the person you hire will give you the best person for any type of sales position:

THE **5** PILLARS

1. POSITIVE ATTITUDE
2. ASK GOOD QUESTIONS
3. SHUT UP AND LISTEN
4. PRODUCT KNOWLEDGE
5. GRIT

1. An undying positive attitude. This is the most important characteristic, because it is what people respond to the most; a positive attitude keeps you going. If you have the right attitude, you are one step closer to the next yes. You must live it and feel it.

2. Exceptional at the art of asking good questions. Anyone who has had some success knows it is not what you say; it is about asking the right questions and listening. Then the prospects will tell you what they want—their priorities and desired outcomes—and you will easily be able to get the correct information.

3. Ability to shut up and listen: Do you have the patience and the discipline to ask and shut up? Allow your prospect to tell you the road map that will show you where you need to go.

4. Understanding of the product: Know why this prospect would want your product/services. Be able to clearly articulate their value and uniqueness.

5. Grit. The salesperson must have the toughness, the willingness, and the discipline to do it over and over again.

How It Works: Hire to these criteria. Using assessments (such as the Wonderlic Evaluation, used by the NFL) helps create a better hiring process. Also have the candidates take a sales aptitude test and a GRIT test.

I suggest that you be very disciplined in the use of CRM, as well as SalesForce. Tracking the activities that take place with each prospect will tell you if you are succeeding.

We developed a call cadence that is effective in the inside sales world. "Front Spin" is one software we use; it allows you to create and craft a roadmap for the sale, which then allows you to build the cadences inside, laid over the CRM, and it does the work for you.

61. When Clients/Customers Are Ready to Buy
By John Clavin

What the Idea Is: Sales teams often include highly technical and intellectual people such as engineers, product managers, portfolio managers, etc. who are aligned with the product and/or service being sold and are passionate about its features. (They may have even actually invented the product/offering). However, they often miss the impact that the offering can make to the prospective client/customer's organization/business.

Why It Is Valuable: I received this advice from Walter Brown, and it is highlighted in his book *Chasing Quota*. His advice is applicable to any sales person, and I have found it particularly useful when selling with teams of highly technical and intellectual people.

How It Works: To help these individuals understand when these prospective clients/customers are ready to move forward with a "deal," I explain to them the following:

Clients/customers "buy" when they can answer the following three questions:

1. Why do it?
2. Why do it now?
3. Why do it with you?

62. Taking an Organization from Early Stage/ Turmoil Through Turn-Around
By John "Jake" Cleveland

What the Idea Is: Taking an organization from an early stage/turmoil status through a turn-around (applies to a wide array of scenarios, from start-ups to companies with a lot of cash on hand)

Why It Is Valuable: It helps the teams understand that a sales rep is not a single player; there are many others involved in the successful execution of a go-to- market (GTM) plan.

How It Works: The Four A's:

ASSESS: Look at the talent you are dealing with, the offering you have, and the territory you are working with, and understand those pieces; then develop a GTM plan that allows for successful execution. You may have to adjust personnel, your expectations, and the timeframe for achieving your GTM plan, as well as where you should focus your resources based on the success/failure of your target use cases. Then rethink your target audience and determine how territory alignment and a channel strategy can enable market-share growth. Here are some questions you should consider:

- What are your current product capabilities versus your roadmap, and how engaged are you with your product marketing and engineering teams?
- What is your internal pre/post-sales-support capability?
- What type of GTM coverage model can you afford today versus in the future?
- Should you leverage alternative channels to achieve your goals faster?
- How well known are your organization and offering?
- Are you leveraging social media?
- Are your use case and value easily understood, or do you need to spend valuable cycles positioning them?
- Do you have the sales and technical content to support your team/channel?
- In today's new world of selling, do you have the capability to reach your target audience, or do you need to leverage external resources?
- How well do you lead development—internal versus external—and can you afford not to?

Regardless of how you answer these questions, don't try to expand too fast and dilute yourself. Understand the motivation, capability, and available cycles of each team and each team member; just because something worked for you doesn't mean it will work for everyone. Once you create the plan, move into the Assist area.

ASSIST: It's about communication—making sure everyone, not just your sales teams, understands where you want to go and what changes are needed to get there. People must understand this is now the direction you are going; and once the decision is made, it's no longer open for debate. It's time to execute. Then you need to be an active participant in those changes. This is where coaching comes into the mix. The most successful way to achieve change is to communicate, over-communicate, and communicate again. Be in front of the desk, not behind it. Be part of the activity. As you deploy, move to the Adjust area.

ADJUST: Adjust as needed the go-to-market activities based on your learnings, your progress in some areas that are resulting in sales, and your understanding of whether you have the right talent for where you are in your product life cycle. Refine your awareness campaigns and customer facing content based on your findings. Don't be afraid to make adjustments, no matter how painful they may seem. Remember that no matter how good someone is, a person who is not working in conjunction with the plan will hurt your ability to execute, and that must be dealt with immediately. Now move into the Achieve area.

ACHIEVE: It is critical that you achieve the goals you have set. Success can breed success within the team just as easily as failure can destroy a team and its morale. Make sure you don't overset the goals to appease others above you; they can be a stretch, but they must be achievable, or they will not create a positive momentum. Along the whole way, you must recognize and reward milestones every week to make sure you spend time on the positive, rather than the negative. There is a time for talking about when things are not working; there is also a time for building moments to help create the ups. People have to want to come to work and get through the issues, share their successes, and be motivated to continue on to succeed; if your team is motivated, you will reap the rewards of success!

63. Leverage Cloud Marketplaces
John Jahnke

What the Idea Is: Leverage cloud marketplaces to give your sellers easy contracts and pathways to big budget (cloud budgets).

Why It Is Valuable: It gives you a way to sell digitally to your buyers. You can do organic user-led/user-discovered purchases all the way up to private offers where you use marketplace as a mechanism for fulfillment. As more and more budget races to the clouds, more and more buyers are starting to buy via marketplaces.

How It Works: Become a partner of AWS, Azure, or GCP, sign a marketplace seller agreement, and then contact Tackle.io, who eliminates all the engineering work required to start your marketplace journey as a software seller.

64. Sales Words of Wisdom
By John Judge

What the Idea Is: Sales words of wisdom

Why It Is Valuable: Applying these nuggets of wisdom will help you be a better leader and sell more.

How It Works:

Interviewing

You need to show that you have a history of being "chosen," and that the people who chose you looked good because of it. Weaving this into your dialog in an interview not only shows the interviewer that they are "not alone" in selecting you as a candidate, but also that they could be the beneficiary of moving their personal career along by choosing you!

Difficult Conversations

Leaders need to embrace the hard conversations, know how to start them, and know how to make them productive. Avoidance of difficult conversations trades short-term discomfort for long-term dysfunction. I have a methodology and training on how to embrace difficult conversations.

Promote from Within

BDRs should become sales reps. Reps should be promoted to team leaders, team leaders should be promoted to managers, and so on. Creating a culture where career growth is not only a priority but a visible reality improves engagement and tenure and limits new-hire mistakes.

98 Percent Meritocracy and 2 Percent Dictatorship

For several years I've made a proclamation about how I plan to run any team I'm responsible for. For the vast majority of time, best ideas, best work, and best results will rule the day, no matter who you are. If you are engaged, work hard, and deliver results, you will be noticed. Every once in a while I have to be a leader, make a call, and expect the team to fall in line. I don't do that often; but when I do, it's the law.

Objection Handling

I have a proven methodology for handling objections that works. (I got much of it by pulling from the ideas of many others.) Here it is: acknowledge-clarify-collect-challenge-redirect or reply.

Instrument Your Business

What are your leading indicators to success? Find a way to measure them. Know the conversion metrics (demo to close, etc.) for the team and for every individual on the team. Publish them with full transparency. Data then drives your coaching. You'll have more predictability to your marketing and sales funnel. It must be automated in your CRM—*no* spreadsheets!

Take the Time to Show You Care

You especially need to do this during the COVID-19 pandemic; however, it's always needed in a well-run team. Do the right thing, and you earn trust. Do your best every day, and you will demonstrate a commitment to excellence. And don't just take the time to show you care about your people because they crush quota, but also because they are human beings who appreciate being cared for.

65. Organizing Your Time and Schedule
By John McCarthy

What the Idea Is: Organization of your time and schedule is essential.

Why It Is Valuable: Organization saves your brain for deep cerebral contemplation, strategy, productivity, etc. that are essential to track and act on in a timely manner. Do not waste your capabilities trying to remember mundane or minuscule tasks.

How It Works: Thirty years ago, while attending an EMC training and education sales meeting, I happened to fill one of my optional tracks by walking into a Franklin Daily Planner meeting; it changed my professional career.

The concept was simple: write everything down. Capture life's details, both professional and personal, in your planner in a notes or reminder section. Keep these records to review and refer to over time as needed. Obviously, over my career Franklin Daily Planners have been replaced with digital tools, but I still utilize a mix of 80/20 digital to written.

Thoughts

Organization = efficiency = productivity = effective time utilization. Time is the critical element. You can't create more hours in a day or more days in a week, but you can improve what you do with your time.

I'm not impressed with hard workers; I am impressed with smart workers.

There is no one silver bullet. It's the little things that add up to success. The glue—the accelerator of building sales success—includes attention to detail, timeliness, urgency, and professionalism; the need to react with accuracy is critical.

66. Five Best Practices for World-Class Sales-to-Presales Relationships and Performance
By KC Choi

What the Idea Is: In my thirty-plus years of doing presales—from being just one salesperson to leading global teams—I have learned a few things along the way about what makes world-class teams: motivated and well-trained talent who are eager to delight customers and achieve breakthrough performance. (By the way, I've always hated that term *presales,* so from this point forward I'll refer to those in the profession as solutions engineers or solution architects.)

Why It Is Valuable: Much to my surprise, solutions have become more complex, not less complex, over my thirty-five years in technology. This may not necessarily be true in terms of pure technical complexity, or "speeds and feeds." However, the ability to tie together everything from the edge-to-core-to-cloud to the on-premise versus hybrid cloud with a focus on business outcomes is a tall order for any sales organization. It's more important than ever for the roles and responsibilities of these two complementary functions to be better articulated, leveraged, and optimized. Before I get to that, let's focus on three basics—training, compensation and recognition.

How It Works:

- Training. In my experience, 90 percent of the best SAs/SEs are motivated first and foremost by knowing they are the best trained and educated for the job at hand. Yes, money/compensation plans are important, but not as important as having the latest certification, hands-on expertise, and the ability to demonstrate that expertise. It's not only their personal knowledge that's vital; it's also their ability to tap into a deep well of knowledge from their peers, mentors, R&D functions, and shared services. If sales has a dollar to invest, I would spend 60 percent of it on training/education. (See below my recommendation for the other 40 percent.)

- Incentives. Yes, SEs/SAs love to make money (who doesn't?), but most love what they do because they are "geeks" at heart. They love the tech, the pace of tech, and the feel of tech. The best incentives I have seen are those associated with this passion. Instead of money, give out something that is rare in tech—a signed iPad from Woz, a rare Sony PlayStation 5, a few laps around the track at racing school, etc. This kind of reward coming with a nomination by the sales team/account leader really seals the love bond between the teams. Some of the best incentive programs I have done through the years had all these characteristics. Spend 20 percent of the available sales investment on this. Advise your sales partners (ISVs and third parties) to do the same.

- Recognition. Everyone loves to be called out. For the account executive, it's about the big deal, the marquee customer, the big transformation.

For the SE/SA, it's about architecting the best solution to work as it should. For senior SEs/SAs it should be about helping those with less knowledge or with less experience to be better. Recognize sales leadership often and with precision—the same precision these technical sales professionals demand of themselves and the products they are representing. Do so, and you will be rewarded with a wing-woman/man who will not leave your side. Spend the balance of sales investment (20 percent) on this.

- Role-playing (putting yourself in difficult situations). I can't stress enough the importance of doing this as a team. It's not enough for individual endorsements. Sales is a team sport, and practicing as a team under the witness of a jury of your peers is essential. Plan as if every sales engagement is an EBC (executive briefing center) level event. Analyze feedback from customers and your peers from every EBC event. Do as many as you can; set a quarterly goal. If you just have one account, set a goal for how many LOB/functions you will reach. Practice the art of finishing each other's thoughts before you start and finishing each other's sentences.

- Leverage your entire portfolio of SE/SA functions. When I first started my SE career at IBM and then Compaq, it was a one-to-one or one-to-few mapping. The idea of an account manager having "my SE" was prevalent. I still see some of this today. The reality, or optimal reality, is that the art of system engineering/solutions architecture is a function, not a person. Many teams I have built and led include tremendous shared service functions that optimize costs, skills, and location; make the field teams more productive and responsive; and look "bigger" than they actually are. These are not "outsourced" teams but are fully included in the team structure. Also, solution center and inside SE/SA teams are critical in delivering customer value. Make sure you use them at the right time—especially your solution center resources—as they should be used early in the cycle (demo) or for heavy lifting (POC), but only if needed. Avoid POCs if at all possible, unless it's a true "proof of concept." Most concepts have already been proven; re-use what's already been done. These teams should be on your account organizational charts, team calls, and meetings. I can't tell you how important they have been to the success of the organization I have had the honor of leading.

I hope these experiences generate better outcomes for you in the age-old symbiosis of sales and presales. (I still hate that term.)

67. The Power of a Follow-up Email Process
By Keith Roseland-Barnes

What the Idea Is: Harnessing the power of a follow-up email process.

Why It Is Valuable: This process accomplishes multiple things:

1. **External:** This process shows the customers you are hearing them. It provides them with a documented history of your interactions, agreements, commitments, timing, value, pricing, etc., which may help with their approvals. This process is designed to allow them to read and react to your summary—and *correct* you so you are always on the same page and there are no surprises on either side. It also gives them an easy way to bring additional people or *new* people involved from their side up to speed, allows them to share details with procurement once at that stage (speeds process), and helps with the creation of internal briefing documents for executive awareness or approvals.

2. **Internal:** It's a great way to provide detailed documentation of the entire sales cycle, which helps with reviewing successful sales cycles to share within your organization or with a post mortem (a loss), meeting prep, account pass off, commitments made, etc. It provides a way to go back and review/adjust toward alternative objectives to solidify a deal. It also keeps everyone honest with all details, "asks," limitations, and timing. Each email is "assumed correct" unless corrections are sent.

3. **Mutual:** These notes keep you both on the same page and ensure you are at the same point in the journey. It also allows you to refer back and understand changes in requirements or expectations and people, and it helps with detailed deal reviews. Finally, it serves as a great way to inject a mutual close plan that is built throughout the sales process.

How It Works:

- After your introductory call, send an email summarizing the call and listing key findings and actions. This is an opportunity to set expectations for future steps as well as ask for information. It also allows you to set up the next meeting, when you will go deeper into their objectives.

- After your first meeting, send an email listing requirements, the solution use case, and technical limitations. This is one of the most valuable places to leverage this tactic. You have the ability to clearly articulate the "pain" you are solving, with potential impact. If you do this right, it will be an opportunity to get your champion and others to agree to the impact your solution can have (and start to set up your pricing and negotiation).

- After POC planning, send an email summarizing and keeping everyone on the same page with measurable success criteria, responsibilities, and expectations around timing, work, and level of effort.

- After the negotiation phase, send an email listing concrete "asks," barriers, and "non-starters" as a way to document and gain agreement on a full set of "asks" from your customer. By summarizing the "asks" properly, you gain agreement early on what you are working toward.

- The customer chose you or your competitor for a reason. After a closed sale, call him or her to express gratitude, understand why, and discover what the expectations are (that were communicated internally as 'the reason' for the decision). Or, if you did not win the sale, call to understand where you missed it on requirements or expectations and why you lost. This is a great way to avoid repeating the same mistakes.

By deploying this process, you will see an increased closure rate. You will also begin eliminating errors, develop stronger sales strategies to work with clients, and see increased accountability among the team to ensure everything stays on task for a project.

The added benefit to this whole process is that when you are at the end of your deal cycle, your customer has everything they need to justify the process they went through, the conversations that happened, details shared, objectives given and expected impact your offering will have on their business. This should help them speed up the internal approval process.

68. Three "Wow!" Sales Best Practices
By Ken Grohe

Wow No. 1:

What the Idea Is: When your product is a complex one, record a two-to-four-minute session with an employee or a customer like the one at this link:

https://www.youtube.com/watch?v=JRBo2UusDcI&t=19s

Then work with FiveRR to make it a whiteboard explainer video. See how Weka.io does it at this link:

https://www.youtube.com/watch?v=nl5YGhcYlN0

Why It Is Valuable: This type of presentation allows your prospects to grasp the *aha* or *wow* of the product at their own pace.

How It Works: For the best results, put bumpers on it for branding and post it on your company's YouTube channel. Have all employees share it with their prospects in their emails or as follow ups for them to share within their organizations.

Wow No. 2:

What the Idea Is: Have your sales force memorize your seven best *wow* business impacts and rehearse them every Monday, Toastmasters style, on Zoom. Here are some examples:

- Seven of the Fortune 50 companies in the US are using Weka for their AI initiatives.
- Weka reduced infrastructure costs at Genomics England's (the largest installation of Isilon in EMEA) 70PB installation by 75 percent while scaling their data lake by 5x.
- Weka has been validated as the world's fastest file system on independent benchmarks from IO-500, STAC, and SPEC.
- Leading vendors in Compute, Networking, and Storage have invested in Weka, including NVIDIA, HPE, Mellanox, Cisco, WDC, Seagate, and Micron.
- Leading pharmaceutical companies brought their latest treatment for Alzheimer's and CF (each have a cost of development of $3.2B) to market one full quarter earlier due to Weka.
- The largest autonomous vehicle company was able to be first in time-to-market by reducing their training time from two weeks to four hours.
- Two hundred scientists at a leading University now have forty hours per week each in parallel to use their 4 Cryo-EM microscopes versus only fifteen minutes each per week.

Why It Is Valuable: This best practice allows the company to have consistency of message, even if the slides and other parts of the message may stray, while also keeping the team focused on what's really important to the executives they are calling on. It makes the field team game ready and well practiced.

How It Works: To create a *wow*, ask your customers six months after they install what the business impact really has been and what they would lose if your solution went away.

Wow No. 3:

What the Idea Is: Create a weekly video blog of sixty seconds or less, sharing sales tips. Post your video blog every single week at the same time (in my case, each Friday at noon, which is why I call my weekly video blog #LunchTimeFriday).

Why It Is Valuable: You will create a loyal following when you focus on creating value for the viewer!

How It Works: On a recent #LunchTimeFriday video blog, I did forty-three pushups for Kathy Ireland's Team 43 challenge, in support of the National Pediatric Cancer Foundation. Every day forty-three children are diagnosed with cancer, and she challenged those who would join her Team 43 to do forty-three something—pushups, jumping jacks, etc.—and give $.43, $4.30, $43.00, $430.00, or even $4,300.00 to the foundation. Here is a link to the video showing me doing the forty-three pushups in my backyard in California for her show:

https://www.linkedin.com/feed/hashtag/lunchtimefriday/

kathy ireland Worldwide

69. Always Lead with the New Product/Solution or Acquired New Technology/Solution
Kevin Delane

What the Idea Is: Always lead with the new product/solution or acquired new technology/solution.

Why It Is Valuable: For technology companies to grow, they constantly have to expand their platform, acquire new platforms, or internally develop an additional platform. Great leaders or performers always lead the company on the new platforms. It is important for the company to be successful in the new areas; generally if you lead the way, the money will follow. It is hard to get a successful sales team to add new platforms if the existing one is successful. It is also very expensive for companies to keep adding "specialty salesforces." The best AEs and leaders always hit the new platform metrics.

How It Works: The best way to deploy this is to be a lifelong learner. Embrace new platforms or solutions and learn how to sell them just as you have been selling the flagship product for the last few years. Realize that hitting your number but not selling the new solution is not what the CRO wants you to do. They want you to crush it by selling everything and hitting every metric. I know this is basic; but in my twenty-five years of introducing new acquisitions, products, or solutions, I have seen that it is a constant battle to get every AE/SE to embrace selling all of a company's offerings. Always sell or lead your team to be number one on the new offerings!

70. No Lone Wolves
By Kevin Haverty

What the Idea Is: There should be no lone wolves in sales.

A lone wolf is a salesperson who doesn't like or want to collaborate. Sales is a team sport. The more valuable your solution is, the more important team selling becomes. This includes leveraging resources inside your company to help you sell, such as your technical resources, a solutions engineer, financial resources, an industry subject-matter expert, the direct management team, and the executive leadership team. This could also extend to other sales teams around the world if it's a global company with multiple buying influences in more than one location. It also extends outside your company to the partner community. Leveraging partners always adds complexity, but it also often extends the reach of the sales team to higher levels in the organization or augments the offering of the manufacturer.

Why It is Valuable: The value of not being a lone wolf is the results you will see. In the wild, the lone wolf simply cannot successfully hunt the wolves' favorite prey: big game. Instead, lone wolves generally hunt smaller animals and scavenge. The same is true for salespeople.

How It Works: There are two reasons sales reps leave the efficiency of the pack and go the lone wolf path. The first is over-confidence. They think they have it figured out and they don't need help. I don't care who it is, all sellers will be more productive and successful if they leverage their resources and get the team selling with them. Every sales campaign should have a virtual team working on it, and the role of the sales rep is to lead this virtual team. This includes motivating all team members, creating and documenting the plan, and keeping the sales campaign on track. The other reasons for leaving the pack and going the lone-wolf route falls on the opposite end of the spectrum. These reps are under-confident and don't want to have their weaknesses exposed. They want to stay under the radar and hope to not get noticed while they try to figure it out.

At ServiceNow we do a few things to remind both sales reps and managers to avoid this trap. I often say, "The lone wolf is extinct at ServiceNow." We also have some fun with the image of a lone wolf with a red circle and slash through it, Ghostbusters style. So it's up to you. Do you want to feast on gazelle, giraffe or bison, or are you happy eating rats and squirrels?

71. Vision, Strategy, Execution, Metrics (VSEM) Approach to Growing Your Business
By Kevin Purcell

What the Idea Is: My Vision, Strategy, Execution, Metrics (VSEM) approach to growing your business.

Why It Is Valuable: The approach starts with a common vocabulary for making decisions to drive sales growth.

Vision: communicates a sales team's shared view of success

Strategy: represents important decisions for where and how to apply resources to accomplish the vision

Execution: outlines critical initiatives, programs, or actions that support each strategy

Metrics: shows how the team measures success and agrees to be held accountable to the execution plan

How It Works: A sales leader requires collaboration from the team to build the VSEM model so everyone owns it. Fostering a culture that encourages collaborative behavior, putting processes in place to help people work better together, and assembling a portfolio of integrated technologies that facilitate collaboration are key to successfully deploying the model.

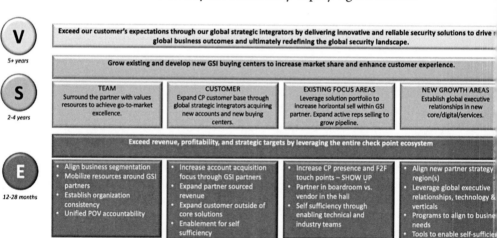

72. Building a Better Interview System
By Kevin Scannell

What the Idea Is: Building a better interview system.

Why It Is Valuable: I have built large organizations for over three decades, and the one thing that has always bothered me about hiring managers was the interview process. For years, I have heard my managers and others talk about clever, cliché-type questions they loved to ask candidates. I believe the interviewing leader must actually be on a power trip when he or she asks demeaning questions to the candidate.

My pragmatic approach to management is this:

- What do you ask your reps to do every day? (Surprisingly, some don't even know.) In my last role I was rather maniacal about reminding the reps and their managers how they were measured—every day. After all, I believe reps lose track if you ask them to do too much, so I tried to make it really simple:
  - Can they drive activity?
  - Do they know the right thing to say when they get in front of someone?
  - Are they likeable? Do they present themselves well? (Make the prospects like you—people buy from those they like.)
  - Do they bring in deals when they say they will come in (predictability)?

How It Works: I may have said it a little differently to my reps, but it went something like this:

- **Drive activity that results in ten customer-facing meetings per week** (activity). I don't care how you get there, but making ten calls is a must! Figure it out; that's why I hired you.
- **Evangelize the message with passion!** Know your brief, your product, your competition, and your market—well! Have passion when speaking with clients. If you don't, I promise they won't respond.
- **Build relationships with clients with extra-curricular activities** (ball games, steak dinners, nail appointments, etc.) Nine to five doesn't cut it. I've built my best relationships on my boat fishing 100 miles offshore, at Fenway Park, and at restaurants the customer loved. (Even eclectic options can be good. Spoiler alert: it's not about you; it's about what your prospect/client likes!)

I had one clever female in my organization tell me when I came across her expense for a nail salon appointment for her and her female client,

"Sometimes ladies would rather get their nails done than go to a ball game!" Brilliant! My wife thought this one was awesome. I agreed. Out-of-the-box activities are great if the customer wants to do it. One rep took his customer to a motorcycle expo for Harley Davidson. I'd hate to compete with that rep. Customers only spend time with people they enjoy being around. Make sure you remember that when a rep can't get a customer out for drinks, dinner, a ball game, or a remote executive briefing, it could be a red flag.

- **Predictability on the forecast.** We leverage qualifying processes that help eliminate roadblocks in sales campaigns. Whether it's Miller Heiman or MEDDIC, I like them all; but some are more relevant, depending on what you're selling.

Now, if these are my four expectations, doesn't it make sense that my entire interview process would be to validate that this candidate had the experience and the history of doing these four things well? After all, what else really matters? I know if these four things are executed well, good things will happen.

Give me a candidate who is not a job-hopper (someone who averages less than 2.5 years at every job) and I'll determine if he or she is a good fit within twenty minutes.

Time is money, and more time is more money. So maybe some of those questions other managers ask, like "Do you like whiskey or rum?" are irrelevant. Perhaps asking the candidate to "sell me this pen" is not quite the best way to spend your time. It's possible that focusing your interview on relevant themes would be more meaningful. Stop the cliché-type interview questions and talk about the things that matter.

This method has saved me thousands of hours across thousands of interviews. The answers really mattered and were extremely relevant.

73. Inside Sales Is the New Trend
By Kristen Twining

What the Idea Is: Inside sales is the new trend.

I started in technology sales right before the introduction of the quad core processor—roughly fourteen years ago. I began selling infrastructure to Enterprise companies and continued to build my career on virtualization, consolidation, the explosion of data, and the shift to cloud. I have sold to global, large, midsize, and small companies while holding various individual contributor, field sales, and leadership roles. It's been an incredible adventure and a roller coaster of a ride.

I started my career in the summer of 2006, straight out of college. I recall in my final interview with the hiring VP of sales, whom I asked what, specifically, I needed to do and the time it would take to hold his role. That was a bold question, to say the least, but I strongly believe my ambition and passion to excel is what landed me the job. I grew my career quickly, rising through the ranks and securing a director role within my first five years at the company. I was on a fast track, and it was like being in a time machine headed toward a future I initially thought would take me a decade to achieve. I continued to achieve upward mobility and achieved vice president at the twelve-year mark.

The interesting part is, after all my field sales roles and experiences, my VP role was for inside sales—something I knew very little about. I thought back to that interview in the café and laughed, as I would have never thought I'd lead an inside sales organization. Heck, I felt like a prodigy for having skipped over inside sales and going straight into the big leagues. And now here I was about to lead a team of 300 passionate future leaders of the company, and maybe even the technology industry itself. What I didn't know then was that I was embarking on a journey that would not only accelerate my career, but establish my brand and my future, all while igniting a passion inside me I never knew I had. I quickly began to realize the shift in the industry, the transformation in front of me, and the fact that I was absolutely in the right place at the right time in the right leadership role.

Why It Is Valuable: Back in 2017, field sales was still the dominant route to market in most large companies; however, inside sales was growing and growing fast. A 2017 *Forbes* article stated that field sales made up 71.2 percent of the sales force, while inside sales were at 28.8 percent of the sales force. However, they projected that inside sales was set to increase by over 2 percent YoY. In addition, survey results showed that large enterprises had a stated goal of increasing their inside-sales-to-field-sales mix to 40 percent.[3] It was clear that a shift was underway.

Over the past two years, with the added factor of the recent pandemic forcing us all to think differently about our sales models, I have positioned myself as a leader directly responsible for change, focusing on spearheading, selling, and positioning this shift as an inevitable go-to-market strategy for success. For example, you may be looking at reducing the cost of field sales focused on growth and expansion in the small-to-medium-size business segment, or you may want to build a world-class talent pool of future leaders for your corporation. Either way, growing your inside sales organization and their accountability will directly impact your bottom line, your talent and recruiting strategy, and your overall company culture. Bringing in inspiring, passionate, and fresh talent who have an open mind and an eagerness to learn helps you mold your sales force into what you want it to become. And that is invaluable.

How It Works: So where do you start? I believe that demand generation is one of the most important and critical roles of the organization. Inside sales has many areas of focus, but demand generation should be the primary activity. There are many variables of the spectrum here. From what I've seen, there are large legacy organizations that are undergoing a transformation, where they are trying to figure out how to shift more of their model and cost structure to inside sales. Then there are smaller organizations building inside sales organizations from the ground up, trying to achieve a cost balance of inside versus outside right out of the gate. In both cases, the primary focus is either on leveraging inside sellers for demand generation in driving net new and expanded market opportunities, or for growing markets that are more transactional and volume based, in which a highly skilled, expensive resource is not required. In each instance, this not only proves to be cost effective, but serves as an incredible growth opportunity for progression and promotion within the company. This in turn can lead to higher talent retention and lower attrition.

In addition to the cost and talent benefits, you are building a skill set for your organization that is fundamental for success: prospecting. This is not an easy skill and one that many sales reps mistakenly believe they will graduate out of as their careers progress. One of the things I love most about leading an inside sales organization is enabling these individuals to build foundational skills that will pay themselves back in dividends if properly maintained and exercised throughout their career. This is something you can't necessarily teach, instill, or reignite in experienced, well-tenured sales reps.

So here we are in 2020, forced to look at new ways to accelerate growth given the pandemic, the economic climate, and the uncertainty of the future. As virtual selling becomes more prominent, inside sales will be the conduit for success. We have seen steady growth of inside sales roles, and that growth will continue. In fact, as I look around, everyone is an inside sales rep right now. Field reps have had to fundamentally shift their mentality, their focus, and how they manage their day. This presents a challenge to their productivity with the transition from always traveling to working from home. Managing time effectively and maximizing your time spent on selling while remote when you have been used to face-to-face interaction can be difficult. A recent article from SalesForce.com says, "Today's sales professionals spend just 34 percent of their time selling."[4] I will counter that by saying that a business development rep, for example, has and continues to spend upwards of 70 percent of their day prospecting, because they have to—it's their main source of income and KPI achievement. Many field sales reps are looking to better understand tactics and best practices from their traditional inside sales rep peers. Field sales reps are forced to prospect more, sell over the phone, and in many cases are engaging in blitz days, outreach campaigns, and leveraging tools and platforms to manage their activity and opportunity generation on a daily basis. This is absolutely a shift; a new mindset for field sellers, however, is fundamental to the success of those organizations that are enforcing and encouraging this shift. I tell my inside sales team that the world is looking to you for guidance and best practices; this is your time to shine and to make your mark.

To summarize, inside sales is not only the current status, but it's the trend. It's becoming more competitive to secure the best and brightest talent, and it's becoming the foundation for talent, demand generation, and a more cost-effective source of revenue growth. Most importantly, it happens to be one of the most rewarding leadership roles. I am passionate about my job—not just because it is strategic to the overall organization, but because it is fun and exciting. I have the opportunity to work alongside up-and-coming, inspiring, ambitious, and self-motivated individuals every day. What I love the most, however, is having the opportunity to mentor, develop, and coach individuals to realize their ambitions and career goals. I always say that I am the kindergarten teacher of sales, and that I am setting the team up to get out of the nest to spread their wings and fly. And as an extra added bonus, you never forget the name of that formative teacher who begins your journey and whom you ultimately become.

74. Sales: Value Realization
By Larry Irvin

What the Idea Is: Everyone does an ROI and various forms of analysis to show what benefit the customer will receive from the service/company. However, they rarely follow through to see what the actual impact was for the customer. Go back six months to a year later and run those analysis numbers again to see what really happened; most of the time it is better than projected. As Randy always says, if you're in the elevator with the CFO for thirty seconds, what would you say your value is? It should be focused on how you helped them generate revenue, save money, or stay out of jail in the case of compliance issues.

Why It Is Valuable: This simple action will cement yourself as a partner who supports your customers, because you show the real value they have received. Showing they have greater returns on their investment will set you up for further deals—it builds credibility, trust, and other values that are important to a client.

How It Works: To get all the information you really need, you may want to do some research for the norms of various costs for this company size/industry. Start with having the customer validate the numbers so you can get closer to the actual big picture. Internally, the numbers you put together can be used to justify the investment, which helps you in preparing for the ask from their decision maker. I've seen situations where the champion has come out with a promotion based on this process.

The proof is in the numbers; extracting the additional revenue for follow-on value realization helps the customer justify additional spends with the company. Follow up is the big key here. It provides a reason to stay in touch, which drives good customer relationships/service.

75. Team Building: Analyzing Candidates During the Interview Process
By Larry Irvin

What the Idea is: Behavioral interviewing; you are trying to understand how people would do things in the context of your company based on their previous behavior. Ask them to tell you what they have done in their previous positions.

There are four dimensions you want to analyze with a candidate:

1. Motivation: they have it or they don't have it; it's in their DNA.

2. Personal characteristics: their thinking processes, their ability to differentiate right from wrong, and their moral and ethical compass (Will they do literally anything, or are there things they know are not ethical that they stay away from?) This is non-negotiable.

3. Coachable traits: knowledge of the security space can be taught.

4. Sales skills: if they have the skills to do this part, again the knowledge piece can be taught. Depending on the role, you may find someone junior in his/her career—a candidate who is motivated but not so strong in other areas, but who shows a massive upside. You may be willing to take the risk of the additional time/training needed to build your ideal sales avatar for the company.

Factors vary depending on the need—is it crucial and immediate, or is it a matter of longer range planning where you are building a team?

Maintain a succession-planning mindset, where you are always thinking of how a candidate may fit into a necessary role in the future.

Why It Is Valuable: It supports creating a strong team and considers potential for succession planning as a part of hiring.

How It Works: Some documentation will be needed to make this process work. You want a 360 view of the candidate, so you need to have multiple people interviewing the candidate, all asking different questions from all four of the categories so they get different views. Don't share your personal thoughts to influence the others prior to their interviews, or you will taint their perception prior to the procedure. Debrief after all interviews are finished to get feedback from the other interviewers. A debriefing may reveal good points that support your view of the candidate, or it could possibly uncover things that contradict what you had in mind, which would give you a good reason to review your notes again.

This process measures:

- How long it would take for the candidate to get to full productivity
- How long it would take for him/her to make a material impact on revenues
- Whether the candidate would work well with the team through a sales campaign process

At my company, we measure:

- How we evaluate people and performance within the company
- Revenue and other aspects, such as team contribution, territory development, business basics (managing expenses), and customer success

We use this to set expectations and do performance evaluations based against it. It has become a part of the culture of the company, in all roles.

76. Solving Business Problems for Your Customer
By Lionel Lim

What the Idea Is: It is my personal belief that sales is less about selling and more about solving business problems or needs. The earlier in your sales career that you realize this and begin investing your focus and time accordingly on building your personal reputation as a trusted advisor to your clients, the more successful you will be in your career.

Why It Is Valuable: Customers want to work with trusted advisors because they benefit from it. If you have a good reputation and customers know you can help them solve problems and achieve success, then getting appointments, filling your qualified opportunities pipelines, being predictable, and making your targets year after year will follow as a result.

How It Works: Build credibility by following these steps:

1. Know your product. Know its strengths and limitations inside and out.

2. Know your industry

3. Understand your clients' industry, their challenges, and their business drivers

4. Do more questioning and listening than talking and selling

5. Underpromise and overdeliver

6. Remember, it is okay to walk away from an opportunity if you know you cannot meet your client's needs. It will preserve the relationship for the long term.

77. Golden Rules for Running a Sales Team
By Marco Mohajer

What the Idea Is: Every great sales manager should have a few golden rules that govern his or her team.

Why It Is Valuable: It allows the salesperson to expedite the sales cycle by focusing on "time," "cost," and "importance."

How It Works: Here are three very effective golden rules I've used for guiding my team over the years:

1. "Dumify" it. In other words, the fact that you know your subject does not mean your customer does. Studies have shown that a single sales call could cost as much as $500 or more, so make sure you are meeting with the right audience; then target your message to that specific audience. For example, you should never talk the same way to a CFO as you do to a VP of Apps.

2. Know your audience. Understand why they are meeting with you. Learn about their business before you walk in. Read their K-1. Know what the customer's top three strategic initiatives are for the year. Understand their pain point and hone in on it. Most sales people just want to talk. In my book, the one who speaks less *wins*.

3. Know when to call it quits. Many reps get happy ears and *think* they have the deal. They lack the ability to understand the metrics and want to believe they have it. *Cut your losses and move on.*

78. Designing a Sales Compensation Plan in a Data-Driven System
By Mark Roberge

What the Idea Is: Designing a sales compensation plan in a data-driven system.

Why It Is Valuable: The compensation plan design is typically delegated by the CEO to the head of sales, and the head of sales tends to use the plan from the last company where he or she worked. Unfortunately, this is a missed opportunity for the CEO to drive the high-level corporate strategy to the front line of the business. The compensation plan is arguably the best tool the CEO has to align strategy with execution. I rarely see organizations take advantage of this opportunity.

The opportunity is even more important as the world of IT and software shifts toward a subscription economy. Selling on-premise software decades ago used to entail a long sales cycle, and it involved placing millions of dollars of equipment into a basement and then spending months training the organization how to use it. It didn't matter if the software worked or was easy to use. The purchasing company was stuck with it. However, in the world of cloud, subscription, and freemium, this context no longer exists. The buyer can access and begin using software over the internet, often for free. Using the software is easy. However, so is canceling. As organizations realize this, they begin to define customer retention as their most important metric—even more important than new revenue acquisition. While some customer retention issues are rooted in product and customer on-boarding, most are rooted in sales—specifically who salespeople choose to sell to, the expectations they set with customers on what needs to be done to be successful, and what level of success should be expected. As CEOs realize the importance of customer retention to their organization's success, they have an opportunity to align sales compensation with this metric.

How It Works: From a high level, sales compensation needs to be aligned with lifetime value, not total contract value. I'd rather have a salesperson sign a one-year contract for $100K and the customer renew for ten years and provide positive references than have a salesperson sign a customer for a three-year contract for $100K per year who never uses the product and does not renew. Unfortunately, most sales commission plans, which are often rooted in TCV, pay the latter salesperson more than the former.

Unfortunately, it is not as simply as paying a salesperson on a retainer for the LTV. If we paid a salesperson 10 percent of the contract for as long as the customer is on board, two negative outcomes can occur. First, we want sellers to be rewarded (or penalized) as close to the good (or bad) behavior as possible. Paying sellers on the annuity fails here. Second, sellers can become lazy. If they have built up an annuity of customers and are getting 10 percent each year, they can stop hunting new customers and still make a lot of money.

Instead, organizations need to identify their leading indicator to customer retention. This leading indicator is a factual, inspectable event that ideally occurs in the first sixty days of a customer's lifespan. If the event occurs, there is a high statistical probability that the customer will be around for many tears. If it does not, the customer will likely churn at the next renewal time. Leading indicators can be as simple as product setup or product usage. Once identified, the sales compensation plan can compensate sellers 50 percent of the commission when the contract is signed and 50 percent when the leading indicator is achieved.

Few organizations understand this concept. Modernizing sales compensation strategy is a substantial competitive advantage opportunity.

79. Adapt Great Leadership Advice from Those Who Have Been Successful
By Mark Stephenson

What the Idea Is: Get great leadership advice from those who have gone before and paved the way to success.

Why It Is Valuable: While John Wooden is known for his team's unprecedented winning of ten NCAA Championships in basketball and seven in a row, few realize that he worked for over sixteen years to perfect his approach, tinkering with every detail before his team won its first NCAA title. Similarly, these are not shortcuts to greatness in sales or sales leadership; rather, together they construct a detailed focus on continuous improvement that require a lifetime of learning. This approach is knowable, it's workable, and you can do it!

How It Works:

Wooden's Twelve Lessons on Leadership and What They've Meant to Me:

1. **Good values attract good people**. People are attracted to candor and authenticity. They like plain-speaking people who mean what they say and do what they say.

2. **Love is the most powerful four-letter word**. What do you do when it's not easy to do it? Giving feedback is like this. Giving feedback to help someone in life or career is an act of love. Wooden was the master of providing feedback on and off the court. His players loved him (sometimes later), but often for a lifetime.

3. **Call yourself a teacher.** Wooden taught English at UCLA. His instruction was detailed and methodical. Many comment on Wooden's ten-of-twelve-year National Championship run, but few know that he perfected his teaching approach and updated his "Pyramid of Success" for over thirty years before UCLA won its first National Championship.

4. **Emotion is your enemy.** Any strength over done can be a weakness. Passion often drives us, and we must believe in what we are doing; but professionals are focused, analytic, and measured to be bold.

5. **It takes ten hands to make a basket.** In sales as in life, make sure you are working for a company that you have a vision for, and then give it all you have—anything less is squandering your opportunity.

6. **Little things make big things happen.** Wooden taught his players how to put their socks on in the first practice every year, so they would never get blisters in a game—sweat the details of what can go wrong so it doesn't!

7. **Make each day your masterpiece.** In their deals, career, and life, sales people often "play checkers" (one step at a time) versus "playing chess" (many steps at one time). Play chess and win more.

8. **The carrot is mightier than a stick.** The stick is not lasting. Capture people's hearts *and* minds and you have talent for sustained exceptional performance.

9. **Make greatness attainable by all.** Show people what the activities look like to be great, and enable them to get there themselves.

10. **Seek significant change.** No one is excited to be mediocre. Do it right or don't do it. Besides, there is "margin in the mystery."

11. **Don't look at the scoreboard.** Everyone is great at tracking the results, but few are good at clocking the actions/activities it takes to be great and win with regularity.

12. **Adversity is your asset.** Create a crisis of opportunity for people to take the action that is in their best interest; they often need the catalyst for change.

Qualities It Takes to Develop a Winning Team and How I Value Them:

- **Industriousness:** The saying goes, "The harder you work, the luckier you get," and nowhere is this truer than in sales. Indeed, the truism "Work finds those who get work done" also underscores the fact that in sales one of the most direct correlations is between effort and output.

However, we must clarify these statements with one that Wooden is famous for saying: "Never confuse activity for accomplishment."

- **Friendship:** People want to be around people they find connection with, and they ultimately buy from people they like.

- **Loyalty:** I have a son who went to West Point, where first-year cadets have a very tough year as a "Plebe." It's basically a year of hard work, hard talk, and not much sleep. West Point is a leadership school at its heart, and its practices have been honed for over 200 years; its leaders understand you must first know how to be a follower before you can one day become a leader. Loyalty is earned; it's not something to be traded or trampled on. Trust is a close cousin to loyalty and is essential for effective and lasting relationships as well as high-functioning teams.

- **Cooperation:** Others have now realized that teamwork is a critical element you hire for, and no high-performing team can go without it.

- **Enthusiasm:** Enthusiasm can and should be "catching" with your prospect and clients and is absolutely essential for you to have in everything you are representing.

- **Self-control:** As Randy Seidl is famous for saying, "Never miss the opportunity to say nothing."

- **Alertness:** Always be ready and sensing new information that can be seized for advantage or completeness.

- **Initiative:** The harder you work in sales, the "luckier" you get.

- **Intentness:** Be present and focused in all things, and you will have the advantage.

- **Condition/Practice:** Wooden's practices had an intensity and focus about them that caused players to often remark that playing the actual game was "easier."

- **Skill:** Skill is the critical first element of consistently hiring great talent. What skills are you looking for? Be as specific as possible. You would not put a "point guard" at the center position in basketball. The tighter your hiring spec is, the more you will recruit folks who can have impact per your ramp quota.

- **Team Spirit:** This is now often referred to as "culture." If you have been with a market-leading, high-performing team, you might take this for granted—but you never will again after experiencing a bankrupt culture.

- **Poise:** Poise can be gained by having command of your solution, its application, and the process of qualification. Being prepared always helps as well.

- **Confidence:** Confidence comes from being prepared and being conversationally fluent in your solution, your customer, and your draft.
- **Competitive Greatness**[5]**:** Know your competition; however, Wooden's focus was on knowing your game plan above all others.

80. Developing a Sense of Urgency in Your Teams
By Marty Sanders

What the Idea Is: Developing a sense of urgency in your teams—getting teams to act and think like every Friday is month-end, every month-end is quarter-end, and every quarter-end is year-end.

Why It Is Valuable: Quarterly Business Reviews and sales activities from five to fifteen years ago no longer meet the velocity requirements of today's business. The markets, our customers' requirements, and macro events are moving way too quickly for these old ways. What I have found is, deals called out in the QBR will rarely match the actual deals that drove the number. Although you may still achieve the quarterly number, the deals are likely very different.

In today's world, you will find that half your business in that quarter will be created in that quarter or it was rehashed from a previous quarter. So why have a QBR? Forecasting becomes highly unpredictable as well. In today's fast-paced world, we need a high-performance culture that embraces a sense of urgency. The other benefit of operating in a high-performance culture is better linearity in a quarter.

How It Works: How do you move to a high-performance, sense-of-urgency culture?

1. You have to move from quarterly BRs to monthly BRs, and these MBRs must be supplemented by weekly commits and weekly reviews in addition to first-level manager and sales rep one-on-ones.

2. You have to create buy-in for treating every Friday like month-end, every month-end like quarter-end, and every quarter-end like year-end.

You will want to look for certain personality traits and work habits in order to find people who can thrive in this environment. This requires profile testing (looking for desires, will to succeed, and lots of back-channel references). Try to find people you can motivate by the mission, as opposed to those wanting a job or career. Sell the mission to them.

Driving compression with your team: A $100k deal closed the first week of the month has $100k a month productivity; a $100k deal closed the fourth week of a month has $25k-a-week productivity. Get managers and reps to understand the value of how much this compression matters. There is significant value in moving a deal up by a quarter, a month, a week, or even a day.

To maintain this sense of urgency in the culture requires significant appreciation and recognition. You need to reward the desired behavior within the team, because it is hard for people to maintain that pace. It's imperative that you recognize it. Let them know they have to get comfortable being uncomfortable, acknowledge it is difficult, and then remind them of the mission. Keep constantly reinforcing the vision, and have radical transparency and honesty about the process.

This is a tagline I live by: *Hire right, sleep at night; people matter.* All the above is contingent on hiring right.

81. Managing New Enterprise Reps Calling on Large Accounts with Long Sales Cycles
By Marty Sanders

What the Idea Is: Managing new enterprise reps calling on large accounts with long sales cycles. One challenge sales leaders have in hiring enterprise reps to sell a product that has a long-term sales cycle (six to twelve months) is determining how to know if they are doing a good job in their first three to six months. You are potentially paying them an expensive, non-recoverable draw, and yet you have to wait another six months to see the final results. How do you judge how they are doing along the way if they are not posting any revenue?

Why It Is Valuable: Leadership needs a scorecard or other mechanism around activities that can be measured and validated to show consistent effort toward continuous activities in pursuit of the long-term contract. This also helps identify roadblocks and provides cues to a weakness or lack of effectiveness in an area that can be addressed and quickly remedied.

How It Works: Study your KPIs and establish measurable activities such as these listed below:

1. Number of net new meetings
2. Number of second and third meetings
3. Proposals generated
4. Executive briefings
5. Getting senior leadership on calls

6. Project identification

7. Validated pipeline names and numbers

8. Number of marketing events attended

Set targets for each one of these activities, and measure using colors such as red, green, and yellow to identify the status within the metric, with the ultimate objective being moving all the red activities into the green category. Reference the spreadsheet example below:

count/Action	Account	Account	Account	Account	Account	Account	Account	Account	Account
Identified Initial Stakeholder									
A. Executive/Econ Buyer									
B. Operations									
C. Cloud Architect									
D. DBA's									
E. Emerging Tech Architect									
Identified Focus Channel Partner									
Identified Relevant SI's									
Identified Azure Lead									
Completed Initial Company Discussion									
Company Presentation									
Company Demo									
Identified Use Case									
Identified Pain									
). Modeled TCO/ROI									
. Introduced our Sr Exec(s)									
. Executive Sponsor Meeting									
. EBC									
. POC									
. Solicited Proposal									
. Unsolicited Proposal									
. Identified Funding									
. Close									

82. First Discovery Call Meeting Framework
By MaryBeth Vassallo

What the Idea Is: Assigning a system to prepare for the first discovery call with a potential client.

Why It Is Valuable: It includes a standard process to be used for each discovery call, ensuring a higher rate of success in moving to next steps and closing business; it also helps create stronger projections for sales forecasting, because everyone is following the same duplicatable process.

How It Works: Follow the five steps outlined below to build your customized process for your company. By tracking the use of this system, once in place, you should be able to show higher closing rates, a better bottom line, and more opportunities flowing into your pipeline.

Step 1: Position of Cold Outreach.

On this call we will understand your goals and how we can align to help solve _____; and if there is a mutual fit, we will figure out the best next step from there. That may be a more detailed call or a catered demo that highlights your company.

Step 2: Template for Invite

Agenda Template for the Calendar Invite

- Company Name/YourCo Initial Discussion

Agenda

- Introductions
- Understand roles and responsibilities
- Nexthink introduction
- Understand "the company's" environment, priorities, and challenges
- Discuss next best step

Participant information

Company Name
- Prospect 1, include title
- Prospect 2, include title
- Etc.

YourCo:
- Sales rep
- BDR
- Solution consultant

Step 3: Sales Research and Preparation

Read the annual report, review LinkedIn, news, and social media

Look for business (and/or) personal alignment to make a connection

- Have a prep-call
- How are we starting the call?
- Review and align on agenda expectation with prospect
- What is our goal of the call?
- What questions to ask

- Understand:
  - Who are we talking to?
  - What information do we have?
  - What information do we need?
- Slides: Prepare messaging aligned to extract "the pain." This needs to be *crisp* and *clear* positioning based on information gathered
- Use time management! Allocate the last five minutes to close for next steps
- Next step goal?
  - Demo, further discovery

Step 4: The Discovery Call

- Overview of prospect
- Introductions
- Why are we talking?
- Role/responsibilities
- Understand their projects, tools, environment (i.e., functions that may be outsourced)
- Explore the current process, challenges, and how to improve
- Ask for goals, initiatives
- Understand the **decision makers** and team organization
- Give an overview of Your Co
- How we help IT departments deliver great digital workplaces by increasing *employee productivity* while dramatically *reducing operational costs*
- Give a customer example
- Use open-ended, probing questions to find alignment for a "catered" demo
- Close for next steps
- Further discovery call
- Catered demo

Step 5: Post Call (Internal)

- What is our next step?
- Qualification check boxes
  ○ Assess/authority
  ○ Need/pain
  ○ Defined next step
- Salesforce update
- Sales accepted (opportunity created)
- Sales rejected (Be specific! What is needed for further qualification, why not a fit)

83. Salesperson Interview Process
By MaryBeth Vassallo

What the Idea Is: Create a targeted process to define your best salesperson avatar and hire to that model.

Why It Is Valuable: It increases the chances of a successful hire, shortens the learning curve, lessens turnover and turnover costs, and develops a stronger sales force, and it can create flow for succession planning within the sales team.

Using this systematic approach helps you create a strong sales team that operates in the desired culture and creates better results.

How It Works: Follow the guidelines in the generic template provided to customize a process that fits for your company's priorities and goals.

[Please visit the website *salescommunity.com* to see a PDF called Vassallo Sales Interview Process.]

84. Sales Process Flow Chart
By MaryBeth Vassallo

What the Idea Is: Use a specific flow to create a systematic approach to following a prospect through the flow of the sales process.

Why It Is Valuable: The teams will all follow the same process, and information is documented and available for all to review as needed. You will also have better qualified leads, with stronger investigation into identifying more opportunities that may be available to the team.

How It Works: Develop the system based on the steps outlined below; create metrics to measure the outcomes.

You will create a better pipeline and more opportunities for sales, as well as duplicatable systems and processes

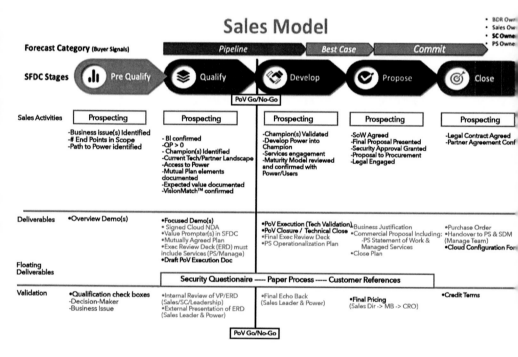

85. Australia
By Michael Burnie

What the Idea Is: Start-up, selling, and GTM strategy for Australia

The size of the market and a varied and sophisticated customer base combine to make Australia an ideal location to offer new and disruptive technology products and services.

Why It Is Valuable:

Australia is a mature, technologically advanced, forward-thinking country with a highly skilled and experienced workforce that encompasses a unique blend of European, Asian, and North American cultures.

These characteristics, combined with a technology-hungry, solutions-driven customer base, makes Australia a strategic location for technology start-ups that offer unique, value-add, and new technology.

Australian spending on information technology products and services is expected to reach around $100 billion in sales in 2021.

Spending on Technology by Segment, Australia, 2018-2022 (Millions of Australian Dollars)					
Segment	2018	2019	2020	2021	2022
Devices	12,443	12,013	11,953	12,027	12,116
Data Center Systems	3,174	3,088	3,061	3,063	3,051
Software	14,590	16,053	17,702	19,460	21,228
IT Services	32,954	34,401	35,891	37,439	39,021
Communications Services	28,011	28,381	29,222	29,627	30,243
Grand Total	91,172	93,936	97,829	101,615	105,659

Source: Gartner (April 2019)

70 to 80 percent of technology sales and installs come from three cities on the east coast:

1. Sydney
2. Canberra (federal government)
3. Melbourne

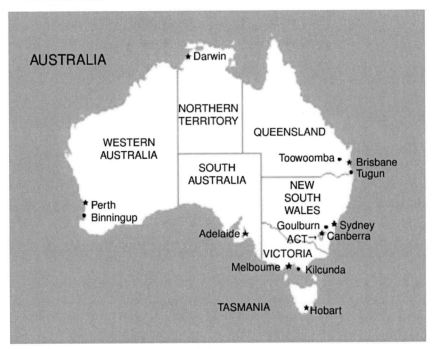

This makes for a quick, low-cost entry into the market. In fact, many vendors have for decades treated the Australian market as a testbed for go-to-market strategies for numerous products. If they get it right in Australia, then it is easily replicable in various other global markets (the US, Europe, and Asia). What works here will likely work everywhere.

How It Works: The sales channel in Australia was traditionally a direct-sales model to very large enterprise and government entities until the late nineties. When the number of vendors, products, and new markets increased, the model transformed into a non-direct, two-tier distribution/reseller model. Orders are fulfilled by the VAR and passed through to the VAD, who takes care of logistics, shipping and imports, and financing.

The vendor supports the reseller in all aspects of the sales cycle—from providing training in a consultative and high-touch sales approach to going on joint sales calls and providing technical and marketing support—with a very involved HQ, corporate executives, and product and marketing specialists.

Under this sales model, the start-up vendor can limit the number of staff required in a direct sales model or multiple city offices.

Sydney is the recommended location to effectively cover all three cities.

Signing up multiple resellers is acceptable, with a focus on horizontal, vertical, and specialized markets. The vendor's sales, marketing, and SE work with multiple resellers by assisting with identifying opportunities and providing technical and marketing support.

Presenting qualified opportunities to partners is an essential first step to enable them to gain confidence in the offering and get their mindshare. This should be supported by building a strong automation toolset from the start, using a CRM such as SalesForce.com and an ancillary channel management tool such as Channeltivity, thus significantly simplifying the handling of issues of scale later. It is also critical to have a functional and documented partner program (preferably online) where partners can register deals and have access to training and product resources.

It is highly likely that the partner program for a start-up will look very different from that of a more mature company. I recommend that the focus initially be on competencies—where a partner has experienced staff in selling the offering *and* has the potential to implement it successfully with a referable client. Reference selling in Australia is very crucial. (Competing businesses will usually use the same technology as their competitors.)

As the start-up matures, a number of these things (such as the partner program) will also mature; however it is critical to have a solid foundation from day one with the essential basics in place.

For a list of Australian distributors and the vendors they represent, go to this link:

https://www.arrnet.com.au/distributor_directory/

86. Sell the Value
By Michael Burnie

What the Idea Is: Sell the value. What does that accomplish? It allows you to set the narrative and differentiates your product and services from the others. It allows you to define the market, set the parameters, and shift the goal posts in your favor. Selling value should focus on financial and business benefits/savings and additional benefits and ROIs, versus focusing on price or discounts. The process of value selling can apply to anything from specialized products and services to competitive and commodity-priced products and services.

Why It Is Valuable: Let's use the example of selling a pen. This idea was made famous from the movie *The Wolf of Wall Street,* where in one scene a number of people in a sales conference were asked to sell a pen. They all failed, because they tried to sell what they thought was a product with no perceived value.

Yes, a pen is a commodity product, for which the only perceived value is writing and pricing; it has a singular function. Most consumers don't really think about the pen and its real value per use.

How It Works: Now if we were to sell the pen purely on value, it might go like this:

The real value of this pen is to document life events. Here are just a few examples of how the pen can be used:

Learning to write

Signing contracts and agreements

Signing for a driver's license or a marriage license

Signing peace accords

Signing a constitution, laws, and amendments

As a graduation gift

You get the idea. Now the pen is valuable. The **value** of the pen will outlive the pen **product**. The moral of this idea is that no matter what product or service you are promoting, value exists—from a basic pen to a unique device. What would you pay for the pen you received as a gift for your graduation—it would be priceless.

Never lower your price. Add value!

87. Success
By Michael Burnie

What the Idea Is: "Success has many fathers; failure is an orphan."—President John F. Kennedy

Successful people build each other up. They motivate, inspire, and push each other to succeed.

Unsuccessful people just hate, blame, and complain.

Why It Is Valuable: Being **successful** means the achievement of a desired vision, favored outcome, and planned goal. The dictionary describes **success** as: "Attaining wealth, prosperity, and/or fame."[6]

How It Works: One of the biggest keys to **success** is to love what you do. You should be motivated, inspired, professional, and have a commitment of support from your organization from the outset and all along the way. Successful people won't wait for something to happen; they make it happen.

Here are some of the ways to start the journey:

- Align yourself with successful people.
- Use and share best practices (what's worked, winning strategies, etc.).
- Use all available resources:
    ○ Marketing, executive management, etc.
    ○ Sales management, engineering, finance, etc.

- Focus on your strengths, not on your competitor's weaknesses.
- Every time you mention your competitor's offering is time you take away from talking about your products and their value strength. Don't sell for the competition.
- You are your biggest competitor; be your biggest winner.
- Ask for the orders; don't wait to be awarded and/or offered. Have some chutzpah.
- Rejection is an opportunity to keep trying, and a loss is not a loss unless you give up.

Love to win more than you hate to lose, or hate to lose more than you like to win.

If you do fail, don't hate it too much; it's the only factor that indicates that you are on the path to success.

88. Trust, Transparency, and Accountability—
Pillars of a High-Performing Sales Culture
By Mike Durso

What the Idea Is: Trust, transparency, and accountability are the pillars of a high-performing sales culture.

Why It Is Valuable: Whether you are a CEO or an SDR, these pillars are valuable at every level of any organization. Trust, transparency, and accountability lead to a culture where individuals understand exactly what is expected of them. These pillars also foster open and honest communication, which has tremendous value to any company. Ultimately, these pillars will create a strong and positive culture, low attrition rates, and employees who are empowered to excel at their job.

How It Works:

Trust

Sales has been, and always will be, about building relationships. Yes, things in and around sales have changed. Tools have gotten better, strategies have evolved, and driving value is more important than ever; however, building relationships is still paramount in complex sales cycles. Simply delivering what you say you are going to in the time frame expected is becoming a lost art. The people who consistently do that are also the ones who have built the most trust with their customers, based on a true relationship. Building relationships internally is equally as important. We have all worked on a team or for a leader where there is immense trust. Knowing your leader or your team fully trusts you allows for empowerment through the chain of command. That empowerment allows for true development. It also allows you to do your job confidentially and without uncomfortable oversight.

Trust is the cornerstone of building these relationships. Without trust up and down the stack internally, and without trust from your customer base, your success will be limited.

Transparency

Transparency builds directly from trust. Transparency has forever been what all reps and first-line leaders want. Bad news is okay or a decision against me is okay, but be transparent, honest and up front. Transparency leads to a proper forecast, and transparency leads to having customers who will build career-long relationships that have depth. Transparency leads to honest feedback and real, actionable coaching. Transparency leads to process improvement and eventually an execution machine. Transparency leads to proper organizational change and a team that is focused on getting better every day.

Accountability

If you have established a relationship based on trust and being transparent, accountability is the natural next step. Many of us were first attracted to sales as a career due to the competitive nature and the idea that "we are keeping score." Holding your team accountable or being held accountable is part of sales. Being held accountable and accepting responsibility for your performance (good or bad) is part of being a good leader. Accountability is also quite important with your customers. If you have established trust and been transparent about what you are both working toward, it is expected that you will be able to hold your customer accountable to do what they have committed to and vice versa. This is a delicate subject, but it's another thing top reps do consistently. I'm sure how to do this effectively is covered in greater detail in another part of this book!

As you can see, these pillars all relate to each other. They are tied together and apply to every step of a sales cycle and every internal situation. Next time you have an internal conflict or a sales cycle goes a bit sideways, ask yourself, *Have I truly established trust, transparency, and accountability in my team?*

89. Building Trust with Your Customer
By Nick Oberhuber

What the Idea Is: Building trust with your customer.

Why It Is Valuable: Building trust with your customer is absolutely critical before a customer will buy your solution. This is easier said than done.

How It Works: You can build trust in multiple ways. One that works well is to become a passionate advocate for the product you are selling. What does that mean? It *does not* mean learning the key messages that marketing tells you to learn. It *does* mean truly understanding how your product works technically, why it is unique, what problems it fixes, and how it is deployed. Without a deep understanding of these issues, you cannot develop a passion. You can try to fake passion, but a customer will sniff that out right away.

I believe good sales professionals should be able to run their own first calls and often their own second calls without help from systems engineering (SE). Some salespeople kid themselves into thinking they don't need to understand the technology they sell that well because that is where their systems engineer fits in. Don't let yourself be duped into having that wrong attitude. The SE will not be on the call when you finally reach the customer after many attempts at 5 p.m. on Friday afternoon on their way home, when they tell you the reason they have not called you back is they do not believe your solution meets their needs.

In addition to knowing what your product does, you should also know your key competitors and how they work, as well as adjacent systems and complementary products. And you need to know them well enough so you really understand your customers when they tell you about their challenges. Customers have been burned too many times by sales people who promise their product will solve their needs, but they overpromise and under-deliver. For a customer to even open up and share their challenges with you, they need to believe you will understand their challenges. If they do, they will share; and if they share, that goes a long way toward their beginning to trust you. One way customers test you to see if you are knowledgeable and trustworthy is listening to your responses. If you ask for additional clarification rather than just answering "yes" to their questions, it shows you understand where you fit and where you do not.

Another important reason to understand your product, your competitors, and your adjacent products is so you can ask intelligent questions. Trainers often say to sales people, "God gave you two ears and one mouth; use them proportionately." Well, that works well if you show up and a customer just starts spilling their guts about what they want, what else they are looking at, etc., which almost never happens. You need to ask the customer questions. The quality of your questions will show the customer whether you know your stuff or not. The better your questions, the more likely the customer will open up and tell you about their challenges and goals. If you do not know your stuff, your questions will be weak and you will not be able to guide your customer toward your solution with the questions you ask. It is a virtuous cycle. The more you know, the better your questions; and the better your answers, the more likely you will be able to build trust. When the customer trusts you, your chance of winning business goes up exponentially.

90. Diversity in Building Teams
By Paola Doebel

What the Idea Is: Building diverse teams is an intentional action that requires a strategy and framework. It is a focused effort that requires a reassessment of the process to hire talent. Diversity is multi-dimensional. It is a prism of attributes that ultimately contributes to the team like a patchwork quilt perfectly sewn together to make something beautiful. It includes age, culture, socio-economic background, religion, educational background, ethnicity, nationality, work experiences, and many more attributes that contribute to how a person approaches a problem or challenges, generates ideas, and interacts with others.

Why It Is Valuable: Building diverse teams is about capturing and harnessing the power of human potential and the range of ideas that come from all of those different perspectives. Executives focused on growth and competitive advantages cannot simply ignore all the ideas left behind because they did not prioritize multi-dimensional diversity and perspectives on their teams. Sales leaders also need to adapt to the changing personas of their customers and clients. As clients and customers become more diverse across the prism of potential attributes, the sales leaders and representatives that support those customers and clients need to mirror those changes to stay relevant and relatable.

How It Works: I understand there is always pressure to hire, especially for gaps and key roles, but the goal is ultimately to build the most capable team responsible for the future development, direction, and execution of the company's strategy and mission. I fundamentally believe that the best companies of the future will figure out how to harness the power of the brilliant ideas that come from diverse teams. That all starts with the very first step, which is the hiring process.

The first step in building teams is reassessing your hiring process and candidate pool. In hiring across multiple countries over the course of the last several years, I have developed the framework for a process I believe yields results in both finding the best candidate for the role and ensuring diversity in the pool of candidates.

1. Advise your talent acquisition team that interviews should not begin without five to seven solid candidates.

2. If you are hiring for a USA-based role, at least two of the candidates should come from a specified diversity, protected class. There is a psychological reason for at least two candidates. In 2016, *Harvard Business Review* released a study that said "If there is only one woman in your candidate pool, there's statistically no chance she'll be hired."[7] The study found that unconscious biases, despite specific programs, simply get in the way of diversity hiring. The study had a real impact on my perspective of candidate pools and hiring. While it was specific to hiring women, I assumed the same unconscious biases would apply to any other diversity candidate in the pool. To defend against these unconscious biases, I require at least two diversity candidates in the pool (more than two is great, but two is the minimum).

3. As I worked through the hiring process, I realized I was also falling into the trap of "standard hiring procedures," which means we all

start with a pool of candidates and narrow that pool down to the top two to three for a final round. The problem is that diverse candidates were getting eliminated during the process, which dropped the number back to potentially only one candidate. This made it more likely we would miss hiring a great candidate because of biases that had nothing to do with actual performance or potential. After further reflection, I changed the framework. To ensure we keep a diverse pool of candidates, I require that all candidates that start the process go through to the final round so every candidate has the same shot to perform during the process and every interviewer is required to assess the full pool of candidates equally.

4. I also spent time reassessing the interviewers. We needed to think differently about both the pool of candidates and the pool of interviewers. Diverse candidates require diverse interviewers who will approach the role, the candidates, and the questions from a different point of view. I think about interviewers from two dimensions:

   a. Diversity of role. A person's skill set and function shape their point of view about what defines success in a cross-functional role. I realized that we needed interviewers from various functions to triangulate on the best candidate.

   b. Diversity of the actual person. To the best of my ability, I wanted diversity of roles and people. The other way to mitigate unconscious bias is diversity of interviewers.

5. Finally, I reframed the actual process, which I believe combined with the above yields the best results. The first interview is with talent acquisition who is helping shape the final pool of five to seven candidates and ensure all candidates are level set on the role. The second round can be one of two things, depending on the role and level:

   a. With the hiring manager—thirty minutes only to level set on the role so all candidates are clear on what defines success as they go into the full process. No candidates are eliminated.

   b. Straight into a panel interview. I believe panel interviews are incredibly important, especially for sales. A panel round tests the candidates' ability to think on their feet, answer questions from a range of people with varying motivations, and control the conversation. The panel interviewers should be clearly defined in advance, and their role on the panel should be clear. They should be peers, come from cross-functional teams, and be diverse (as previously noted). If possible, I like to have a wild-card interviewer on the panel—someone from a cross-functional team who is in a diverse class, and who is known for their unique or unconventional perspectives. Those types of people, if you have them, help level the playing field and fish out attributes and stories from candidates that others will simply miss. There should be no more than four people on a panel. Each member of the panel should understand what they are trying to "test." Competencies can include: technical acumen, cultural fit, market knowledge, executive communication skills, customer engagement and comms, complex deal closures, etc. If possible, questions should be discussed and provided in advance. After the panel interview, interviewers should come together for a debriefing session to finalize their thoughts and feedback on the candidate, which will be provided to the hiring manager. The third round will either be the panel or should be a peer of the hiring manager from a cross-functional team, if possible. Having other leaders interview candidates is an important perspective to consider. It also helps the hiring manager guard against his/her own biases. The final round should be with the hiring manager, who is by then armed with all of the feedback from the previous rounds. If I am the hiring manager, my preference in this round is to give the candidates a final chance to address with me their specific concerns and feedback.

c. Prior to making a final decision, especially for leader and executive roles, I recommend a discussion of the candidate with the key peers who participated in the panel interview. Get everyone aligned on the decision and articulate how their involvement contributed to the final outcome. It is also a good way to address any concerns that may exist.

This process utilizes more resources and more time from the organization; but if the leadership and the organization are committed to building great teams fit for the future of business and changing customer demographics, than this is a small sacrifice for a significant return.

91. Creating a High-Performing, Diverse Team
By Paola Doebel

What the Idea Is: So you've built a diverse team; now what do you do? Achieving the first goal of building the most capable and competent team for the future required time, effort, and a thoughtful process. However, for the leaders of those teams, the work has only just begun. Simply putting people on the same team under the same leader does not mean they will work together, share ideas, or contribute in impactful ways. Creating a trusting environment of diverse team members who care about each other, respect each other, and value each other's contributions, even when they don't always agree, requires a leader who intentionally and thoughtfully manufactures a positive growth environment. It takes time, planning, and focus. As a leader who had to do this very thing, I spent as much time thinking about my team as I did my business. I knew there was something almost magical that could be created, but not easily replicated, if I could I crack the code.

My first real diversity challenge was bringing together a team of people (male and female) who lived in eight cities across six countries who spoke ten languages and were from four very different religious affiliations. While many leaders will not have a challenge of that magnitude, the problem is the same. It boils down to the first critical question: How do I get this team to trust each other? Once trust is built, the next question/ obstacle is: How do I get this team to depend on each other? If trust and dependence are built, then the team is now more than just a group of individuals with interesting and unique backgrounds. It is a unit working together to achieve a mission. When that happens, the unit can accomplish and achieve unbelievable results. At that point, the diversity of the unit becomes a powerful and valuable tool, because the unit can approach almost any problem or challenge with enough ideas and collective skills/ tools in their toolbox to find resolutions and solutions faster and more creatively than their competition.

Why It Is Valuable: Unless strong leadership builds trust and dependence among the team, diversity alone can be as destructive as it can be productive. The very differences and range of attributes that can bind a team and make them a powerful unit can pull the team apart if leadership is not intentional in its efforts.

How It Works:

1. First, the team members need to trust the leader. In the most diverse team scenario, which likely means the leader is also considered diverse, the relationship starts at the most basic exploratory level. For the leader, that is real work. I approached each of my team members with an open and inquisitive mind. How could I value their perspective and contribution if I really did not understand the root of the idea, the feedback, and the input? I had to put aside my

assumptions and learn about each of them, both individually and collectively. I studied history, culture, and religion. I read books, visited museums, tried new foods, and asked genuine questions. I learned about Chinese medicine, Muslim holidays, Japanese cultural evolution, the impact of the ancient maritime silk road, and the history and impact of trade and colonialism on South Asia, as well as many other fascinating topics. I genuinely wanted to understand the lens through which my team saw the world and approached their roles. That authenticity was obvious and helped me build trusting relationships.

2. I cannot put a time limit on the process, but it does not happen overnight. It took dedicated time, an authentic desire to learn and understand, and many hours of engagements with my team on many of these topics.

3. The leader needs to intentionally create/manufacture opportunities, projects, and programs for each team member to own that contributes to the success of the team, drives productivity, or enables efficiency for the benefit of the group. Each team member should be required to interact, coordinate, or collaborate with other team members to complete their project, program, or effort. The best projects or programs are long-term responsibilities delegated to a single team member to own for the benefit of the entire team, because they require consistent and regular interaction over a long period of time. The team member should also have a regular cadence to read out progress, either via email or on a staff call. Activities like this help drive tactical, non-threatening, consistent engagements that are beneficial for the group as a whole when they are completed.

4. The next step is to pull the team together to decide on longer-term strategic projects to be worked by subsets of the team. These should be for the long-term benefit of the business. Each project team is required to work together to develop, structure, and execute the plan. It is important that the leader oversee some of this work to ensure the team is working together and enabling equal participation across all members. A regular cadence of read-outs and progress updates to the broader team is important. I also recommended that each read-out be led by a different member of the team to ensure each member of each team is put in a position to lead and vocalize the work and progress of the group. Final presentations prior to execution should require all members to have a speaking part.

5. It is also critically important that the leader of the team build an environment where the team is comfortable to speak freely and openly without fear. This becomes more challenging the more culturally diverse the team is oriented. I recommend understanding and learning how to engage each member in a meeting in a way that is culturally sensitive but enables them to express their thoughts and points of view openly. A good start to this process is to speak with each team member in a one-on-one setting to articulate the goal and desire to have the team contribute openly. Ask how best to ensure and engage that team member in an open forum. During those moments of open team engagement, the leader has to be very attentive and observant of the group dynamics to ensure the engagement is orchestrated and moderated in a productive way without overly controlling the discussion. The more this happens and the more the team trusts each other, the easier it will become for the leader to initiate the discussion and allow the team to take it forward.

6. Most large companies do feedback sessions at least one time per year. Those feedback surveys are important and should be taken seriously, especially as new leaders with new team members are learning to work together. A best practice to garner the most productive results, especially from highly diverse teams, is for the leader to nominate a team captain to lead a discussion about the results without the leader present. Using myself as an example, I would look through the results and focus on a few key questions that I thought were important for me to understand in more detail and ask for ideas to help improve. I knew the team would not tell me directly, so I employed the team captain idea. On behalf of the broader team, during a follow-up staff meeting, the "team captain" would read out a summary of the discussion and provide ideas. The "team captain" for a discussion like this has to be a senior team member who is highly respected by all members of the team.

7. Leading diverse teams and building trust and dependence is about more than just work programs and strategy projects. Most leaders do team-building sessions as part of the process they use to build camaraderie. I did not believe that team dinners or simple outings were enough to build real trust and understanding. I knew from my own process in learning about individuals that I had to create a learning and cultural appreciation environment. As the leader of a global team, I was able to bring the team together in person one to two times per year. We chose a different location for each meeting, based on

where the team resided. The "host" team members were responsible for our cultural deep-dive team-building experience. They had this amazing moment to teach all of us about them, their history, their culture, their homes, and their backgrounds. These sessions were unbelievably powerful unity-building experiences. We did UNESCO world heritage tours, street food tours, tea ceremonies, and calligraphy classes, to name a few—all organized and led by members of the team who showed such great pride in their homes. We all learned so much about each other beyond the numbers and the facts.

8. We collectively celebrated each other's holidays and recognized their importance in each other's lives. I still receive "happy Thanksgiving" emails from team members in Asia and "merry Christmas" notes from team members who do not celebrate Christmas. It is a beautiful thing to experience people who care about each other's important moments, even when they don't participate in them themselves.

Building and leading diverse teams structured for the future of business is a leadership challenge. Positive results are not a foregone conclusion unless leaders create and foster an environment that leads to those results. Success is determined by:

1. Engagement of the team with each other in group settings

2. Completion and execution of short and long-term projects

3. KPI success and business outcomes, achieved by a growth mindset and collective participation

4. Progressive improvements in employee surveys about their leader and the engagement of that leader with the team

5. Future performance of team members (Are they getting promoted and progressing?)

6. Whether team members continue to be confidants and allies, even when they move to other teams

92. First Date
By Paul Salamanca

What the Idea Is: You're on a first date and your date says "I'm not looking to marry you at this point. I just want to get to know you." You'd probably say, "Of course! Let's first see if we're even compatible. It's just a first date."

This is the same reaction you should have when your prospect says to you on the first meeting, "I'm not looking to buy anything. I'm just interested in hearing more about your company."

Why It Is Valuable: Over my career as a sales rep, I would say almost 90 percent of my customers have said this to me on the first meeting, and by the end of the meeting they were agreeing to meet again. So don't let that affect your meeting. You're qualifying them as much as they're qualifying your company. If you don't see a big enough pain where you can help, then it's okay to not date again.

How It Works: You should really be worried if the prospect *does* want to marry you after the first date. The person may say something like, "Send me a quote right away" or "I want to make a decision ASAP" or "Just show me the demo and give me a quote." When your prospect moves too fast early on in the sales process, it's a red flag, just as it would be if someone asked for marriage on a first date. You need to slow things down to better qualify whether it's a real opportunity or if the prospect is only looking to get a second price for another solution he/she has already decided to purchase.

No matter how cool you think your technology or product is, no real enterprise deal will want to marry you after one date.

93. Building Big Teams and Relationships: Adjusting for Today's World
By Pete Friedman

What the Idea Is: Here at NetApp, I wear two hats; I am responsible for the Cisco Alliance globally, and I lead the FlexPod Business. FlexPod is a Converged Infrastructure solution developed in partnership with Cisco. The FlexPod solution has been in the market for over ten years and is sold through our channel partners to end customers. My team consists of a group of business development managers and solutions architects. Each of the business development managers is responsible for growing the FlexPod business in a specific geographic patch. To be successful, it is imperative that the business development managers build big teams in territory to help them scale their reach. My goal is to help them build big teams to gain market share. Let's start with this simple analogy: We are born with two arms and two legs. Scale those numbers to 4 x 4, 6 x 6, and so on, and suddenly you have many working on your behalf.

Why It Is Valuable: FlexPod is sold through channel partners; therefore, it is important that my team work closely with the partners in their respective geographies. To help scale the business, my team will educate, enable, and motivate our partners to drive the FlexPod solution. Primarily working with the ecosystem in Cisco, we identify the cross section where both of us would win in working toward a mutual goal.

We get a force-multiplier effect when we tap into our friends at Cisco, gain credibility with them, and get reinforcement from these partner and eco-partner relationships.

In order to maintain consistency and ensure maximum results, it is important to have a process to help build and grow the FlexPod business. For example, while there are dozens if not hundreds of potential partners in each geography, it is important to work with the key partners who will help grow the business and to not spread resources too thin. Again, the larger the team the business development managers have working on their behalf, the larger the pipeline and the more opportunities they will enjoy to sell FlexPod solutions.

How It Works: We spend a considerable amount of time with our own teams, making sure everyone understands what the solution provides and how it makes them relevant. They must also understand how we can leverage the partner community to get an uplift and gain more access to the customer as well as more opportunity outside our traditional buyer.

People are often moving so fast to get a home run that they cut corners. Instead of going to the basics and following the process, they will go to first base and then skip to third base.

We focus on following all the steps to stay on track with the process. Using their mental checklist to see that the prospect can be identified as the right customer for them, they ask themselves several questions: Is there an opportunity? Is there a match in what they are trying to accomplish with the solution we can bring? Can we maximize the time and return?

Here are some of the tools in their bag that help them with successful sales strategies: strategic account planning sessions, workshops, and listening to the voice of the customer. Then we make sure the teams come together. The goal is for the customers to state their needs and desired outcomes. Teams huddle and plan out strategy to provide the solution. They need to build a baseline of trust and understanding, and everyone comes together to build that out.

Here are questions that must be answered from the partner perspective: Are they resourced? Are they enabled? Are they motivated to have these conversations on behalf of the customer? Do they know the real wants and outcomes for the client and for their team?

I have found that sales are so complex now that not every company can provide a solution for every customer. Partnerships and strategies can provide the fix for that. Understand all the resources that are calling into the customers. Build that out, and continue to network and expand on those relationships.

In today's scenario, circumstances have created much more of a virtual world over the last ten to twelve months. It's much more difficult to build widespread trusted relationships via Zoom and telephone calls. We used to do a lot of customer events and trade shows so we could meet people within those environments. We are working to get back a little more face-to-face opportunities. Now we are having to do a lot of calls and demonstrate trust and credibility through actions.

NetApp has recognized that these are unprecedented times and that doing business as we once knew it has changed. In order to adapt and accommodate these changes, NetApp has been keenly aware of work-life-balance challenges and stress overload and therefore has implemented policies to support and address the new working structure.

94. The Sales Cycle
By Peter Baglieri

What the Idea Is: The sales cycle is a journey. Know when to talk business and when to go off topic to other interests, personal, etc.

Why It Is Valuable: The value here is that technology/business can be boring, especially now, when people are glued to their terminals or phones in the same room all day. Going off topic is an opportunity to get closer to someone and develop a relationship based on all the things that really matter for the long term, vs. just the transaction. You'll learn more about other people, what makes them tick, what their hobbies are, family situations, their passions, etc. This can only help you when negotiating, dealing with tense issues, asking for their help, and moving the ball forward.

How It Works: I deploy it sometimes when the other person least expects it; it's good to call someone when you *don't* need him/her. That's how you build good will. One of my most unique and best gifts is my ability to get business executives out of the office to attend unique events, including F-1 Racing, golf, the US Open Tennis Championships, Italy car rallies, etc.

95. Hiring Practices for the Sales Person (For Earlier-Stage Companies)
By Peter Bell

What the Idea Is: Probably 90 percent of start-up companies have wrong hiring practices for their sales people. They believe they want a superstar, but most superstar sales people do not want to work in a new start-up sales company.

Ideally, the founder/CEO should be a sales person. If the people who founded the company can't sell their product, it is unlikely they can get someone else to. **They must have a candid self-awareness of where the company is and its ability to attract and develop talent.**

Why It Is Valuable: If you want to build a repeatable sales machine, you need to have a recipe. Invest in training and in measurement, then repeat.

How It Works: Make an honest assessment of where the company is and its ability to attract talent that is appropriate to the stage of the company. Then hire someone with the right attributes, but not necessarily all the experience, and invest in training that person.

You can test the accuracy of this concept by assessing whether your first or second hire is more successful (i.e., which person is hitting expectations that were set for him/her, as measured by the sales manager and the salesperson?).

96. Performance Management for Leadership
By Peter Bell

What the Idea Is: The "spend" is normally between sales and engineering. People usually look at engineering as very scientific. Sales is more often looked at with a "free-wheeling, we-will-give-it-a-shot" mentality, and people often underestimate the cost of misfiring (risk).

If people invest in a start-up, they get their product ready and then hire sales people. Those first few people often do not work out because their image becomes tarnished and others will not want to work with them. (Why would they?)

You need to get it right from the very beginning. Look at sales development with the same lens and discipline as you do your product development part of the organization, and spend as much time in one as you do the other. Lay out the same chart for sales as you do for product, and have equally good systems/processes in place.

Why It Is Valuable: This concept allows you to measure your investment and make changes that are data driven.

How It Works: It is transparent; the sales team roadmap is shared with the team and reviewed with the team on a regular basis, at whatever cadence is appropriate for your particular company.

You'll know it is successful when you look at the investment and see the ROI. Look at what it costs to win a customer vs. what the customer spends over time. Applying his type of thinking will enable you to be more accurate in your metrics.

There are also some cultural aspects that apply. Your sales team members typically enjoy working for you, they stay longer because they care about the company, and they will be more successful overall because they believe in the company and can sell it better.

It's about the dollars. You will see it manifested in the numbers; when you lose a sales person, it is very expensive to go back to rehire and retrain, and your cost is much higher.

97. Sell Yourself, Sell Your Company, and Then Sell Your Product
By Peter Bell

What the Idea Is: People have to want to do business with you as a person, then they have to want to do business with your company, especially in areas where product offerings may be similar. This applies, no matter what stage your company is in (start-up or well established).

Why It Is Valuable: This truth transcends industries and scales from small to large.

How It Works: It's important to share up front what is unique about you and your company. Sales is a big part of the culture of the company. In the past, culture was an internal component; however, it is now visible to the outside world and often determines how the company is perceived by the customer, thereby becoming a determining factor in their buying decision.

This is basically a test to see if the reps believe enough in themselves and their company to "drink the Kool-Aid."[8]

This concept resonates well with salespeople and sales managers. In the world we live in today, with recurring revenue business, people buy into the company before they buy in to the product. They want an enduring relationship, and they often measure it by the long-term success of the salesperson and the company. That's why it's important to differentiate your company and your product.

You have to train your sales force to do this, and then test it (using written and/or oral tests). You can also use role playing. Of course, this is developed internally on a per-company basis, as it is tailored to the specific company. You can have different successful companies with very different cultures.

98. Understanding Your Strengths and Weaknesses
By Peter McKay

What the Idea Is: Understand your strengths and weaknesses to become successful in sales.

When I first entered this business, I didn't have a lot of sales training; I was a controller for a company. I looked for ways to increase my knowledge and ended up connecting with different people who were good at their craft. I started asking questions and learned how to solve problems.

Why It Is Valuable: If you want to get better, you must get feedback and develop a thick skin to be the best. It takes self-confidence and a forthright manner to overcome insecurities, be able to take advice to discover your strengths and weaknesses, and then turn your weaknesses into strengths. This comes from an attitude of serving. I have always tried to be easy to talk to and have attempted to quickly get people to like me. This enables a more casual discussion and more open dialog. People want to work with and help people they like. Get them to like you as quickly as possible.

How It Works: Where should we seek advice/feedback? Almost everyone likes to be asked for their expertise and advice, and it is a win for both the asker and the asked.

When I made the transition to sales, I didn't know how to sell. To learn the skills I needed to be successful, I sat next to the best salespeople I could find, listening to them as they had conversations with clients. When I learned as much as I could from one person, I moved to another, studying the best to become the best.

I didn't have a pipeline at the start, so I had to build one. I needed to find out how to get people on the phone, prospect, and work my way around a company. I struggled here until one day, during a bike race, it hit me. I was doing well in the race, right up until the moment I got to a hill and slowed down, when everyone passed me. This had happened before, so I figured out how to overcome my weakness by tackling that issue. I worked and worked the hills, increasing my strength and endurance until it became a strength and not a weakness. I decided to apply this to sales as well.

I practiced and practiced; I went into a conference room by myself, got on the phone, and started working (making my mistakes as I went). I continued until I refined the process and got good at it. The next thing I tackled was getting better at ROI assessments and business spend justification. Again, I sought out people who were the best at it and learned from them. I created a constant focus of playing to strengths and improving weaknesses. Once I was on a strong track for eight or nine months, management asked if I wanted to be promoted to work with a bigger team; then I had to work on those weaknesses as well. I worked to uncover the blind spots, being open to feedback from anyone who could help by sharing the things that might not be his/her strengths.

In the early days of Synk, the culture was very molded around "caring deeply." We cared about everyone and didn't want to hurt anyone's feelings, so we never said anything "bad," even though that may mean holding back on the necessary help for the person. If someone did give us constructive criticism, we could become defensive and be tempted to fight back and not accept the really good feedback that could truly make us better. When we did that, we never improved.

It's interesting to see how things have evolved since I started my career vs. now when I am nearing the end of my career. In the beginning, we would take the best sales reps and do the personality assessments, using all the tools we could find to determine what made them successful, and then create a profile to hire to. What we got were people who were the clone of the manager—those who did exactly what the manager did. In tech, everyone wanted everyone else to be the same (i.e., we wanted very limited diversity).

As I moved through my career, I determined that there was something to be said for diversity—in thinking, styles, and personalities. The diversity factor has brought about a need for different skill sets and sharing best ideas, because selling today is very different than it was ten or twenty years ago. The process is different and requires all of us to think differently about what "good" looks like now.

Here are the things I look for now when hiring new people: we still need openness, creativity, hungriness, and the need to be assertive, but we are now seeking all aspects of diversity. It is much more critical today for leaders to find and develop diversity by gender, race, cultures, etc. One of the biggest transformations for me has been becoming aware of the unconscious bias training we did for many years that was a big part of the VMware approach to diversity. I and others around me were unconsciously using actions/words that did not foster a very diverse and inclusive culture, and we didn't realize they were exclusive until someone pointed them out to us. Since then, I have become very conscious of these issues when building the right culture for our company.

99. Sales Management Best Practices
By Peter Quirk

What the Idea Is: Sales management best practices

Why It Is Valuable: Use these best practices to effectively lead your team and exceed expectations.

How It Works: These are best practices I've gathered over the years I've been in sales management:

Lead by example, be persistent, and drive the message through that will exceed your goals.

- Clearly define the goals and the steps you will take to win.
- Measure results.
    - "If you can't measure it, you can't manage it." –Peter Drucker
- Overcommunicate.
- Follow through on what you say you are going to do—keep your word.
- "Target ten sales calls a week." –Randy Seidl
- Do not procrastinate; just get it done and move on to the next step.
- Time is your enemy; manage it well.
- Follow through with what you say you are going do.
- Be early for appointments.
- Be organized; plan your week, and review every Sunday evening before the week starts.
- Listen more than you talk.
- Understand your customers' business and personal needs, and create solutions that help them advance, both personally and professionally.
- Understand your employees' business and personal needs, and align the positions available to advance them, both personally and professionally.
- Practice your presentation skills.
- Keep your LinkedIn up to date.
- Look into a mirror while you are on the phone. Your facial expressions will come through on the call; smile and be happy, and your customer will hear it in your voice.
- Be confident, well dressed, and prepared for all meetings.
- Have an agenda for all meetings.
- Do not waste the customer's time.
- Send a follow-up email with next steps the same day or evening.
- Network, network, network!

- The more you know about your employees and customers, the better you can serve your customers and lead your employees.
- Network with your competition.
  - Know your competition
  - "Keep your friends close and your enemies closer."—Godfather, Part II
- Be the first one in the office and the last one to leave (if and when you have an office again).
- Treat everyone with respect; treat them the way you would want to be treated.
- The people you see on the way up the ladder are the same folks you will see on the way down.
- "You are not as good as you think you are, but you are not as bad as they say you are." –Lou Holtz
- Be honest.
- Be to the right of right.
- Be accountable, take responsibility for your actions and for the people on your team, and don't blame others for your mistakes; learn from them and take risks.
- Protect your people, but hold them accountable. (Be loyal, but objective.)
- "Run to the fire; bad things don't get better with time." –Meg Whitman
- Gray is good sometimes, but do not go over the line.
- Be a lifelong learner.
- If you are comfortable, you are dying and on the way to being irrelevant.
- Become comfortable being uncomfortable.
- Read a diverse portfolio of business information, news feeds, and books you enjoy
  - PodCast, WSJ, Economist, The Daily, etc.
  - Listen to the opposing side and learn.
- Be recruiting all the time.
- Always have a bench.
- Stack rank your reps.
- Turn over 10 percent of your sales team every year.
- Always be available to the customers and respond quickly; let them know they can count on you.
- An angry, upset customer is a good customer, because they are still talking to you and giving you a chance to fix the problem.
- Keep a good life balance between work and family.

- Spend the company's money like it's your own money—don't waste it.
- Build a diverse, inclusive team.
- Whether you're hiring men, women, someone of a different race, technical talent, or sales talent, ask:
  - Do they fit culturally with the team?
  - What are their goals?
  - Will they make us better and challenge us, but not be too disruptive?
- Be committed and represent what you believe. Don't avoid conflict; don't be a pushover—be respectful but hold your ground. Know when to back down or push forward.
- Selling is a combination of art and science.
- Plan—daily, weekly, monthly, quarterly and annually, both best practices and goals.

Weekly:
- Meet on Monday evening to plan the week; send out the agenda the Friday before the weekend and resend on Monday morning.
- Have no internal meetings Tuesday through Thursday at a minimum, as that is prime selling time; be in front of customers.
- Have a recap call every Friday with the managers or reps, depending on your role, to discuss how the week went.
- Do weekly training on relevant subjects, products, and sales.

Monthly:
At the end of month one, know your pipeline in the current quarter. You need to have 60 percent commit coverage at the end of month one. You have to have a solid commit for the quarter and understand any risks to your current commit and what the upside is. Are there any game changers in the funnel? What executive support may be needed to reach quarterly commits, etc.?

Quarterly:
- Have quarterly business reviews.
- Look at YOY compares, QOQ compares, and YTD performance. Review all segments/BUs. In Q1, provide an initial yearly plan. In Q2, recap the prior quarter/quarters and focus on current quarter activity, review business and sales goals, and set the commit for the current quarter.

Annually:
- Align sales FSC, margins, and sales goals with the overall financial plan for the company. Build plans around:

- Internal partners (i.e., different BU's and specific targets; I can provide examples)
- External partners, distribution, VADS, VARS, SIs.

100. In-Quarter Close Plans
By Phil Castillo

What the Idea Is: In-Quarter Close Plans

Why It Is Valuable: It increases close percentages and helps streamline communications, roles, and efforts.

How It Works: Build a straightforward internal close plan for strategic or larger opportunities. Define the opportunity name, type, revenue, and/or average recurring revenue costs. Write a quick one-to-two-sentence description of the project. List the key stakeholders and their roles for your internal team as well as for the external customer/partner team and their roles. Then make a list of key milestones/actions, owners, and dates, and keep it constantly refreshed.

Some CRM tools have pieces of this, but having a simple form like this makes it easy to update and streamline your forecast and other internal conversations. It also provides a way others can provide feedback and show potential missing steps or things to care for in the deal closing.

While this is an internal document, it can be sanitized and used as a "JEP" (joint engagement proposal) to share with a customer for an ongoing agreement on key steps needed to complete a project/purchase.

101. Sales Leaders: Having a Model for Success
By Phil Harrell

What the Idea Is: Sales leaders have to have a model for success that defines the critical processes, infrastructure, metrics, and talent required to drive predictable, repeatable, and scalable revenue growth.

Why It Is Valuable: Sales leaders have to not only be able to achieve revenue targets, but they also have to be able to understand and explain the system they're using to make revenue production repeatable and predictable. This last point is critical. Even if sales leaders meet quota, CEOs and boards of directors (BoDs) get concerned if the sales leader can't demonstrate that the results were achieved through the use of a systematic approach.

The modern sales leader must rely on more than just hiring top talent. They must also install processes, infrastructure, and data so they can plug new sales reps in, help them quickly be productive, and ensure broad-based performance, versus relying on a small set of star performers to make the numbers every quarter. A system that outlines the model for success helps sales leaders sleep at night, because they know: 1) the reasons for success, and 2) their sales team is executing within a system that will ensure that a majority of them help produce consistent results.

How It Works: Think through all the critical processes, infrastructure, and metrics that are required for your sales operating model and what you need in the following areas:

- Sales strategy - Identify the most attractive opportunities to grow revenue.
- Organizational design - Select an organizational structure optimized for efficient growth.
- Talent management - Design a talent strategy that will enable you to find and keep top sales talent.
- Demand generation - Ensure adequate pipeline development in target markets.
- Sales execution - Ensure value-added, consistent execution on opportunities through to close and post close.
- Sales productivity - Utilize science and data to identify ways to iterate and improve.

Set up the infrastructure required from the technology side, automate as much of the processes as possible to avoid human error, and gather the right data. Apply data and science to the art of sales to help your team succeed.

102. What Do the Best Reps Do?
By Phil Harrell

What the Idea Is: What do the best reps do?

The best reps do two things better than average reps: First, they generate high levels of activity with prospects and customers by minimizing the amount of non-core selling time. And second, they qualify very carefully by asking good questions to diagnose the situation and understand the prospect's problem so they can evaluate whether they can solve it. If they determine they can't solve the prospect's problem, they walk away early before they've invested valuable time and energy.

Why It Is Valuable: Time is a sales rep's most precious asset. Great reps know they can't afford to invest their time in deals that won't close if they want to consistently make their numbers. A sales person's job is to determine who is ready to buy and whether they can solve the customer's problem. By asking the right questions and listening to the responses, they can qualify the prospect or, if necessary, disengage early before spending too much time on something that is outside their wheelhouse of solutions. It's important to spend time working on deals that are real and with people who can buy so reps can get a good return on their time.

How It Works: Every day when you get up, you have to think about making sure you are doing the right things that lead to success—getting in front of the right prospects and asking the right questions that help you diagnose the problem and provide a solution. If you can't solve the problem, it might even mean you recommend that a prospect go to a different company. It's about being very strategic with your time. It sounds like a difficult thing to do, but you can do it with practice and good coaching from someone who will work with you to help you go to the next level.

103. Relationships
By Piyush Mehta

What the Idea Is: Building a trusted relationship is extremely important in all aspects of your life. This is also true in building long-term relationships with business partners and customers.

Why It Is Valuable: By building trusted relationships, you will be more successful at selling. These relationships take years to cultivate and are the result of delivering on commitments.

How It Works: Here are my key points for successful selling through building trusted relationships:

1. **Know your customer.**
   Know what vertical your customers reside in, what their strategic objectives are, and what the disruptors are in their industry.

2. **Put yourself in the customer's shoes.**
   How long have the CEO and upper management been there? What commitments have they made to drive a transformation to their business? Do they have empowerment and budgets to drive their strategy? If so, *who is leading that charge?* How is this empowerment distributed across the globe?

3. **Get through the right doors to build the right network.**
   Do those who are empowered know your company, and do you have the relationships to get in front of them? If the relationships exist, great. If they don't, do you have the *network to build* those relationships, or can you get friendly intros to the right people?

4. **Align your solution with your customer's goals.**
Research and understand the end goal. How does the end goal align with their strategy, and what business value and the outcome can you drive that *differentiates you* from the competition?

5. **When doing business, expect to run a marathon and not a sprint.**
Engage, as frequently and as wide as feasible within the organization. Driving any change is a marathon and not a sprint. There needs to be a strategic approach to the entire journey, but then a sub-strategy is required for each mile. Agree to a win criteria and clearly define what both sides achieve if accomplished. *Ask for the business,* as they won't give it unless you *ask! And ask big!*

6. **Be nice. Build friendships!**
Business relationships are as *much about trust* as anything else. If they trust you and like you, they will do business with you. If you are artificial and just there for the order, then it will be short-lived. Can you call or text those empowered within your customers on their cell phones? Do you know their family or what's going on in their personal lives? Were you there when they needed a friendly ear and it had nothing to do with a deal?

Happy selling!

104. Motivation/Reward
By Prentiss Donohue

What the Idea Is: At a high level, there's a core philosophy regarding motivation/reward for sales folks. Despite the popular contention that everyone is "coin-operated," that's not my experience. In addition to recognition and reward, top performers need three things:

- Purpose (their own company, the customer outcomes, the time to value for any given project, etc.)
- Mastery (their own skills, knowledge of the customer environment, their expertise in the industry, etc.)
- Empowerment/Autonomy (This is the hardest in large enterprise software companies, but orienting around the AE is key, and letting them know they have air cover/responsiveness from the organization is critical.)

The need for purpose, mastery, and autonomy (which is reinforced in Daniel Pink's book *Drive*) is at the center of having a front-foot sales team to help drive growth. Deploy with clear communications, ongoing enablement/training, and reference cases. Top performers resent low achievers in their midst. It's as important to the organizational effectiveness to clear out low performers and instill a sense of "beating-the-budget-is-the-price-of-freedom" mentality as it is to put air under the wings for the high-achievers—along with recognition. Celebrate the stars, big time.

105. Long-Term Mindset Outweighs Quarter-End Performance
By Riccardo Di Blasio

What the Idea Is: In today's world, the majority of salespeople are obsessed with quarter endings. At the end of the day, Wall Street makes the stock move up or down based on your quarterly results. Since your quarterly results are a consequence of a long-term focus, you must learn to look beyond them.

Why It Is Valuable: If you are leading a public company with stock, the analysts/bankers/investors are manically focused on the quarter; consequently, you will drive your organization on a quarterly driven culture. I'm going to say something a bit provocative—the quarter is not the main objective; a great quarter is a consequence of many, many things done right. Your current quarter results are the outcome of actions and initiatives you took six to nine months ago.

How It Works: Being therefore focused on the strategy first, ask yourself, *Do we have the right amount of data, the right segmentation, and the product positioning for each of the segmented market verticals?* Once you have that, ask, *What is the best organizational structure we must form to support the execution of the model we have designed? After the organizational model has been designed, what are the skills we require from our sales organization to get the needed results?* Money can't be the only priority; it is a consequence of a lot of endless days and sleepless nights as well as a lot of training and study, research, assimilation, and mistakes below the waterline that the outside doesn't see. If you nail all these things right, you will have a great quarter.

Many of the leaders in our space are quarterly driven, because that is how the capitalist system tends to value sales (you are as good as your last quarter)—using a very short-term mindset. Companies like Amazon do not focus on just the immediate quarter and how it impacts the stock. Bezos doesn't care, because he is focused on the long term. You must be very self-confident and have the courage to not listen to investors and Wall Street. Keep your focus on your North Star, and keep focusing on the long term.

If you focus on all the right elements of the equation, the success of the quarter will be a consequence.

106. Selling is Not Just an Attitude—It's a Precise Science
By Riccardo Di Blasio

What the Idea Is: People tend to believe that selling is an attitude—that you need to know the industry, have a rolodex, have a lot of tools, and know the product, which is all true. But at the end of the day, it is all about the data.

Why It Is Valuable: There has been a big acceleration in the use of data in the last few years because of the better tools that are available. I have been manically focused on using data over the last two decades because of the availability of better information and analytics. Today we can be data driven and led by data whenever we need to build a go-to-market strategy or make a decision.

Tools and sales organizations are still being managed mainly by perception; even how you score the performance of the sales professional still involves a lot of perception and not enough data. When you push the envelope by adopting the newest and best-of-breed technology, which is often AI driven, you can really crunch all the data you have in your sales organization. Whether it is coming from within your company or you get the data from marketing, it will really be very useful in helping to give you a dashboard across the operation.

How It Works: We need to move past using perceptions and gather all the data available with the tools we have at hand. Use AI and any other methods available to you to implement strong analytics into your decision making, because it will help you understand how big your market is and all the different market dynamics. You can translate that into your market and into your product speech. Data can actually be a great supporter of your efforts when you are doing that. The more data analysis you have, the more precise and correct your outcomes will be.

107. Enterprise Sales: It's Not about Selling— It's about Enabling People to Buy
By Rich Napolitano

What the Idea Is: In an enterprise sale, it's not about selling; it's about enabling people to buy.

Why It Is Valuable: When they think about selling into the enterprise, people are often confused about what it takes. At the end of the day, it's about understanding the nature of the clients, their business, their pain points, their risks, their hopes, and their dreams.

Enterprise clients are sophisticated business and technology people. They actually object to being sold to. However, they are open and profoundly interested in being educated and learning about what you have to offer.

How It Works: Selling to these clients is more about listening and education than anything else. Detailed account plan templates from Miller Heiman or MEDDIC are often used to streamline this process and create consistent systematic campaigns.

The sales process is not the lone-wolf activity of a sales hunter, but a coordinated campaign where the sales manager is the offensive coordinator calling the plays throughout the game to ensure a win. Salespeople can err here, when they allow it to become too much about personal ego and not about team involvement. They will not be able to take down the big accounts without the support and participation of a team. Using product sales as an example, some people who should be included in that team are the founder, the CTO, and the lead product manager. You may often have a VP of engineering substituting for the founder in much larger organizations.

In conclusion, the enterprise sales enablement is about educating the prospect using a systematic and coordinated sales campaign that allows the client to choose to purchase a solution rather than being sold something. When done correctly, enterprise sales wins are the major leagues of professional sales and result in lasting relationships for many years.

108. Mutual Accountability: How It Becomes a Basic Component of Success
By Richard DiGangi

What the Idea Is: The term accountability sometimes carries a negative connotation—a blame mentality, along with an assumption of guilt. That's not it at all.

Why It Is Valuable: You understand how both you and your customer will be held accountable for your efforts to achieve agreed-upon success. Accountability involves the ability of a person to provide a focus on an initiative, make the necessary decisions, and garner support from his/her customer to achieve success. The biggest misstep of salespeople is doing an inordinate amount of work for little to no reward.

How It Works: You must think strategically about your business and the people involved.

Do you understand your customers' businesses?

Do you understand your customers' goals?

Do you understand your customers' metrics?

Do you understand your customers' compensation or measurement?

Have you agreed (clearly) on the rules of engagement and what the goal is?

What does success look like or resemble?

What steps have you agreed on that each party will take to achieve this success?

What would you do in order to guarantee success?

Are there penalties for not doing what was agreed upon?

Jointly agreeing on mutual efforts and success is a recipe for success. Mutual accountability is something that needs to be practiced in order to be successful. Anyone who excels in a sport, or whatever their craft of choice, practices. It requires more than just minimal practice when the mood hits; it requires a clear, focused, and disciplined practice that analyzes the process, questions the results, and continually looks for ways to improve on what they are doing.

109. Self-Awareness
By Richard DiGangi

What the Idea Is: Self-awareness is one of the most important aspects of sales success.

Why It Is Valuable: Having a conscious awareness of your actions is very important. Know yourself, understand your strengths, determine how to improve your weaknesses, and eliminate blind spots. Not understanding how you are viewed can hinder your success. Not understanding what is around you can also be a hindrance. If you do not know what you want in your life, you cannot determine the path to get there. Self-awareness is understanding your own emotional intelligence, and it leads to better decision making. It can make you better at your job and a better communicator in the workplace, and it can enhance your self-confidence.

How It Works:

Take a look—what do you see in the mirror?

What do you believe about yourself?

Do you believe in your desires?

Do you believe you have the right to success?

What do you deserve?

What is your definition of success? What do you want in life? From your partner? From your customers?

Do you possess self-regulation?

Do you have motivation?

Do you have empathy?

When someone else looks at you, what do they see?

How are you viewed by others?

Do you exercise social skills?

Do you have a positive outlook or negative outlook?

80 percent of energy is wasted on negative outlooks/attitudes; it's easier to be negative than positive, but it is a choice we can consciously make every moment.

Do you want to change your self-perception? Then shift your mental attitude:

Shift From:	To:
Negative mental attitude	Positive mental attitude
Focus attention on yourself	Focus attention on the client/other person
Limiting beliefs	Resourceful assumptions/beliefs
Risk averse	Bravery/courage to take risks
Blame mentality	Personal responsibility

110. Creating a Viable Compensation Plan Process
By Richard Dyke

What the Idea Is: Management must be able to properly compensate a sales team, and it must be able to motivate desired business outcomes with proper incentives (cash/prizes/recognition).

How do you get your sales team excited about a new comp plan? Each time an announcement is made about a new compensation plan, the sales team is likely to be worried about incentive income because they could believe something will be taken away. There is a lot of paranoia around each new comp plan rollout.

Why It Is Valuable: Every quota-carrying sales team wants to bust open the comp plan and make a lot of money; they want to overachieve! Sales teams don't like complex plans that involve too many tricky "trip wires" or contingencies that could crush their potential upside. They don't want to feel that the company is working against them.

The vast majority of sales teams genuinely care about their company's revenue growth, health, and business goals and objectives. They also want to be held accountable and motivated to overachieve these objectives. Team "buy-in" is required, and transparency helps seal that team commitment.

Ultimately, you want the entire team to be fully engaged and highly motivated. When that happens, you get a lot more creative thinking and man-hours on the job, along with more excitement around the opportunity and the upside. When the comp is all properly aligned, the customer-facing, quota-carrying go-to-market team does a lot of good for the company.

How It Works: At a high level, identify the top three to five company growth objectives (they can span a variety of different business objectives) and document them with the senior executive staff so there is a high-level buy-in for the following year's business goals.

Once that is done, the senior executive leader of sales needs to "look in the mirror, examine his/her convictions," and verify and accept the viability and objectives of these goals.

Then the sales leader should choose a small team (a committee) of top sales performers. Sales teams can be made up of personnel outside of sales. For example, sometimes the SE (pre-sales system engineer) reports to the sales representative, but in more recent years the voice of the SE is much more dynamic and important. If that SE's voice is not represented, you will lose an important factor/contributor of information.

The key is for this committee to include at least one high-performance team member with a history of being upset/agitated with the comp plans/goals in the past, so you have someone with an objection to some points of the plan. Controversy is good for the discussion and helps bring clarity to the end results. This is also the team who should present the comp plan to the company, if possible (or be a part of the presentation).

This sales-team committee should feel special/honored; fly them all into a great location (to corporate or to a resort), arrange for nice accommodations, provide a team dinner in a nice atmosphere, and make it a great event for them, with a higher-end appeal.

Dedicate at least two separate sessions to the development process. Begin with two or three hours in the morning; then have a break to give the team time to attend to calls/current business needs, followed by another two- or three-hour session in the afternoon. Follow that with a meeting between the senior executive sales leadership and the sales-team committee so they can review the progress on compensation and motivation and freely express their thoughts.

A very important part in this process is for the two separate sessions to be a "blank page" and unsupervised. Provide the sales-team committee with the high-level company objectives/goals (the things they must keep in mind). Then, as a committee, they must determine how to best motivate their sales team to reach these goals. Coach the committee to use data to help guide their case (i.e., internal historical sales data, outside compensation metrics, prior comp plans, other verified data from the field on what is working for other organizations, etc.).

There should be no expectation that whatever they write is set in stone; but there should be an expectation that it will go forward for review and approval. If it makes sense to the CRO or head of sales, the feedback will be put into the final plan. One or two good things will come out of this; it is a sales plan from the team and for the team, with their comp and upside first in mind.

The final segment of the process is to have the sales-team committee present the entire plan to the entire team. This has worked out well over the years. It eliminates a lot of anxiety. When salespeople are selling salespeople, you probably get a better plan, because they push themselves harder than you would. Ideally, you always want to have the compensation plan drive the right behaviors.

111. Effective Training/Motivating, Training/ Testing, and Certification of Training
By Richard Dyke

What the Idea Is: There is an accreditation process for sales education that gives salespeople clout, empowerment, and credibility toward their everyday efforts, sales acumen, and stature. (This credibility should be verified by score/status.)

Why It Is Valuable: When you go through the process of basic company sales education, especially in organizations at the start-up level, there are a lot of holes in the program. There is a critical need to solidify company messaging. It must be crisp, clear, consistent, and standard throughout all the teams. Consistency is crucial, as everyone in the whole organization should be "speaking the same language," not just the sales team. Through this process you will root out any confusion. Any nuances that are not clear must be rooted out; there must be one voice. You are ultimately looking for repeatability through all layers.

How It Works: If you need to develop your own system in a start-up, it's best to choose a theme to work with. Baseball has a great hierarchy and structure, so it is a good theme to use in running the program. With a theme, you can motivate at different levels with different awards and incentives for the certification process. If you don't have a learning management system (LMS), it will be somewhat manual. In today's environment, you will want to have online testing, updates, and online access to learning and education. You will want to have two tracks: technical and sales. The salespeople should go through both tracks. The SEs should go through the technical track and have the option to go through the sales track. Another school of thought is that both the salespeople and the SEs should do both tracks.

Start the program off by giving everyone a numbered jersey (keeping with the baseball theme) with the company logo to reinforce that they are on the team, and give them a written description of the program. Then verbally go through the training at each level. Using the baseball theme, entry level is at first base, and participants get an additional reward of a batting glove, a wristband, or something similar. They get to go to second base with additional training/certification, and they receive a new reward. They go through the same process to get to third base, where they get a higher level of education and a greater reward. When they get to home base, they may get a bat with an insignia and a certification for completing the program. If they participate in advanced training beyond that, they will get greater rewards. Advanced training would involve much deeper testing on the knowledge base and additional certifications.

One part of the training requires the participant to hold a verbal Q&A testing signoff. The sales rep must be able to verbally give a clear description of the product and the company in a conversational forum.

112. Maximize Effort and Results: Pushing Beyond First-Level Management Goals
By Richard Dyke

What the Idea Is: Maximize effort and results, pushing beyond first-level management goals.

Why It Is Valuable: This helps to call out or eliminate "sandbagging the number" at the district management numbers level to give much more accuracy and consistency to forecasting reports, pipeline, and revenue growth.

How It Works: Sales leaders work to go through business reviews with their sales teams, but they cannot always participate in this process with all the teams. Set up a format for goal reviews with the levels of high, medium, and required deal numbers (worst case scenario). Ideally, the absolute worst-case goal should add up to be more than the district commit number for the team.

When I could not always make the district meetings, I would make sure to attend the district dinner meeting that night, and I would order a magnum of champagne or wine. I would have the meeting leader bring a Sharpie marker to the dinner and have all the salespeople sign their name to the bottle, date it, and add their commit number and their worst-case number.

I found that the worst-case individual number was often at least two times better than the worst-case district number. This magnum carafe then became a trophy and a battle cry. If you do this, be sure to take pictures of it to share; reference it during the campaign time, and use it during the award ceremony later. In the end, the carafe could be given to the sales manager or sales leader. This is just a fun idea to help drive individual performance commitments to tie to the greater district objectives!

113. The "Seller's Journal"
By Richard Geraffo

What the Idea Is: The "Seller's Journal"

Why It Is Valuable: I have kept a "Seller's Journal" for over fifteen years. Each and every time I meet an executive, CEO, or innovative customer, I make a journal entry to capture my "learnings." I find myself often referring back to the journal when I need a refresher on critical business topics.

How It Works: Here's an example: I met Mark Hurd during my studies at the Stanford Executive Program. I listened to Mark describe what he thought the "role of a CEO" was. I captured his thoughts and put them in the journal.

As another example, I also have in my journal the definitions of "strategy" and "execution" and why they are different.

I have also captured the most interesting "interview questions." For example, if you were trying to understand how the candidate thought about building their teams and what they considered critical attributes, you might ask, "If you had to build a team of only three people, who would you hire and why? What is the profile of each?"

My latest entry in the journal is, "Try to fail but never fail to try," a quote from Coach Adrian Williams-Peloton.

114. Be Proud of Being a Salesperson
By Rick Ruskin

What the Idea Is: Be proud of being a salesperson. I am a chief sales officer, and I want people to know my exact role when we meet.

Millennials sometimes think the title of "salesperson" is not prestigious enough. They may think people will not want to deal with them because all they are going to do is ask for money. The problem seems to be a mix of ego and money (they want to make the high dollars, but they also want their peers to recognize their value). They need to be proud of what they do. In most companies, the highest paid people are the salespeople. Top salespeople are held in high esteem.

Why It Is Valuable: It's good for you to know your role in the business, and for the clients to know you are serious about generating business for your company and you're not just there to educate them.

This brief story illustrates the point of being clear on who you are and what you do:

The team went to a potential customer to present for a multimillion-dollar deal. They walked in and prepared to meet with the chief technical officer. He was late. Everyone was already positioned on either side of the table, ready to begin. When the CTO finally arrived and looked around, he said, "I don't want a sales pitch today."

From the other end of the room, I closed my folder and replied, "We are here today to talk about our technology and make sure we are meeting your requirements. We have outlined them to make sure we are working within your budget. But make no mistake, I am here to sell you something; and if that's not okay, then we don't need to have this meeting."

There was absolute silence for a few moments as the CTO returned the stare and then said, "All right, go ahead." We made the sale. It could have backfired, but letting people know your role and why you are there is crucial to the success of the meeting.

How It Works: You must maintain the right attitude about being a salesperson on an ongoing basis.

115. Make Training a Way of Life for Your Company
By Rick Ruskin

What the Idea Is: Training is never complete; it cannot be a one-shot deal. Business, messaging, and the competitive landscape are always changing, so training needs to be done on a regular basis.

When I start a business, one of the first things I do is set up a training regimen that includes:

- Proper onboarding, with weekly, monthly, and quarterly tune-ups.
- A combination of live practical training and proper industry certifications.
- Live training in onboarding, plus quarterly training, and maybe an annual sales kickoff with most of the time spent training.
- Training, role playing, and in-character presentations. We put them in uncomfortable situations, and in roles selling to peers and the management team. (If they are good there, then selling to customers is a piece of cake.)

Let's look at a sports team as an example: They train all the time for months before their season ever begins, and then they train all week for a short time of actually performing. They practice every scenario and are never surprised by what they see on game day. It's the same situation with sales.

Why It Is Valuable: You want to set a goal of having your teams be the best prepared, no matter what team they face. With the proper training, they will be ready for any eventuality and can face anything.

How It Works: You must be very detailed about planning; create a calendar for all the training cadences for the year. Once you lose credibility, it's almost impossible to regain it. So you don't want your people to interact with a prospect until they are ready. Try to make it fun; have final exams and internal certifications that they have to pass in order to get out with the clients. Give awards, prizes, and positive reinforcement. You don't have to be a jerk to be tough.

You can measure your training program by setting the plan and measuring against that. Make sure you have completed your plan, and test your people to make sure they are ready for battle.

116. Perspectives and Philosophies: Leading from the Front
By Rick Ruskin

What the Idea Is: No matter how big your company gets, you need to be on the sharp edge of the business, meeting with customers, and getting out and working with your team members.

Why It Is Valuable: You have to set the tone with a mindset that says, *I am going to work harder than anyone else*. It keeps you sharp, because you are out there with your team, hearing everything. Don't ask your team members to do anything you won't do yourself.

I have been a sales executive (as a vice president, etc.) for many years and have four million frequent-flyer miles from selling around North America—I have actually been involved in closing business on the ground in forty-two states—as well as thirty other countries. My people know I am in it with them, because I understand their issues and challenges; and I understand who they are because of the way I work with them.

How It Works: You must develop the right attitude and do whatever actions it takes. It's important to create a cadence—tell people where you will be and when, and they will get things done. Set the expectations that you are coming to town to close business and help them get their next set of deals in motion. And if they are sales pros, they will make your trip meaningful.

The proof of the value of this concept is in the overall success of the organization. There are different metrics for each type of business; and depending on the metrics outlined for the company (long-term growth, for the quarter, etc.), set your personal goals and then the goals for your team, and plan from there.

117. Change Management: Exporting Best Tech Sales Practices to a Traditional Industry
By Robert Chu

What the Idea Is: Change management—exporting best tech sales practices to a traditional industry (in the specialty chemicals sector).

Nine years ago, after the acquisition of my previous division, I joined a specialty chemical company out of northeast Tennessee. Eastman was a nearly 100-year-old company with a portfolio of products spanning from auto glass to plastics to the intermediate products that went into film, acrylics, coating, and many other components of fibers, garments, food additives, etc.

I joined this company because the head of HR and I were colleagues at Gateway. Eastman was looking for someone to head up two of their Asian Pacific divisions, with a focus on China. The assignment was based in Shanghai, their AP headquarters. They needed someone with an injection of account management discipline and rigor, and predictability in sales forecasting as well. My value add was that I brought a level of velocity and a drive for constant change, rapid product intros, and phasing out existing products to customers.

Why It Is Valuable: The principles, systems, and processes used in the IT sales world can be applied to other industries.

I had no experience in either the chemicals industry or the energy industry, other than as a seller to that segment from my days at Dell, Gateway, and 3Com. The interesting draw for me was to provide a level of change management to the sales organization at Eastman in the AP region. The sales cycles there were very long, and products and solutions had existed without change for many years—sometimes decades—unlike the tech industry with its constant changes.

In the first quarter after I joined, I was able to attend sales calls with direct customers and key partners and observe the cadence of the sales-forecasting process as well as the overall reporting back to divisional headquarters in the US. I was also able to observe the sales tools that were available for the reps, including call sheets, preparation for executive call briefings, and forecasting tools. I also participated in the account management of existing sales training as well as online tools for account information.

These were my observations after one quarter: "There is a very random-ized and unstructured approach in forecasting, account plans, call-sheet scorecards, follow up, and accountability on forecasting at the Asia level as well as on a global level." The company was evaluating SalesForce.com before I joined and wanted to eventually bring their processes online with this SaaS product. Sales training and account management training had been done three years prior with inhouse trainers from the US headquarters.

Our conclusion was that the team needed a new approach in terms of account tracking, customer information, and prospecting in order to be compatible with the company's move to SalesForce.com. We evaluated a few vendors for conducting a comprehensive account management training program for the forty sales reps and managers in the two Asian divisions. This was to be a pilot for the AP region; if it was successful in implementation and adoption, it would be rolled out across the entire AP region for Eastman, and eventually globally within six to nine months. After narrowing it down to two short-listed companies that we believed would be the most conducive for a mature industry such as chemicals, we started this journey with Miller Heiman.

At the same time, we wanted to introduce change management with the teams, which would include sales forecasting cycles on a weekly cycle versus a monthly cycle—what Eastman was using at that time. One particular division that was most compatible with the weekly cycle was a commodities chemicals group called OXO Alcohols. Their intermediate products were pegged to the price of oil and subject to change on a constant basis (moment to moment). The weekly process was much more conducive versus reviewing the products and trends on a monthly basis. We were able to increase the responsiveness of competitive pricing with customers and partners, reduce decision time from headquarters, and capture higher margins and selling times; we were no longer trialing the market. As we began bringing our company to a forward position in marketing, it almost became an arbitrage position in the market. We utilized daily calls with the US team to decide on the best regions to sell products in with the highest margins and the best prices. We adopted many of the principles brought to us by Miller Heiman, and this was one of the successful outputs from the change management plan. (The blue sheets system was instrumental in allowing us to attract the status of direct customers as well as key partners.)

How It Works: All teams at all levels, from top to bottom, went through the Miller Heiman training for a week. I participated as head of the division to make sure they had executive buy in. We ran in parallel with SalesForce.com training, taking two paths—the automation of sales tools and a new style of managing customers from end to end, from prospecting to closing and tracking. We were able to institute the cadence to the one-week schedule during the end of Q2, only five months into my joining the company;

we rolled it out in Q3 and were able to deploy SalesForce.com in the middle of Q3, starting with inside sales. We then reviewed all the accounts and helped the sales reps and the managers with data integrity and consistency in the inputs; after a quarter of teething, as well as change management, we were able to direct the teams to move from written communications. (Everything had to be documented within the SalesForce.com tool.) Basically, within two quarters we were able to create accuracy and efficiency within the group.

The daily war room calls contributed to our success. We could see improvements in the average selling prices, margins, and speed of decision. We were allocating supplies to the most optimal price/margin mixes in AP. Other groups that were much more stable than OXO Alcohol began to see our success. By the year's end, we had instituted SalesForce.com and were able to implement the Miller Heiman processes into our account management, which allowed us to have a consistent format in terms of presenting account plans and preparing for sales calls within all levels of the organization. Each call, no matter what region, was now using the same information and practices; this became a powerful tool that allowed for very effective customer/partner calls.

118. The Microsoft Server Incubation Business in the Asia Pacific Region, 2003-2006
By Robert Chu

What the Idea Is: This is a description of challenges the Microsoft server incubation business faced in the Asia Pacific region, 2003-2006 (which was a catalyst for growth in the fast-emerging Asia Pacific markets) and how those challenges were resolved.

I worked at Microsoft from 2003-06 as the GM of the Windows Server Business division for the Asia Pacific region. Our unit was the data-center business unit serving SMB, the public sector, and large enterprise customers. The portfolio included seventeen Windows Server software products ranging from server operating systems (Windows Server) to email/collaboration (Exchange Server), database systems (SQL Server), security, storage, and small business server systems. Over 85 percent of the Asia Pacific business unit revenue was driven by the three main products (Windows Server, Exchange, and SQL Server). The remaining 15 percent was derived from the remaining fourteen products, with only the SBS (Small Business Server) having a meaningful revenue of about 4 percent total.

Why It Is Valuable: This was our challenge: The Server business in 2003 was approximately $400m, with an annual growth of 7 percent during the past two years. Our 2004 target was an aggressive growth of 10 percent. While the business was tracking at the rate of the overall hardware server growth rates across the region and generally increasing market share against key competitors (Linux OS with Server, Oracle—database and Lotus Notes—email), the overall growth was essentially gated by the hardware server growth. The growth was also affected by taking substantially larger market share from key competitors in the main sectors of database and email systems.

How It Worked:

2004 Plan. In order to reach or exceed the revenue goal of $440m, we needed a new growth strategy beyond just relying on growing with the server market and acquiring material market share from competitors—with the three main products. Thus, the focus had to be on the remaining 15 percent of the Windows Server family, with an even more micro-focus on the largest (and potential growth) of the three products among the fourteen.

Our team evaluated the market growth projections of the three server segments within the region and concluded that enterprise storage, SME servers, and security firewall systems were growing at rates that were at premiums to the overall 6 to 7 percent server growth rates. These segments aligned with the Windows Storage Server, the Windows Small Business Server (SBS), and the Windows Internet Security Acceleration Server (ISA).

The go-to-market motions. The Windows Storage Server was primarily driven hardware attached to two key OEM server and storage partners, Dell and HP. The largest markets were in Australia and Korea. The industry segments were in manufacturing (Korea and Taiwan) and service providers (Korea and Australia).

The Small Business Server was a partners-driven business sold by distributors and SIs focused on businesses in the mid-markets of about 400 to 500 employees. Top markets were in India and Australia/New Zealand.

The security firewall segment (ISA Server) was also sold primarily via specialized security SIs with experience across both hardware and software firewall solutions and via traditional distributors. The largest markets were in Australia, Korea, and India.

Our Server Business Unit was comprised of forty storage sales specialists in each of the markets across the Asia Pacific, with a revenue/head of approximately $10m/specialist. This number was higher in the developed markets of Australia/New Zealand, Korea, Singapore, and Hong Kong, and lower in emerging markets of SE Asia such as Thailand and Malaysia and the large markets such as India and China. These specialists supported the mainstream Microsoft enterprise and SMB sales teams. They had to possess strong technical knowledge of all the seventeen Server products. In reality, however, they essentially spent 90 percent of their time on the three core Server products—and reactively on the fourteen smaller revenue products, mostly on a deal-by-deal basis with partners and OEMs. Thus, there was a lack of proactive focus and specialization on the fourteen products.

Proposal. With the market data and anticipated growth segments (by country and industry verticals), our team proposed a 2004 plan for the three key smaller Server businesses, which was an "incubation" approach. We pitched the proposal to the Server BU HQ team in Redmond and settled on a growth target of about 20 percent for the incubation Servers (Storage, SBS, and ISA) out of the fourteen total. We also received funding for three sales specialists and a lead manager (coach/player) of the incubation sales team. The agreement was to scale the incubation business from $60m to about $72m year-to-year, with each specialist having quotas of at least $15m each by year end.

Planning and Execution. With the approved plan and funding, we began to recruit the specialist and leader of the group. With the Storage Server as the main focus of the three incubation businesses, a manager (coach/player) was hired from HP Storage who had experience on the OEM Storage and Server business. He carried the entire $72m incubation business quota, but he also played a dual role supporting the storage server sales directly. The other three server specialists were hired from the storage, security, and SMB server sectors to support their specific product lines. We began a two-step process of internal evangelizing the three incubation products among the main storage specialist community and the Microsoft general sales teams during the first quarter of FY 2004. Our main approaches were via training, funding for large POCs, and my role of reaching buy-in with country managers and regional segment leaders, followed by visits by Microsoft HQ staff for customer/partner calls almost monthly (to product line leaders). External evangelizing was achieved with joint seminars with HP and Dell, partner training, demand generation campaigns across SMB segments, and manufacturing verticals in Korea and Taiwan.

Location and experience of the regional specialists. The entire team had to support all the vast Asia Pacific region/markets, so we tried to place the individuals in the markets where they could have the highest impact. We specifically required industry experience with the Storage product they supported (security expertise for ISA Server, enterprise storage for Storage

Server, and SMB channels for SBS). We hired the security specialist in Sydney, Australia, given the large and growing firewall market there. The Storage Server specialist and the team leader were hired in Singapore (Asia HQ), as Dell and HP had their Asia Pacific regional counterparts there also. The Small Business Server specialist was hired in India, given the potential and size of this key emerging market, and as other in-county specialists in developed markets such as Australia and Singapore were able to work more independently.

Results. We achieved $74m for the incubation business (with a $72m plan) and also overachieved on the overall revenue for the server business at $455m (with a $440m plan) in 2004. The incubation team continued to grow for the next two years with rates of 22 percent and 18 percent annually. At the start of 2005, we hired two more storage specialists to focus on sustaining the incubation business growth, and an additional three at the start of 2006. After about a year in the incubation business and reaching a certain critical mass of revenue (achieving revenue targets), each of the storage specialists were transferred to the country-based storage specialists team.

Lessons learned:

- There is no single one-size-fits-all strategy. Focus on the incubation businesses across two approaches in Asia Pacific. The developed markets such as Australia and New Zealand are very similar to the US—in market adoption, marketing/sales strategies, adoption of new technologies, and maturation of channels/customers (and some are even more advanced in Australia/NZ).
- Emerging markets. Focus on specific industries/segments—probably one or two that you can place your limited resources bet on for the highest impact. For our Server incubation business, we narrowed to SMB in India and manufacturing in Korea and Taiwan.
- Investing in the Server incubation business resulted in a "Halo effect" for the overall core Server business, with faster growth and higher attach rates to the Windows Server, Exchange, and the SQL Server. It also extended the overall value proposition of the MS Windows Server to the partners and direct customers (for single vendor, TCO, and top-bottom data center solutions).
- With a large company such as Microsoft, gain buy-in for your plans early: HQ, regional Asia Pacific leadership, existing team, and partners/customers. Communicate maniacally on progress and achievements. Always include the country teams when sharing wins as regional best practices.

119. Adapt to Survive
By Romi Randhawa

What the Idea Is: We must continually adapt to survive.

Why It Is Valuable: There is no one "aha" moment in a reseller's life. They are always ongoing. We continue to evolve as our industry changes. Most resellers are always shifting along with their customer demands and OEM needs. Sometimes those shifts are very expensive to adopt, and sometimes the market is not ready for them. But every successful reseller has been able to navigate through the dynamics of their customers' demands and OEM needs.

I sold my previous business because we could not perfect the timing of cloud adoption to offer our customers. We were offering it too soon, and customers were hesitant. Today, that model is well accepted, but it is a challenge for a reseller to play in it. Hardware sales are still keeping lights on for most partners. Partners who adopted the quick transition to services and cloud, mixed with hardware sales, are the ones surviving well today, even though they are still challenged with keeping up with the growing cost. As a partner grows in sales and profitability, they have to re-invest most of that money into evolving into an even bigger and better partner.

Enterprise clients are consolidating, and CFOs are demanding local buying because of the tax advantages it brings. OEMs are pushing more and more in-country, as they can better support the clients with local teams. Governments are trying to keep the money in their GDP versus importing and losing all the money IT companies are spending.

How It Works: I started Epodium with a very simple philosophy. We wanted to deliver the technology quickly, efficiently, and globally. In the end, good technology has to be delivered on a platform—either internally or on the cloud. We built our footprint in over thirty-two countries to help enterprise customers acquire technology in a very simple way. We built our own tool that allows them to view their global catalogue and manage their procurement. Our sales footprints are in most of the countries where we touch and manage local deals. We have partnered with all major OEMs and distributors to bring consistency in the sales process.

We built direct sales and partner channel sales. Our goal is to bring ease in global procurement to partners and enterprise customers.

For us, this is certainly an "aha" moment.

120. Assessments: Knowledge is Power
By Sal Maita

What the Idea Is: They say knowledge is power, and when you are in sales you want to have as much knowledge as possible. You need to know everything you can about your organization; your products; your competition; the current marketplace; economic, political, and social trends for your industry; and opinions about your business from independents. But of course you already know all you need to know about your customer. Or do you?

Without some level of intimate knowledge about your clients and a deep understanding of their business and requirements, it's difficult to position yourself to win their business. The best way to attain that "all-you-need-to-know" status is to build out a strong assessment practice.

Why It Is Valuable: Assessments take time, they slow sales cycles, and they are a hassle to get everyone to agree to. But when you do assessments well and lead with services for your clients, you end up not only knowing the detailed requirements, but you also have something even more valuable to your customers. You have the road map of where they are going next, and you are the person or organization best suited to help them get there.

Getting enough information about your customers' environment puts you on equal footing with them. It creates a bond and sense of trust that enables you to cross the line from being a salesperson to being a business consultant for their needs.

Now just having an assessment tool doesn't mean you're going to be able to win all the time. You have to have the service solutions to help back those assessments up! All this hard work is worth it when you perform assessments and get to show off your team's technical prowess. Your revenue and margins will increase, and your customer satisfaction rate increases as well. If you know what the customers want, help them design it, and then deliver it, you have a much better chance of meeting their expectations and winning together.

How It Works: Depending on your specific business, there are some ready-made assessments for technology views. There are also organizational, leadership, and other types of assessments to help your specific segment of the market. The key to success is having the right assessments and methodology to help your clients get the most out of the time spent with you.

Analyze your products and services to determine what information you need from your client to help you provide the best solutions. Then develop a standardized process that is easily duplicated by each of your sales teams, and you will be able to have a much more consistent pipeline of qualified prospects to close—thus creating much more reliable sales forecast numbers.

Once you have the assessments and services aligned, you end up providing your customer with a great experience that they are sure to return to use again.

121. The Most Important Tool: It's About What You Ask, Whether You're a Sales Leader or in Sales
By Scott Anschuetz

What the Idea Is: In today's evolving virtual selling environment, where the charismatic, well-intentioned face-to-face meeting for building rapport no longer exists, now more than ever, the most important tool in our toolbox is asking the right questions. Now it's not what we *say* but what we *ask* that will create more coachable moments for our sellers.

Why It Is Valuable: It's no longer just about having teams memorize a pitch. In fact, the more they talk in the virtual sales world, the more likely the prospect or customer is going to wander. While the pitch still has relevance, it is only important if it lands with a target audience that understands what it is about. In today's environment, where you must keep people engaged as they are multitasking during virtual calls, you have to come in with relevant, well-prepared questions—and you must have more of them and ask them more frequently. So as leaders, are you reviewing the questions your teams are planning to use when a gap is identified?

How It Works: Challenger came in, and it raised a lot of excitement. Everyone was eager to challenge the status quo, as we have been saying for years, "You can't come in and pitch a product; you have to come in to connect with the customer to fix the biggest problems they are trying to solve." You need to ask questions about problems they may not even know they have. As sellers, we can't leave it up to chance; and as leaders, it's even more important that we ensure we are reviewing, discussing, and refining the questions.

As leaders, we spend so little time coaching our teams on what to ask, because we often spend our time qualifying opportunities. We find the biggest holes, and we give them guidance on what to go after in order to fill the gaps or to become better positioned or qualified. As a result, we very rarely spend time coaching the teams on what we believe they need to ask next. We not only need to think ahead of time about the questions that drive the most relevance; we also need to ask the team to offer up what **they** think they need to ask next. This exercise showcases their capabilities in executing that task, and this is where the real coaching moments appear.

As sales people, we very rarely pause prior to a meeting to think about the person we are meeting with and the questions we must ask to become relevant and meaningful. I believe these six questions focus on the most important key areas to dig into and understand:

1. What is the number-one priority, objective, or goal for that target buyer?

2. What are the biggest problems/challenges they will face in trying to achieve those objectives? What problems can we solve for them, and how do we best demonstrate to them how we differentiate from our competitors?

3. What might they be looking to do? What is the solution they perceive they need? (You can determine how informed they are by the answers you get here.)

4. What would be the impact/value if they solve those problems?

5. Who are the people in addition to themselves who need to say "yes"?

6. What steps do they need to go through with you to be convinced that you can deliver on helping them achieve their objectives?

As sellers, prepare more questions to drive interaction in this evolving virtual world. As leaders, review the questions the teams are considering, use this as an opportunity to identify skill gaps, and up-level their abilities and talents. It all comes down to what we ask, NOT what we say.

If you are looking for a tool/resource to support you, you can find us at *www.visualize.com*.

122. Partner with Your Customer on a Timeline and Execution Plan
By Shannon Seidl

What the Idea Is: Partner with your customer on a timeline and execution plan

Why It Is Valuable: It ensures that the sales rep and customer have the same expectations on a deal. It also allows you to speak to the deal internally at your company with confidence.

How It Works: This can be accomplished by sending a casual timeline in an email to solicit the customer's confirmation or through a joint evaluation plan. The joint evaluation plan should state the dates for each step to be completed, what each step entails, and who is involved. The key is to have an agreed-upon timeline so you get the deal in on time and both parties are held accountable.

123. Quality over Quantity in Prospecting Efforts
By Shannon Seidl

What the Idea Is: Quality over Quantity in Prospecting Efforts

Why It Is Valuable: So often SDRs are focused on the number of dials and the number of emails that they lose sight of quality interactions. Creating specific, repeatable messaging is what develops a quality pipeline that will progress. Quality outreach (pushing to find quality meetings that create a quality pipeline) allow SDRs to experience sales cycles early and often. However, if they get stuck in stage one (merely prospecting) and then progress their career to an AE, they will not know how to drive a sales cycle and move through the sales process.

How It Works: Target personas and industries with a message that is relevant and top of mind. Once a meeting is secured, follow up with next steps and take on some basic responsibilities of an AE to ensure you are prepared for the next role and experienced in progressing a deal cycle.

124. Sales Best Practices
By Steve Alfieris

What the Idea Is: **Hire People Who Know More Than You**
After spending the majority of my career working in the US Federal Government market, I understand that it is an intricate process to reach the appropriate decision makers and close a deal in an efficient manner.

Why It is Valuable: By hiring recently retired military officers, I was certain to have key individuals who knew the needs of the specific department, the government sales process, and the key decision makers.

How It Works: In order to facilitate the government sale and build strong relationships, I decided I needed to hire sales reps from specific agencies to infiltrate the specific agencies (i.e., retired Air Force Colonel to lead the team targeting the Air Force, a retired Army Colonel to lead the charge at Army, etc.).

What the Idea Is: **Build Relationships with the Team**
As simple as it sounds, engage with the members of the sales team and build a relationship with the individuals by learning a little bit about their personal lives and their career goals.

Why It Is Valuable: Accessibility not only stimulates loyalty, it also affords the opportunity to learn small but valuable pieces of information that can promote the sales process

How It Works: Set aside time each day to walk the floor and engage with the team on a personal level. Make sure people are happy doing their job.

What the Idea Is: **Positioning Sales Force for Success**

Individual contributors need to have challenging sales goals that are attainable to be positioned for success. If the sales team members cannot envision the road to successfully meeting their quota, morale will dip, anxiety will heighten, and nothing positive will be accomplished.

Why It Is Valuable: Quotas need to reflect the goals of the company as well as the abilities of the team members and the economic environment.

How It Works: Getting the reps to own the quota will produce successful results for everyone. Make sure that metrics/goals assigned allow success and position every part of the organization to be successful. If it is not plausible to achieve success, sales people will not stay with you. To be positioned for success, the reps must be provided with the support of marketing, engineering, leadership, and partners.

125. New Sales Model (Go-to-Market Strategy)
By Steve Corndell

What the Idea Is: Over the years, the traditional approach has been to have sellers both in the field and in inside sales. Since the call-center model doesn't really scale, a hybrid model has emerged.

Most of our sellers are located in Boston. They're not considered *inside* sales reps; they're just sales reps. We have found that having an open floor model (versus cubicles) enables our newer reps to learn quicker about the technology, products, and campaigns. The sales reps still go on sales calls to meet with customers (usually within range of a quick flight), they still partner, and they still do sales events in the field. But this model has closed the gap on ramp time and on finding different candidates out in the field, and it allows for collaboration between sales, the management team and the sellers. Reps have immediate access to marketing, engineers, customer success, and other pieces they need to be successful. This combination works.

With our model, COVID-19 actually gave us a competitive advantage because we already knew how to leverage the technology others were grappling with. The pivot to virtual was an easy one, and the team has been able to prospect more, learn more, and continue to be successful. Others have been very intrigued with our model, and I have done a great deal of consulting as a result.

In previous models, the reps first went through the inside sales program and then interviewed for an outside sales position, which may have taken them to a different territory where they didn't want to move. Those who have moved in the past now fly back at least once a month to be with their peers and continue learning and developing; they feed off each other's energy. In between visits, we do Zoom Happy Hours by shipping them a bottle of their favorite beverage and scheduling a time to be together.

Culture is very important to us. We have music playing on our sales floor, and TVs are constantly flashing metrics. When reps who are in the leaderboard roster have success, they ring a bell. This model has vastly increased productivity; in fact, we have almost doubled our business, growing 40 percent YOY with this model—with fewer resources! We can do fifteen Zoom calls a day, as opposed to three in-person meetings bookended by commute times.

Why It Is Valuable: The new sales model provides increased productivity and accelerated rep ramp time (i.e., it takes less time for new reps to learn the technology, sales cycles, and metrics they need to hit, because they are exposed to that knowledge every day from being in such close proximity with their more experienced peers). There is better collaboration between business units, managers' inspections are better facilitated, and it contributes to a better, tighter culture.

How It Works: Track everything:

- How well do they understand the technology?
- Can they run a sales campaign without an engineer?
- Can they do a demo without an engineer?
- Can they build a business impact presentation?
- How many pipeline adds do they have a week?
- How many side deals do they have?
- What is their forecast?

All metrics are then gamified for the floor in order to show reps their standing among their peers.

126. Compensation
By Steve Dietch

What the Idea Is: To your "A" players, even though it's more than money (it's also the challenge and the camaraderie), what it really comes down to is how they are paid. They want to know if they made quota and if they are making President's Club.

Why It Is Valuable: It creates a clear line from the products to the compensation plan, and it's simple for the sales person to understand and excel.

How It Works: Culture is important; you have to design your compensation plan within the framework of your company. The easier and more understandable you can make the simplicity of a sales plan and use that to direct energy, the better it can be.

When you have a leverageable sales force across several regions selling fifty products, how do you create a compensation plan that incentivizes people to execute? You need to keep it simple, with just two to three components.

The most important component is that the enterprise needs to figure out what its sales priorities are; it cannot be everything. Make it what it needs to be, with one or two components that are needed to meet goals, then add a new component that needs to help something grow really fast. You can use a carrot or a stick, or both.

You will know it is working if your organization has met its revenue and margin goals and if you meet your quota achieving distribution. It acts as a sort of bell curve; what is the optimal number of reps who need to make quota? Did you set them up for success?

127. Early-Stage Company: How Do You Kickstart Your Sales Engine?
By Steve Dietch

What the Idea Is: How do early-stage companies kickstart enterprise sales with urgency and constrained budget.

Today, early-stage companies are challenged to penetrate the enterprise. Existing enterprise proven vendors and organizational inertia create enormous barriers to entry for companies in the initial stages of existence. Investors have limited patience and look to CEOs and their sales leaders to "hack" the typical long enterprise sales cycle—demonstrating traction as quickly as possible and establishing a solid foundation to meet key milestones that drive a successful next round of fundraising.

Successful early-stage companies have discovered that relying solely on their own pipeline development is tough. The lack of personal senior executive connections at target companies is a significant challenge. Selling high in an enterprise is key to not only creating the right sales momentum, but is mandatory to accelerating the sales cycle. Anything below vice president, where there is lack of budget ownership/signature authority, is most likely going to drive a less than stellar result. And if it is successful, it will take twice the time, versus engaging at the executive level.

So what's the answer? Is it building out a strong direct sales force? Probably not. This takes time, it's hard to recruit, and it's extremely expensive for an early-stage company. Is it using reseller partners to generate pipeline and drive deal closure? More than likely, no. In the early stages of a company, there is a lack of understanding about how to sell the product yourself. Engaging a partner to do the end-to-end selling before the company's own salesforce gains a solid understanding is not recommended.

The better approach to "hack" the sales motion is to use what we would describe as sales advisors. These sales advisors are former executives or consultants within your target verticals who possess strong connections to senior executives at companies that fit your ideal customer profile. Early-stage companies enlist these individuals to provide introductions to executive committee members to kickstart the sales process. In exchange, these individuals are compensated with lucrative commissions if the introduction results in a closed deal.

Why It Is Valuable: You are building a high-quality pipeline with zero dollars out of pocket upfront. The company only pays if the introduction results in a deal.

How It Works: Based on your segmentation and ideal customer profile (ICP), identify an initial handful of advisors (former executives in target markets/companies, consultants, agencies) that have strong executive-level connections. There is no downside to recruiting as many advisors as you can, given the cost only materializes if a deal closes.

Once you've established a group of advisors, you will need to create program guidelines on deal registration and roles/responsibilities. It's important to hold regular pipeline reviews with your advisors to keep them up to date and aligned to the company's priorities.

128. Deal-Close Timeline
By Steve Sullivan

What the Idea Is: Deal-close timeline for sales team (rep and SE) in large enterprise/complex sales engagements

Why it is Valuable: This timeline allows first-line sales managers to validate *all commit pipelines* for accuracy and timing.

How it Works: For each committed opportunity for any given quarter, the sales team would map out a timeline, from start to close, for all high-six- to low-seven-figure commit engagements. It is designed to be mapped out at the beginning of the quarter and shared internally for review (to the rep, SE, and supporting cast), and then shared with the customer to get his/her buy-in on the deal timeline for 100 percent transparency. In this way, you and the customer are working toward the same desired outcome. The milestones should be customized per the company's sales process. The definitions of each milestone should be self-explanatory to avoid seller and/or buyer confusion.

A picture is worth a thousand words:

129. Quick and Easy Forecasting Questions
By Steve Sullivan

What the Idea Is: Quick and easy forecasting questions for first-line sales management.

Why It Is Valuable: Information gained from these questions allows first-line sales managers to inspect and validate all commit pipelines, which allows for predictable and accurate quarterly forecasts.

How it Works: Make sure each sales team can answer the following seven forecasting questions for all committed deals:

1. Budget: Have you confirmed budget approval for the month or quarter?

2. Compelling event: Is it ours, or is it the customer's?

3. Internal Champion: What is his/her track record? Is there one?

4. Trial Close: Have we attempted? With whom?

5. Decision Maker: Have we met, and is there a meeting planned?

6. Does this project require PoC/testing? Have appropriate internal resources been involved and is there a validated solution?

7. If no PoC/RoR is required, has the technical approval been given?

A quick and easy check for the team is: why <your company name> and why now?

130. Start Each Quarter with a Focused Sales Communication and Operations Plan
By Steve Sullivan

What the Idea Is: Sales leadership (such as CROs and sales VPs) for earlier-stage companies (less than 500 employees) should start the first month of every quarter with a focused sales communication and operations plan for all employees.

Why It Is Valuable: You will have simplified, *transparent* leadership who will focus the sales team (and company) on key company initiatives for the upcoming quarter and on the criticality of their involvement and focus.

How It Works: At the beginning of a new quarter:

- **Week 1: Quarterly kickoff (QKO).** Review the past quarter's performance, what worked well and what didn't, what was learned, and one or two of your most impactful customer success stories (wins the company employees can feel good about contributing to). Also review new employee contributions and wins, goals for the new quarter, targeted win opportunities, hiring plans, introduction of your newest employees (since the last meeting), key engineering milestones, etc.

- **Week 2: Quarterly Business Reviews (QBRs).** Typical QBRs for direct sellers and first line management focus on sales commit and upside, challenges, what worked and what didn't, help needed, and five thought-provoking questions to get the sales team focused on strategic ideas for growth. Be sure to include audience representation from all walks of life to educate on the nuances and importance of customer engagements and revenue.

- **Week 3: Partner QBRs.** Choose your top partners and your potential high-growth new partners and do a two-to-three-hour QBR with each strategic partner (a field channel team function with a consolidated report should be completed by the end of the week). Review the scorecard (how we are doing, improvements we can make to the relationship, etc.) and high-profile deals, pressure test new programs that are or will be rolling out for feedback, etc.

- **Week 3: Sales All Hands.** This will be your first bi-weekly sales all-hands meeting, where you will chart progress and celebrate the wins. (Repeat every two weeks.)
- **Week 4:** Start sending out "Anatomy of a Win" reports celebrating large wins or first wins by a new sales team. Format is important; hit the high points (the problem identified and how it was solved, a list of customer constituents, a funny story along the "win" journey, "expand" potential, etc.) Use these win reports to highlight key behind-the-scenes contributors (deal MVPs from engineering, operations, etc.).

131. Consultative Approach
By Steve Tepedino

What the Idea Is: Curiosity is a big asset. Take a curious approach to understand how things work, what problems your customers really have and how to solve those problems, and what it is like to be the customer.

My company is a reseller, and this approach allows us to understand the problems and come up with solutions to solve them. We have found a way to accelerate our success, and the value prop is to be more successful or successful at faster pace.

Over time, you will be able to understand more how your customers operate, based on their title/role/experiences. Earn a seat at the table with curiosity and knowledge (finding out how their business works, what their day is like, etc.). This allows you to create a portfolio of solutions that you can offer to them to help formulate their success. A good consultative sales person is always a catalyst for success.

Customers always want improved service; that doesn't mean it isn't good already, but it can always be better. I firmly believe if you want a customer's share of spend (market share), you need their mindshare first. You must be compelling and demonstrate how your product/service is the best answer for the client out of all the right answers available.

Why It Is Valuable: Taking the approach of what interests my customer fascinates me. We must apply what they teach us to what is important to them. When we can connect the dots and begin to recommend ways to accelerate their success, we will get the mindshare, and market share will follow. Then we need to think about how we can grow the customer so their experience continues to excel. That gives the reward back to the customer.

How It Works: Good parents tend to make good kids. You have to hire people with a likeable demeanor. Look for those who are ingrained with these fundamental characteristics:

- A genuinely curious nature
- A sincerely caring attitude
- A likeable personality that allows them to engage in these conversations, where they are in the food chain and understand they have a choice
- Willing to make commitments and keep them. Commitment aversion is not a characteristic that will work in this role.

They must also have had direct experience in training and have case studies, and they need to understand that there is a sales process; deals do not close themselves.

To make this work, you must have a plan that goes beyond the first sales call; customer experience is improved if your sales calls are strung together with purpose. The next call must be orchestrated with purpose before the current call ends. They must link together. You can teach this by using stories of where, when, and how it has worked. Be sure to also give examples of times when things didn't work out as planned.

I find it helpful to have visuals around the office that make a point. I have a picture of Custer fighting Indians, and behind him is a salesman with a machine gun, tugging on Custer's coat to try to get his attention. Custer is saying, "Can't you see I'm busy?" I often teach with stories because they are so effective.

Another visual is a picture of Ronald Reagan with Gorbachev, with the caption "Trust but Verify." We should take what we are being told as truth, but then find a way to confirm it is. We have to ask, *What do we actually know, and what do we remember to be true*? Sometimes we assume old information is true over the passage of time, but when we integrate more fact we find it is actually not the same as it was; we have to allow for the input of new data.

The leading indicators that this concept works are increased revenue and higher customer retention. You will also have more sales calls, more sales activity, increased pipeline, and good vendor engagement. You'll be able to form more revenue streams (not one and done), such as infrastructure, services, etc., because you are building relationships over time.

CRM is a fantastic tool for measuring interactions and activity. When sellers think the system is for them, and not for their boss, it becomes part of their process and determines how they manage their day. It creates a different type of interaction.

132. Relationship Management
By Terry Richardson

What the Idea Is: Enhance strategic partnerships through a disciplined approach to relationship management.

Why It Is Valuable: Vendors realize accelerated growth, increased customer relevance, improved relationships across the ecosystem, and improved competitive share through enhanced market and opportunity coverage.

How It Works: Establishing and growing strategic partnerships requires an investment in resources that balance strategic initiatives and operational excellence. In my experience, I realized over a few decades that the following are critical elements that should be adhered to:

1. **Document a Success Plan:** The orientation should be focused on establishing win-win outcomes, with clear identification of the investments and expectations of each party. A common set of goals and objectives, planned actions, and measurement metrics must be established. The expectation should be to mutually review and amend the plan quarterly.

2. **Take a Long-Term View:** Successful partnerships should last for well more than a year, and a multi-year accretive partnership should be the target. It is incumbent on the vendor representative to advocate for the partner internally, and avoid pyrrhic victories that are not in the best interest of sustainable, enhanced relationships.

3. **Focus on Value-Add:** Explicitly identify, document, and validate the value the partner brings to the vendor, the value the vendor brings to the partner, and the joint value proposition the vendor and partner together bring to the end customer. Testimonials and communications should always be focused on value-add and customer outcomes to reinforce the foundation of the partnership.

4. **Review Leading Indicators:** All efforts must be centric toward building incremental pipeline and use pipeline growth as the ultimate measure of partnership health. Steady pipeline growth will precede revenue acceleration and will provide confirmation that the joint value proposition is resonating. I coach my team to be data-driven and action-oriented, and to bias their time toward activities that result in incremental pipeline.

5. **Make It Personal:** Ultimately we are in the people and relationship business. I coach my teams to become acquainted with as many

people as possible (certainly the key stakeholders and top influencers) and to strive to develop meaningful relationships that are beyond the casual acquaintance level. This could be manifested by exploring joint hobbies, conversing about family or other personal topics, and/ or establishing other points of mutual connection. I believe in the adage, "People do business with those that they know, like, and trust."

6. **Work with Urgency**: There is a time and place for every partnership; and given the rapid change and transformation occurring in most industries, it is imperative to act swiftly when partnership opportunities present themselves. Those who manage strategic partnerships should strive to "make the news" versus "report the news" and do everything necessary to keep the focus on the elements of the partnership that provide the greatest ROI for all stakeholders. I have found that the best partner account managers have strong sales backgrounds, and they leverage their ingrained sales skills and successes to maximize the opportunity associated with the partnership.

7. **Lead Transparently**: Results matter, so we must hold ourselves accountable for ensuring partnership goals are met or exceeded. Every quarter, I expect my team to own the results narrative and proactively identify issues that are not consistent with partnership expansion. For each issue there must be an action plan to improve, and successes should be shared internally to shape the proper perception surrounding the partnership. Within every organization there can be, and should be, unexpected leaders who emerge at all levels. Regardless of an individual's role, there is an opportunity to lead with effective communication and by taking the proper actions best aligned with achieving the desired results of a given strategic partnership.

133. Recognition
By Tom Haydanek

What the Idea Is: It goes back to a simple sports analogy. Dan Marino, the quarterback for the Dolphins, once said, "Take care of the hands that take care of you." I have that same mentality regarding my team. The customer and the team always come first, and the rest takes care of itself. Spend less time "selling up" and more time with the customer and your team.

Your ultimate goal is to build, develop, and retain a high-performing sales organization, and recognition is a key part of achieving that goal.

Why It Is Valuable: At the end of the day, all people like to be recognized and valued for their efforts and achievements. When you take care of your team first and they know you have their back, they will run through walls for you in return. This will improve retention and loyalty, and then success just follows.

When I began leveraging a consistent recognition methodology, my team was able to achieve one of the highest performance and retention rates among my peers.

How it Works: Recognition comes in many different forms. It does not have to be expensive, and it does not have to be something big; it just needs to be something that simply acknowledges the team members for what they do. Sales is absolutely a team sport, and it is imperative to recognize the extended team as well for their contributions to the collective team's success.

For recognition to have the greatest impact, you must know your team and what drives and motivates them individually. As a new leader I once recognized an individual at a national sales meeting (as I would have liked to have been recognized), and the person was mortified; unfortunately, I did not understand at the time that not everyone is motivated the same way. It takes time and commitment, but you must understand your team members and what drives them for recognition to have the greatest impact.

I know as leaders we all do recognition; but if it is only done once a year, infrequently, or inconsistently, recognition loses its overall impact.

Here are some easy ways you can recognize and motivate your team to have a positive impact on performance and team success (nothing earth-shattering).

- Provide consistent quarterly recognition of your top performers as well as people in the cross-functional teams that support you who are also instrumental to your success. This may include people in operations, finance, logistics, manufacturing, engineering, etc.
    - o For example, send them a nice bottle of wine or whatever their beverage of choice may be; but in addition, include a handwritten note that is specific to them. I know this takes time and commitment, but the note really makes the recognition more impactful.
- We implemented a Dog on the Bone Award, which became one of the most coveted awards. It simply recognizes an individual or a team that just would not lose a competitive win or takeout deal no matter what obstacles were put in front of them. It was a rawhide bone spray painted gold ($2.00) along with a plaque with the names of all the previous winners. It was incredible to see how this award took on a life of its own and drew a fierce competition to receive it.
- Friday shout-outs. Take an hour on Fridays to make five-minute phone calls just to say thank you to key employees who made a difference that week; it costs nothing and makes them feel special.

- Provide opportunities for a lot of small local get-togethers and include your partners and extended team members (obviously, following today's COVID protocols). Be creative and pull together your own year-end summits. Most companies have started scaling back significantly on these events, and they have become a demotivator at times. By this I mean if the recognition becomes a "popularity" contest versus for specific, clear, and concise performance achievement, it has the complete opposite effect. We have had highly effective year-end summits on numerous occasions, and it has a greater motivational impact that increases loyalty, teamwork, and commitment.

- I know this may sound "corny," but create a birthday club by simply texting "Happy Birthday. Have a Great Day" to individuals on your team. Throughout the years, I have received countless email responses on how "blown away" employees were that I would take the time and acknowledge them on their special day. Texting someone "Happy Birthday" does not cost a thing, and it's a huge motivator.

- The partner ecosystem is a vital extension of your sales team, and recognizing the extended team increases their loyalty and commitment, and motivates them as well. It creates significant scale and leverage that cannot be achieved otherwise. Be sure to treat them with the integrity and respect they deserve.

134. Setting Goals and Developing Your Plan
By Tom Haydanek

What the Idea Is: It is all about setting the bar high. Have a plan in writing that outlines what your goals and objectives are, both personally and professionally. Ask your people to share their goals with you so you can help support them in achieving them, and make this a part of your mentoring and coaching sessions.

One of our top-performing representatives would always set his plan to achieve more than 200 percent every year. In the five-plus years this individual was on the team, he fell below 150 percent attainment only once.

I had another representative who was also successful, but who would only set his plan to achieve just over 100 percent each year. This team member consistently achieved his number; however, it was usually just at 100 percent.

Bottom line, set the bar high, have a plan, and challenge yourself. You will figure out a way to get it done. When you believe it, you will achieve it!

It is imperative to review the plans at a minimum of once per quarter. Too often these plans and goals are only looked at once or twice a year.

At that rate, it is too late to course correct, and the whole concept is for naught.

Why It Is Valuable: It allows you to own your own destiny, both personally as well as professionally.

How It Works: Take action and physically write your goals down and carry them with you to review them weekly. Share your goals with the people who can help you achieve them, and they will also become invested in your success.

If you are waiting for the mothership to come help, you have already lost, because it is not coming.

II
WALTER BROWN DEDICATION
By Randy Seidl

Walter Brown has been a vital ingredient to my success and the success of thousands of others who ever had the pleasure of meeting him or reading (and marking up) his books that several of us have given out. I first had the pleasure of meeting Walter in the late 80s when I was at EMC. At the time, we were a bunch of young yahoos; and when Frank Keaney and Mike Ruettgers came to EMC, they quickly realized our sales teams needed better processes and discipline. Walter brought all that to us and more. I can remember creating tools still being used today by many of us: territory notebooks, call planners, numerous evaluation templates, and lots of other great gems you can read about in both of Walter's books. EMC had a great sales reputation, and Walter was a big piece of that. Mike Ruettgers, previous EMC Chairman and CEO, told me: "I would consider Walter the father of direct technology selling and a main pillar of EMC's success."

As you will read in the dedications provided by Brian Bell and Ken Dougherty, Walter really gave of himself personally, and it was amazing how he could simplify such a complicated profession. I had countless sessions with Walter, both face-to-face and over the phone, as he helped me as well as my sales teams. I always admired his calmness, his thoughtfulness, his ability to listen even when he knew it was misguided information or just BS, and his providing feedback in a way that everyone wanted it and retained it.

I also remember bringing him to a managers meeting I hosted in Maryland while I was at StorageTek. It was about 2005. He was as sharp and informative as ever, and he had my team on the edge of their chairs soaking in all of his great wisdom and asking numerous questions. Whether he was presenting to a group or doing one-on-one coaching, he was truly a shining star.

Up until he passed, we would still connect and meet up when he and his lovely wife Sarah would come to Boston or go to their mountain retreat in Woodstock, VT. I miss Walter.

I would also like to thank Sarah for her friendship and for allowing us to continue to carry Walter's torch and his wisdom as we strive to coach sales talent to learn more so they sell more. Thanks, Sarah!

WALTER BROWN DEDICATION

BY BRIAN BELL
Technology Partner, Rally Ventures

It was 2003, and I was now in charge of a fast-growing sales team for a VC-funded enterprise tech company—and I had limited sales experience, since I had spent the majority of my career flying jets in the US Air Force. I heard about this guy who worked miracles with tech company sales teams across the country. I read his book *Chasing Quota*, which is about a two-hour read—it has few words, but a big meaning. I immediately thought, *I need to meet this guy, and he needs to meet with my sales leaders and tell me all the ways I am screwing up!* I somehow tracked him down—he was basically living on a mountain top in Woodstock, Vermont, off the grid, with no electricity or phone. He said he was retired and didn't consult anymore. Regardless, I sent him a plane ticket to Minnesota (where my company, Compellent, was based). He showed up, gave me my report card (the good, the bad, and the ugly—like I wanted it). And our relationship grew from there—Walter was a mentor, one of my best friends, and the grandfather I never knew.

I have given out hundreds of copies of *Chasing Quota* to new and veteran sales managers—with a signed note and my business card. I feel a bit like a Walter Brown disciple. :) I still believe to this day that first-level sales leaders (and first-level leaders across a company) are the secret ingredient to high-performing teams. The first-level leaders are in the trenches with the team and have to translate company goals into actions—and have to coach, evaluate, support, hire, and fire all the talent that works at the company. They are among the most important keys to success in every organization.

In his final note to me in his last days of life (after a courageous fight against pancreatic cancer), he was as pithy as in every page of Chasing Quota. "Please do not be overly concerned about this sudden turn of events, as life for all of us is really a short journey with an uncertain outcome. And my journey, until recently, has been first class."

Enjoy the words from my friend, Walter Brown.

WALTER BROWN DEDICATION

By Ken Dougherty,

Vice President of North American Sales, Enterprise Preferred at Dell EMC

The first ten years of my twenty-five-year career were spent carrying the bag as a sales rep, covering some large enterprise accounts such as Citizens Bank, Putnam Bank, and Bank of America. My first sales manager job was with StorageTec (I was the youngest sales manager there), where I was fortunate to be able to work for Randy Seidl. I've since been in sales management for fifteen years. And at the very beginning of my sales management career, I had the good fortune of meeting Walter Brown.

Walter met with me to do a deal review in Waltham, Massachusetts. We went through a subset of opportunities he was advising me on, and our relationship began and grew from there. In the last fifteen years, throughout my sales leadership career, there has probably not been a day that I haven't had Walter in my mind. His book *Chasing Quota* sits on my desk, and I refer to it at least daily, if not weekly.

Walter really helped me understand that sales is a complex business, but there are some very basic and simple tenets that must be followed. One of the key things he taught me that I've used for my entire career is to measure my sales people often, with the top priority being their ability to forecast accurately. I believe accurate forecasting is the barometer that measures a successful sales professional, and it involves three questions Walter said we should ask:

1. Why do it?

2. Why now?

3. Why with us?

Answering those three questions has been the hallmark of my being able to forecast accurately throughout my career. When I hold quarterly forecasting meetings, I always put those questions on my white board, and I don't allow any of my field reps to commit a deal to a certain time frame within that quarter unless they can answer all three. Over the years, people have come up with many ways to put a spin on the questions—with methodologies like MEDDIC, for example—so they can decipher whether the deal is real.

Walter was able to boil the very complex world of sales down to the wisdom he put in his book. He talked about how to build sales organizations, saying top sales managers do three things well. They:

1. Assemble a team of high-quality people
2. Constantly develop those people
3. Drive them to produce the numbers

To do that, you need to build your team with people you know, like, and trust. Walter taught me that you should never hire a stranger—someone you don't know or someone you trust doesn't know—and to always make sure you continue to cultivate the individuals you hire.

Even though I didn't talk to Walter every day, I can look back over my career and see that when I was struggling with an opportunity, something I wanted to do within my team, or how to manage a challenging situation, I would always turn to his book. There are so many things he referenced— like getting out from behind your desk and going on sales calls with your people—that have always stuck with me. I discovered that the best way I could learn was to be in front of customers. And the best way I could learn about the capability of my people was to go out in the field with them.

Of the 132 pages of Walter's book, I've dog-eared probably 30. And looking back over my career, I can see how fortunate I've been to have his advice. For example, I never took a job unless I could answer the seven questions he referenced in the beginning of his book. He said to be successful, you need a Playable Hand, including these seven cards:

1. A healthy marketplace
2. A competitive offering
3. Enough territory
4. Good compensation plans
5. Supportive management (I've always been very fortunate here, because Randy has been at the top of that list, and a number of other folks have been there and supported me in my career.)
6. Realistic goals (makeable without miracles)
7. Enough time

As he quotes in this book, "Every sales manager I've ever met has too much to do. The best solution is to do fewer tasks but do them well, and leave some tasks for another day." I wouldn't be where I am today had it not been for Walter Brown. He instilled some key priorities in me as a leader to make sure I got my doggie bag and focused on the things that were going to make the biggest difference.

CHASING QUOTA
BY WALTER BROWN

A ROADMAP FOR ANYONE WHO MANAGES SALES PEOPLE

About This Book

This little book, small enough to fit in your pocket and readable in thirty minutes, contains more than one hundred individual rules for managing sales people successfully.

It is written for you if you manage sales people, regardless of your background, and regardless of whether your job title is sales manager, company president or something in between.

Chasing Quota was born when I began to coach sales managers. At that time I believed I had a good command of the subject.

But over the years special insights kept emerging from these coaching sessions until I found that the bulk of what I knew about sales management had been learned since I began coaching.

I gradually refined these insights into a well-tested set of rules (my road map) for good sales management.

But the challenge has never been to get the rules down on paper—years of coaching accomplished this. The challenge was to make them memorable enough to truly change your habits.

That is why I wrote this book.

Table of Contents

CHAPTER I.   WHAT TO DO FIRST

Top sales managers do three things well:
1. Assemble a team of high-quality people.
2. Constantly develop those people.
3. Drive them to produce the numbers.

However, to be successful, you need a Playable Hand, including these seven cards:
1. A Healthy Marketplace
    (Enough action, no dominant competitor, pricing that allows a profit, etc.)
2. A Competitive Offering
    (Good enough to win your share.)
3. Enough Territory
    (Enough action, either actual or potential.)
4. Good Comp(ensation) Plans
    (That will allow winners to make good money.)
5. Supportive Management
    (Maximum support with minimal meddling.)
6. Realistic Goals
    (Makeable without miracles.)
7. Enough Time
    (It nearly always takes longer than you plan.)

If you don't hold all seven cards, then get them.
Or look for another assignment.

Now let's look at some rules for getting started right:
(In the back is a glossary of key terms used throughout the book.)

Take time to see the financial picture.
*   Make sure you know your company's financial status: balance sheets, operating budgets, income statement, etc. You won't understand your management until you can see things from their viewpoint.

Don't be stampeded into growing too fast,
*   because too fast is too risky.
*   If more than one third of your people are unproven (new, newly promoted, etc.) in their current jobs you are probably growing too fast.

Don't have too many direct reports.
*   If it takes more than one hand to count your direct reports, you have too many.

Avoid part-time sales management.

- Probably the toughest assignment for sales managers is to also carry a personal sales quota, because of the constant conflict: Do I sell today, manage today, try to do both or what? Avoid such jobs unless they transition into full-time sales management.

Negotiate your quota well.

- Be smart about this: Do your homework, prepare your position, and sell it hard. Don't let yourself get steamrolled; you have to live a whole year with a bad quota.

Assign more quota than you carry.

- To crush your numbers you have to create a cushion.

Build a common language.

- You can get by with a dictionary of less than 30 words: Suspect, prospect, qualified, hot, closable, in the funnel, etc. But make sure that everyone uses the same dictionary.

Sales Success can be summarized in nine words:

- *Build a good prospect pipeline; then harvest that pipeline.*
- Make sure everything else flows from this simple structure.

Plan ahead.

- Publish a sales team calendar, at least a month in advance.

If you are newly promoted from sales ranks, spend the bulk of your time where you have been spending it: In front of prospects. But do it with your reps now, instead of alone.

- (Of the choices available—salesman, salesperson, sales rep, account exec, etc.—I have opted to use the term 'rep' throughout.)

Carry a bag before you take a sales management job.

If you take the job anyway,

- Climb into a tandem harness with your reps and learn the job in depth.

Don't expect a big inheritance.

- Reps mostly inherit empty pipelines, managers mostly inherit flawed teams. Don't complain about it. The team you build will shine by contrast to the team you inherited.

To be a top sales manager you will need to:

- Read People
- Lead People

- Feed People

And

- Weed People

CHAPTER II. HOW TO BUILD A STRONG TEAM

Grade your reps into A's, B's, and C's.
- Where the A's are stars, the B's are proven producers, and C's are all the others.

Now eliminate the C's (up or out).

A top sales manager has candidates lined up to fill the next open territory.

Stay in recruiting mode.
- Campaign-style recruiting will (at best) only net you the top people from that campaign. Recruit continuously and you will find much better people.

Find people who are made of the right stuff.
- Can play in your league and will pay the price to succeed.

Decide whether you need hunters, farmers, or hunter-farmers.
- In general, good hunters don't farm well, good farmers don't hunt well, and good hunter-farmers are in short supply. Get players that fit the task—or make the task fit the players.

Where have your best people come from?
- Go back to those same sources when you need people again.

It's hard to pick winners.
- So use a high standard.
- Pick people who look like they will be better reps than you ever were.

Strangers are high-risk choices.
- Try not to hire total strangers, which I define as people you haven't worked with, nor has anyone you trust.

Never settle.
- Unless you feel very good about someone, don't hire them. Too many reps never make a sales call as good as their first interview.

Make sure reps go into serious training *from their first day.*
- Issue report cards.

Certify your reps.

- Without licenses they can't drive cars, fly airplanes, practice medicine … and a whole lot more. Why should they be allowed to sell for you without passing some reasonable tests?

Never orphan new reps.

- Make sure reps get a *fast start program*: special attention, resources, support. Make your last call of the day to your newest rep.

Be careful with pro hires.

- A lot of them want minimal training and no coaching: "We're pros and that's why you hired us." Don't listen. Train them and coach them until they prove they can do the job.

Don't confuse training with coaching.

- Training is done in a classroom.
- Coaching is done on the street. One is not a substitute for the other. Both are necessary.

Reps with fatal flaws should be working somewhere else.

- Check your reps, especially your new reps, for fatal flaws: Not smart enough, not hungry enough, not hungry enough, not persuasive, won't take direction, etc. Fatal flaws are flaws that are (a) fatal if not fixed, and (b) not fixable in a reasonable time frame.

Very few reps do well after a seriously poor start.

- If a new rep's track record is poor after a reasonable time, start lining up that rep's replacement.
- And don't let your feelings get in the way.

Always have a bench.

- "Extra" reps, trainers, whatever, ensure that you don't get caught with a full quota and empty territories. Having no bench is like having to fix your car while driving it down the road.

CHAPTER III. WHAT TO DO ALL DAY

CENTER MOST OF YOUR DAY AROUND YOUR REPS:

Your job is to add dimension.

- Ask yourself, 'where do I contribute the most?
- How well would my team do without me?'
- Then ask your reps the same questions.

Get out from behind your desk.
- Spend at least 3 days a week in the street—coaching and mentoring your reps—all the way to quota—and beyond.

Never say anything once.
- A good coach repeats lessons until everyone gets it right.

Don't hesitate to check the quantity or quality of your reps' activities.
- If good, they will be happy to show you. If not, you need to find out. If a rep tries to dodge you, it is always a sign of trouble.

Make sure your reps know where they spend their time.
- Make sure you know where they spend their time.

Some reps know how to light fires, but don't know where.
- Some know where, but not how. And some are always in the dark. When it comes to prospecting, make sure your reps have matches—and know where and how to use them.

You can't harvest what you haven't planted.
- Pipeline additions must match pipeline subtractions. So don't let your reps spend too much time harvesting and too little time prospecting. Follow the same rule yourself.

Measure pipeline buildup, not just sales production.
- It's true that we judge reps on their sales production; but good pipelines will normally yield good production. In other words, good results come from good process.

Hug the right prospects, not the easy prospects.
- Each rep needs a clear prospecting roadmap—a plan for building pipelines. Two or three pages maximum. Regular reviews. Without it they won't find or hug the right prospects.

Reps should also hug their customers.
- Not just prospects—customers.

Review pipelines regularly.
- Start with a rep's best deal, as they judge it. Then second-best deal, etc. If your still enthused after five deals, your rep probably has a decent pipeline.

Don't get swallowed up by the details of a deal.
Prospects buy when they are comfortable with the answers to three simple questions:

1. Why *do* it?
2. Why *now*?
3. Why with *you*?

Be objective.
- Reps invest so much emotion in their deals that they lose objectivity. Your job is to help them find it.

Your best reps are your models.
- Who has the most business in your organization? Learn how they've done it—and copy them.

Remember that reps are optimists.
- How else could they do their job?

Reps are also visual people.
- Use pictures to train them, to persuade them, etc.

Words are important to reps.
- Make sure they learn the right words: To present their products. To ask the right questions. To capture prospect interest. To persuade. To close.

Reps are not illiterate.
- They often pretend to be when it comes to documenting their activities. But they *will* cover the subject orally.

If your reps have good jobs, remind them.
- If not, do something about it.

If reps don't have enough motivation, don't supply it for them.
- Reps need to supply their own basic motivation. It is not a commodity you can lend.

SOME OF YOUR DAY IS NOT CENTERED AROUND YOUR REPS:

Treat everyone like a prospect.
- Your management, your peers, your reps—everyone. In other words, selling is a full time habit.

X -Y = Z
- This is your contract with management, where
- X is what you agreed to sell, and
- Y is what you agreed to spend doing it.
- Whatever happens to X and Y, protect Z.

Never inflate a sales forecast.
- To please your boss. Or your ego. Your management only wants pleasant surprises.

"Adopt" your team's five best deals.
- Stay on top of those deals. Don't hesitate to take over a Top Five deal, if necessary, to win it.

Keep an eye out for the big deals.
- It's hard to crush your numbers without winning some really big deals along the way.

Acquire the habit of winning.
- Share the habit with your reps.

Put your customer's interests first.
- Even ahead of your own short-term interest. Never mind the short-term cost. Over time, this rule is a winner.

Only sell proposals you would buy.
- Here is a simple test: Would you buy a given proposal if you were in your prospect's shoes? Because that's the way a proposal will be judged. Your reps will eventually thank you for demanding this test. And so will your prospects.

Avoid military terms.
- Good selling is win/win, war is win/lose (or lose/lose).

Talk to your competitors regularly.
- What you learn will help you far more than what they learn will hurt you.

Learn to be tough enough.
- Sales managers fail when they won't do the hard stuff.

Take charge.
- Do you run your branch (district/region) or does it run you? Find ways to move from the passenger seat to the driver's seat.

Build a team you can rely on.
- Make today's numbers if you can—but not at the expense of building a team that will crush tomorrow's numbers.

Top heavy vs. bottom heavy strategies.
- When your team is top heavy (more A's & B's) crush your numbers. When your team is bottom heavy (more C's) build a team that will crush tomorrow's numbers.

Find ways to make the job fun.
- Despite the constant pressure for production, if you can find ways to make it fun you can hang in there. And if you can hang in there long enough, you can win.

CHAPTER IV. HOW TO HOLD YOUR TEAM TOGETHER
Be consistent.
- Good sales management is not unlike good parenting.

Make sure your word is good.
- Keep your promises. Keep your threats.

Treat your team like teammates.
- Don't make them work for you, get them to work with you.

Listen.
- You don't need to agree with your reps. You do need to listen to them.

Gut Check your reps regularly.
- You need to know what's on their minds.

Keep things positive.
- A rep's success depends on staying emotionally positive. Your success depends on keeping your reps emotionally positive.

Your reps need regular feedback.
- Both positive and negative feedback. Make it honest. Make it constructive.

Invite Senior Management to your sales meetings on occasion.

Make your sales meetings valuable.
- There are no excuses for holding a boring sales meeting.

Most teams have at least one rep who has all the answers.
- Who probably thinks he deserves *your* job.
- Don't worry about it. You have found your replacement and that's good. See Chapter VI.

Rank everyone and publish the rankings.
- Reps are competitive, so published rankings—who's first, who's second, etc.—drive most of them to improve their position.

Hold sales contests.
- Sales contests motivate reps and are usually worth it.

Make some of the rewards shared rewards.
- Most reps have spouses, or the equivalent, who influence them. You can influence those spouses with shared rewards, such as a week-end getaway for two, team picnics, annual president's club trips and the like.

Hold planning workshops twice a year.
Where you and your reps go offline long enough to think through questions like:

What are we doing well?
What are we not doing well?
What lessons have we learned?
What adjustments should we make?

Be careful about changing comp plans or territories.
- Changes to comp plans or territories usually make reps nervous—or worse. Make sure you see clear benefits. Sell those benefits to your reps.

Try to like your teammates.
- It will probably turn out to be good business. It certainly will make the day go better.

Success has an addictive aroma.
- Work hard to create it.

CHAPTER V.   WHAT GOES WRONG—AND HOW TO FIX IT
You can avoid a lot of problems if you follow the previous 82 rules.
But here are a few rules designed for solving common sales management problems:

If a rep isn't selling:
- Ask yourself: 'Is the problem in *finding* deals or in *closing* them?' One is a prospecting problem, the other is a harvesting problem.

If a rep isn't selling:
- Ask yourself: 'Could I harvest this pipeline? How?' Your answers will probably tell you what's wrong and what to do about it.

If a rep isn't selling:
- Ask yourself: 'Has this rep ever made the numbers?' If so, what has changed?

Never let a rep stay below quota for two consecutive reporting periods without taking action.

Keep your reps out of trouble.
- Some reps are prone to driving their lives into the ditch.
- It is a lot easier to *keep* them out of the ditch than it is to *pull* them out.

Decide which is better: bad breath, no breath or new breath.
- Time and again you will face the same choices: Do you (a) keep a rep who is seriously mediocre (or worse) and get poor coverage; (b) discard that rep and get no coverage; or (c) replace that rep and get "new" coverage. Try to make a decision that will last.

And here are a few more that anyone (including sales managers) ought to find useful:

Don't tolerate bad attitudes.

Don't keep losers.

When your plate is too full.
- Every sales manager I have ever met had too much to do. Your best solution is to do fewer tasks, but to do them well—and leave some tasks for another day.

Think of problems as normal.
- Don't waste energy on why the problem came your way; invest that energy in solving it.

Problem solving starts with problem definition.
- Decide what the real problem is, then solve that.

Prioritize problems (A/B/C) where
    A is threatening
    B is serious
    C is nuisance
    Solve the A's first, etc.

Decide whether you can fix a problem, others must fix it, or the fix must be shared. Proceed accordingly.

If a problem is Serious or Threatening, don't fall into "decision gridlock."
- After a reasonable time, do *something*.

CHAPTER VI. THIS JOB ISN'T PERMANENT, IS IT?
For most of us, first-level sales manager is just one step on a ladder. So, sooner or later we begin to look for a way to take the next step.

I have three simple rules:
1. Crush your numbers.
2. Acquire a strong sponsor (who is higher on the ladder).
3. Find your replacement.

Success does not usually send announcements. Give it time to arrive.

Glossary of Terms

People in the world of sales do not always share a common language. And to the uninitiated our language may be obscure. For these reasons I include this list of common terms, as I use them in the book.

Rep—In this book I use "rep" as a generic term for all the sales apeople under your management.

Crush Your Numbers—Exceed your assigned sales quota by an unusually large amount.

Quota—A mutually agreed-upon standard for sales production over a given period of time. Normally, both reps and managers have quotas.

Prospects—Prospective buyers who would agree that they are in some kind of evaluation or decision cycle with respect to your products or services.

Prospecting—The art and science of finding, and qualifying, active prospects. Otherwise known as building a pipeline.

Pipeline—A list of prospects who are actively being pursued at any given time. In short, "real" prospects.

Harvesting—The art and science of squeezing sales out of a prospect pipeline.

Hunters—Reps who are unusually good at selling to new accounts (versus to customers).

Farmers—Reps who are unusually good at selling to customers (as opposed to new accounts).

Coverage—A measure in quantity and quality of prospecting activity underway in a given sales territory during a given time period.

Carry a Bag—A rep with an assigned quota is "carrying a bag."

Territory—The definition of where a rep can prospect for new business.

Direct Reports—The number of people who can report directly to you.

Pro Hires—Reps who had significant sales experience the day they were hired.

Deal—A specific piece of business being pursued with a given prospect.

Thank You

Over the years, I have been privileged to work with hundreds of bright and interesting people. I learned from all of you. Thank you for the lessons. You are truly a part of this book.

Walter Brown

About the Author

A graduate of Princeton University, Walter Brown has spent his entire career in the computing industry.

Beginning as a system engineer at IBM, he later co-founded a software marketing firm at the dawn of the software products industry, and was subsequently a principal in several related ventures.

Since 1979, Mr. Brown has been doctoring sales organizations exclusively in the computing industry. His clients have ranged in size from a few sales reps to a few hundred and are located throughout the world.

CHASING QUOTA 2
BY WALTER BROWN

A ROADMAP FOR SALESPEOPLE

Some time ago I wrote a book called CHASING QUOTA—a Roadmap for Anyone Who Manages Salespeople. Readers said they liked the book, but a number of them asked me an interesting question—What can I give my salespeople that mirrors the advice you gave to me?

Here is my answer.

Table of Contents

CHAPTER I.   WHO SHOULD BE IN SALES
MAYBE YOU, IF YOU:

- LOVE TO WIN
- HATE TO LOSE
- LIKE MONEY A LOT
- LIKE PEOPLE, AND VICE VERSA
- BELIEVE STRONGLY IN YOUR PRODUCTS & SERVICES
- TRULY HELP PROSPECTS FIND SOLUTIONS
- CAN PERSUADE
- CAN TOLERATE INCOME RISK
- CAN HANDLE REJECTION

CHAPTER II.   NEW ASSIGNMENT—
GETTING STARTED RIGHT
MASTER IT NOW.

- You won't get another chance to learn what you need to know without the pressure for sales production.
- Pass some tests before your training ends because you will surely be tested in the field.

LEARN THY TERRITORY.

- Learn its history, its customers, its potential, its strongest competitors and more.

DON'T EXPECT A BIG INHERITANCE.

- No matter what you were promised, be prepared to build a new pipeline from scratch.

NEGOTIATE YOUR QUOTA WELL

- Else you may have to live a whole year with too much quota.

LOOK FOR SUCCESSFUL MODELS.

- Who are the Top Producers? How are they doing it? What lessons can you borrow from them?

DON'T BE AN ORPHAN.

- If you are working alone, (remote office, remote territory, etc.) take time to build internal relationships, starting with your boss.

SPEND ENOUGH TIME ON PLANTING.

- Early on, before everyone expects you to be harvesting.

SCORE SOME POINTS EARLY.
- Get on the scoreboard to prove that you can.

VERY FEW REPS SURVIVE A SERIOUSLY POOR START.
- Make the early days count.

CHAPTER III. WHAT TO DO ALL DAY—PLANTING
SALES SUCCESS CAN BE SUMMARIZED IN EIGHT WORDS:
- BUILD A GOOD PROSPECT PIPELINE, THEN HARVEST THAT PIPELINE.
- Is that what you are doing?

HOW WILL YOU MAKE YOUR NUMBERS
- From current customers or from new customers? From singles and doubles or from home runs?
- Make a plan and follow it.

HUG THE RIGHT PROSPECTS.
- You need a clear prospecting roadmap—a plan for building a good pipeline. Without it you won't find and develop the right prospects.

HUG YOUR CUSTOMERS.
- Do it often. Hugging customers begets more business and more customers.

MINIMIZE COLD CALLS.
- The more cold calls you must make, the weaker your prospecting roadmap it. Find more efficient ways to find new prospects.

YOU CAN'T HARVEST WHAT HASN'T BEEN PLANTED.
- Plan to plant more than you need.

CHAPTER IV. WHAT TO DO ALL DAY—HARVESTING
WHAT CAN YOU CLOSE NEXT?
- Make this your first and last question every day.

WATCH YOUR PIPELINE, NOT JUST YOUR SALES PRODUCTION.
- Sales are the end product of a process, the better your process, the greater your production.

LISTEN.
- You don't learn much about your prospect when you are talking.

LEARN EMPATHY.
- The more you can put yourself in your prospects' shoes, the more likely they are to buy from you.

SELL PROPOSALS THAT *YOU* WOULD BUY.

- Would *you* buy your proposal? If so, you probably know why your prospects will buy it. If no, why are you selling it?

HELP YOUR PROSPECTS MAKE GOOD DECISIONS.

- Good for *THEM*. Which in turn will be good for you.

EMOTION

- Most prospects make emotional decisions which they wrap in rationale.
- So sell to your prospect's emotions. But supply a rational wrapper.

HOME RUNS

- You need to hit them because it is hard to crush your numbers without some big deals along the way.

GET HELP.

- Help is always an available for bigger deals.

JOINT SALES CALLS

- Making joint sales calls is like dancing in a tight space—each of you better know what the other is going to do next.

DON'T FALL IN LOVE WITH YOUR DEALS.

- Too much optimism means you will stay with bad deals too long. Always add realism to the mix.

STAY OBJECTIVE.

- A good rep invests emotion, which can cause a loss of objectivity. Hold on to yours.

EVERY PROSPECT'S THREE BASIC QUESTIONS ARE

- **Why Do It? Why Now? Why With You?**
- Keep it simple—Sell to those questions.

LOSE RIGHT.

- If you lose, you lose. Leave your relationship intact for tomorrow's business.

CHAPTER V.   INSIDE YOUR HEAD (THE MIND GAME)
YOUR INNER (MIND) GAME IS CRITICAL, FOR EXAMPLE:

- Is your head really into selling?
- Will you step outside your comfort zone to be successful?

WHEN YOU ARE COLD CALLING

- Do you feel more like a pest or missionary?

DO YOU BELIEVE

- In the products and services you are selling? Would you buy them if you were in your prospect's shoes?

WHEN YOU HEAR OBJECTIONS

- Does your belief in your offering underpin your response? Do objections undermine your confidence?

ARE YOU SELLING

- Or helping your prospects solve their problems? Should there really be any difference?

DO YOU TRULY KNOW

- How your prospect gains from your proposal? Do You Care?

IF YOUR ANSWERS ARE TENTATIVE

- Then your inner game may not match your visible game—which will inevitably limit your success.

TO WIN CONSISTENTLY YOUR INNER GAME MUST BE CLEAR, AND YOUR VISIBLE GAME MUST FIT THAT CLARITY.

CHAPTER VI.   LIVING WITH YOUR BROTHERS & SISTERS
KEEP YOUR WORD.

- Keep your commitments—to your customers, to your management, to your peers, to everyone.

COMMON LANGUAGE

- If your team has a common language*, use it.

  *language to describe or evaluate deals, build proposals, dissect sales calls and the like.

KEEP YOUR EXPENSE REPORTS CLEAN.

TREAT YOUR MANAGEMENT WITH RESPECT.

- Most of them will earn it. Most of them will reciprocate. Don't hide from them: they are entitled to know how and what you are doing. They can help you; they are your partners.

GUT CHECK YOUR BOSSES ON OCCASION.

- You need to know what's on their minds.

SELL INSIDE.

- Selling inside your own organization is just as critical as selling in the field.

NEVER INFLATE A SALES FORECAST
- To satisfy your boss or your ego. Your management only wants pleasant surprises.

NEVER GET RANKED AT THE BOTTOM. REPS AT THE BOTTOM ARE AN ENDANGERED SPECIES.

SALES MEETINGS—SHOW UP. CONTRIBUTE. BENEFIT.

TRY TO LIKE YOUR TEAMMATES
- It will probably turn out to be good business. It will certainly make the day to better.

TALK TO YOUR COMPETITORS
- Regularly. What you learn from them can prove more valuable than what they learn from you.

BAD ATTITUDES ARE FOR LOSERS.

AVOID MILITARY TERMS.
- The Best Selling is Win/Win. War is Win/Lose (and often lose/lose)

BE PATIENT WITH FOOLISHNESS
- If it contributes to the sale

CHANGE IS NORMAL.
- Welcome changes. Take advantage of them.

COVET THE NEIGHBOR'S TURF.
- Sales Territories often change hands. Get some of those changes in *your* hands.

CRUSH YOUR NUMBERS AND YOUR MANAGEMENT WILL LOVE YOU.
- Miss your number and they may divorce you.

EXPECT THE OCCASIONAL FLOGGING
- By your customers; by your management. Sales reps are a convenient scapegoat.

SHARE THE APPLAUSE
- When things go right. Take your share of the blame when they don't.

HELP YOUR BROTHERS AND SISTERS
- When they need it.
- It's satisfying.

- It's the right thing to do.
- And it pays big dividends.

CHAPTER VII. WHAT GOES WRONG AND HOW TO FIX IT
PROBLEMS ARE NORMAL

- So don't waste energy on why the problem crossed your path. Invest time and energy in solving it.

DECIDE WHAT THE REAL PROBLEM IS

- Versus the symptoms, and solve that.

IF YOU ARE NOT WINNING

- Is your problem *finding* deals or *closing* them? One is a *prospecting* problem the other is a *harvesting* problem.

IF YOU ARE NOT WINNING

- Is *ANYBODY* winning, and what's different about them.

LIVING THROUGH A DRAUGHT?

- Farmers survive and so may you, by working their plan, staying patient, and watching for rain.

TIRED OF PROSPECTING?

- So are we all from time to time. The key is to keep doing it.

DOES A COMPETITOR SEEM UNBEATABLE?

- Competitors are rarely unbeatable. You just have to figure out how.

THE LEAPFROG EFFECT

- Vendors are always leapfrogging each other. So if your frog isn't in front, then maybe it is getting ready to jump.

BURNED OUT?

- Sales is a game with few timeouts. So take timeouts when you need to, because nobody will call them for you.

CHECKPOINTS

- Checkpoint your next deal once a day, your best deals once a week, your pipeline once a month, your ranking once a quarter and your job once a year.

COMMISSIONS

- Counting them before the deal closes is not smart. And spending them before the deal closes is worse.

KEEP OUT OF TROUBLE.

- It is always a lot easier to *stay* out of a hole than to *get* out of one.

NO WHINING.

- You are paid to make your numbers. If you are not making them, find a remedy. If you can't find a remedy, move on, and don't whine about it.

CHAPTER VIII.CRITICAL SUCCESS FACTORS

REMEMBER THAT 'NO' MEANS 'NOT NOW', NOT 'NEVER.'

A/B/C EVERYTHING

- Customers, prospects, problems, to-do lists, etc. A's are a first priority, B's are next, and C's are all the rest.

PLAN AHEAD.

- In sales, time is nearly always your scarcest resource. Treat it with great respect.

CUSTOMERS ARE LIKE GOLD.

- Make sure they get the Twenty Four Karat Treatment.

TREAT EVERYONE LIKE A PROSPECT.

- Your customers, your management, your teammates, everyone. Selling is a full-time habit.

TRY TO BE A REALISTIC OPTIMIST.

LEARN TO NEGOTIATE.

ROADBLOCKS

- Good sales reps learn to get around them.

SOLUTION SELLING REQUIRES THAT YOUR PROPOSALS MEET YOUR PROSPECT'S NEEDS. RELATIONSHIP SELLING REQUIRES THAT YOUR PROSPECTS KNOW AND TRUST YOU. THE COMBINATION IS NEARLY UNBEATABLE.

CONVICTION

- Prospects can feel the power that flows when you sell from conviction.

WORK HARDEST TO MEET PROSPECT'S NEEDS, NOT *YOUR* NEEDS.

TAKE CHARGE OF YOUR TERRITORY

- Make something happen.

TIME
- In a given situation, is time your friend or your enemy? If it's your friend, coast, if it's your enemy, accelerate.

FIND WAYS TO MAKE THE JOB FUN.

MANAGE YOUR TERRITORY LIKE AN INDEPENDENT BUSINESS

MOTIVATE YOURSELF
- *You* have to know why you're here. Others can only help you *remember* why you're here.

CHAPTER IX.   MOVING ON UP

FOR MANY OF US, SALES IS JUST THE FIRST STEP ON A LADDER. SO SOONER OR LATER, WE LOOK FOR A WAY TO TAKE THE NEXT STEP.

HERE ARE TWO SIMPLE RULES THAT WORK:
1. Crush Your Numbers
2. Acquire a Strong Sponsor (who is higher on the ladder)

THINKING OF SALES MANAGEMENT?
Here are a few simple tests:
1. Would you rather motivate prospects or teammates?
2. Would you rather sell or help others sell?
3. Have you coached anyone? Did you like it? Did they?

GO AHEAD, BE A SALES MANAGER. TAKE A PAY CUT.

APPENDIX: HOW TO FIND THE RIGHT SALES JOB

TO BE SUCCESSFUL IN SALES, YOU WILL NEED A PLAYABLE HAND, INCLUDING THESE CARDS:
- A Healthy Marketplace
- Competitive Products
- Enough Territory
- A Good Compensation Plan
- A Stable Employer
- Supportive Management
- Realistic Goals—Yours and Your Employer's

TO TEST WHETHER A PROSPECTIVE (OR CURRENT) EMPLOYER IS OFFERING A PLAYABLE HAND:

- Are these people *winners*? (Revenue & Profit History)
- Is their Sales Team making its numbers?
- How well do their customers regard them? (a solid vendor has a solid customer base)
- Have you interviewed any of their reps, especially their *top guns*?
- What about turnover? (Good sales teams have low turnover?)
- What support will your boss commit to help you get off to a fast start?
- Do they want you to be a *hunter* or a *farmer*? (most of us are better at one OR the other)
- Do the *details* of the deal make sense? (comp plan, territory, training plan, etc.)

IF IT ALL CHECKS OUT, TAKE (OR KEEP) THE JOB.

- If not, keep looking.
- If you are already in the wrong job, start looking.
- Days spent in the wrong job are long days.

FOR MORE THAN FORTY YEARS I HAVE BEEN PRIVILEGED TO KNOW, TO WORK WITH, AND TO LEARN FROM MANY OF THE BEST SALES PEOPLE IN MY WORLD, THE WORLD OF INFORMATION TECHNOLOGY.

YOU KNOW WHO YOU ARE. YOU ARE ALL IN THIS BOOK.

THANKS FOR THE LESSONS. *wfb*

Glossary of Terms

People in the world of sales do not always share a common language. And to the uninitiated our language may be obscure. For these reasons I include this list of common terms, as I use them in this book.

Rep—In this book I use "rep" as a generic term for *all* sales people under your management.

Crush Your Numbers—Exceed your assigned sales quota by an unusually large amount.

Quota—A mutually agreed-upon standard for sales production over a given period of time. Normally both reps and managers have quotas.

Prospects—Prospective buyers who would agree that they are in some kind of evaluation or decision cycle with respect to your products or services.

Prospecting—The art and science of finding, and qualifying, active prospects. Otherwise known as building pipeline.

Pipeline—Lots of prospects who are actively being pursued at any given time. In short, "real" prospects.

Harvesting—The art and science of squeezing sales out of a prospect pipeline.

Hunters—Reps who are unusually good at selling to new accounts (versus to customers)

Farmers—Reps who are unusually good at selling to customers (versus to new accounts)

Coverage—A measure of the quantity and quality of prospecting activity underway in a given sales territory during a given time period.

Carry a Bag—A rep with an assigned quota is "carrying a bag."

Territory—the definition of where a rep can prospect for new business.

Pro Hires—Reps who had significant sales experience the day they were hired.

Deal—A specific piece of business being pursued with a given prospect.

RANDY'S SUCCESS IDEAS

1. Evaluate Your Leadership Skills

This is a tool I've used over the years, which allows sales leaders to assess themselves on how they are doing in critical areas. I would strongly suggest you take the assessment yourself, then ask those you report to or who work for you to validate your assessment as a reality check. It's always helpful to put together your own improvement plan on any of these areas where you can improve so you can get to a level five in all these areas.

"What Winning Leaders Do"
from Jack Welch's Book *Winning*

Rate yourself on a scale of 1-5:

_____ Leaders relentlessly upgrade their team, using every encounter as an opportunity to evaluate, coach, and build self-confidence.

_____ Leaders make sure people not only see the vision, they live and breathe it.

_____ Leaders get into everyone's skin, exuding positive energy and optimism.

_____ Leaders establish trust with candor, transparency, and credit.

_____ Leaders have the courage to make unpopular decisions and gut calls.

_____ Leaders probe and push with a curiosity that borders on skepticism, making sure their questions are answered with action.

_____ Leaders inspire risk taking and learning by setting the example.

_____ Leaders celebrate. Celebrating makes people feel like winners.[9]

VIP: Use this tool to be the best leader you can be, with the goal of reaching a level five in each area.

2. Do an Audit of Your Life Quarterly
(or Any Frequency You Want)

Over the years, I've acquired two different versions of a Whole-Life Audit that I've used for myself and my sales teams to help us achieve balance in our lives. I borrowed the first one from my late friend and Boston College Professor Frank Ladwig, which is a shorter version of one I borrowed from fellow YPO members and executive coaches, Michael Bloch and Jim Warner. (The original Seven Sides of Personal Development information that Frank taught us in 1984 is included in the appendix.) Both are great tools to use for an evaluation of your life balance. Of course, it is always great to aim high and do your best to achieve 100 percent balance in every area. It's good to be aware of the areas where you're off balance so you can develop your own improvement plan.

I've found it's best to be deliberate when I'm setting goals. For example, if I'm really busy with work, my friends and my body may suffer. If that's the case, I have to make a conscious, deliberate decision about whether I want to achieve balance in those two areas at that particular time in my life, or be content knowing that is a deliberate choice. Someone who is out of work will likely be unbalanced on the money side, yet they may be strong in family relationships and other areas. The point is to be deliberate and self-aware about how balanced you are and either make changes or be satisfied.

Whole Life Audit 1
(Adapted from Whole Life Audit by Frank Ladwig)

Area of Your Life	Word/Phrase to Describe Your Relationship	Working? (Yes/No)	Word/Phrase to Describe Your Six-Month Target
Life Balance			
Money			
Your Marriage			
Your Children			
Other Relationships			
Your Body			
Spirituality			
Sense of Life Purpose			
Yourself			
Approach to Life Today			
Your Work			

Here are some examples of words I've used to describe my relationship with that area of my life. (This was when I was SVP/GM at HP.):

Area of Your Life	Word/Phrase to Describe Your Relationship	Working? (Yes/No)	Word/Phrase to Describe Your Six-Month Target
Life Balance	Out of whack	No	Deliberately content
Money	Balanced	Yes	Keep earning and investing
Your Marriage	Exciting, loving, fun	Yes	Continue to prioritize
Your Children	Love, fun, pride	Yes	Continue to prioritize
Other Relationships	Not much	No	Low priority
Your Body	Workouts bad this month	No	Exercise 3x per week
Spirituality	Connective/Supportive	Yes	Daily prayer
Sense of Purpose	Can see where I'm going	Yes	Execute on my goals
Yourself	Comfortable, demanding, proud	Yes	Don't burn the candle too much
Approach to Life Today	Work-centric, give-get, exciting, happy to help	Yes	Keep going
Your Work	Successful and fulfilling	Yes	Continue to exceed expectations

In the last column, describe in just a few words where you want to be in that area six months from now, or in whatever time-frame you choose.

Whole Life Audit 2

Area of Your Life	A Word/Phrase to Describe Your Relationship to the Area Today	Is It Working for You?	A Word/Phrase to Describe Your Six-Month Target
Intellectual Self			
Emotional Self			
Physical Self			
Spiritual Self			
Sexual Self			
Approach to Life			
Time			
Vocation/Job			
Sense of Life Purpose			
Money/Security			
Power/Control			
Success/Approval			
Contribution/Service			
Partner/Spouse			
Your Children			
Parents			
Siblings			
Other Family			
Work Associates			
Friends			
Mentors/Guides			
Small Group			
Local Community			
The World (Political/Socio-Economic)			
The Natural World			

VIP: Use these tools to make you deliberately aware of the areas of your life that are balanced (in whatever way you define success) and those you want to improve in, so you can hold yourself accountable and ultimately achieve happiness.

3. Adapt Some of These Whole-Life Audit Items to Develop Your Life Goals

Here's an example of how I have turned some of the Whole-Life Audit items into my goals for 2020 and down the road.

Mission Statement: To live an authentic life that God, my family, and I can be proud of. To be happy, do what I want to do, and live in the moment!
Positive Outlook: I wake up positive every day, lead a balanced life, make a difference in the world, love, make money, and have fun by passionately:

1. Focusing on my family relationships, my spirituality, and God
2. Eating healthy, drinking water, exercising, engaging in sports, avoiding toxins, and sleeping seven to eight hours
3. Excelling and developing professionally, on the road to be the Bill Campbell of Boston
4. Proactively managing my network
5. Improving financially
6. Helping/developing my family, friends, colleagues, and strangers; encouraging paying it forward
7. Pursuing mental stimulation and development
8. Reviewing both my goals and accomplishments and furthering my belief in my goals becoming a reality
9. Planning ahead to live life to the fullest so I can get/give the most each day
10. Surrounding myself with people I like, trust, respect, can learn from, and align with
11. Treating others the way I want to be treated
12. Focusing on my priority to-dos in the morning
13. In case of adversity, believing/knowing I can, I will, I must!
14. Living this motto: "Happy to do it!"

Then I can look down my road with confidence and look back with pride, without regret. I will always be my best self, and I will always be myself.

2020 Overall Goals
Top Goals

1. Stay in touch with family and friends and be in the moment
2. Sleep 7-8 hours, exercise every day, lift weights two times/week; maintain weight in the 220's, and drink 120 oz. of water
3. Successful launch of SALES COMMUNITY and publish *Your Go-To Sales Advisor*
4. Give back and serve others: Boston College, St. Sebastian's School, Malta, Harvard and Duke baseball, YPO, and friends

Family
1. Janet: enjoy a great marriage and relationship, always keep her number one in my life, enjoy mutual interests (skiing, pickleball, golf, TV series, tennis, dancing, trips, and going out with friends), maintain great communication (including listening), always be caring and loving
2. Kids: stay in touch and engaged in their lives, support their goals, be loving and nurturing, invest focused time, be a mentor for them, know their friends, play, savor the now, maintain a consistent structure and latitude, stretch their imaginations, discuss their dreams, show them the right way to do and handle things, help them experience the whole world, model how to react and act, share my feelings/experiences, show them how to share, extend deserved trust, talk to them about concerns/blessings/people/life, help them learn to think well, teach them financial responsibility, help them with career advice, go to their games 3. Take trips with kids 4. Take family trips 5. Have birthday dinners 6. Parents: In touch and engaged

Spiritual
1. Pray, thank God daily for everything, remember that gratitude improves my attitude, daily mass 2-3 times per week, pray at dinner 2. Nourish Father Jim relationship 3. Serve in Knights of Malta

Health/Physical
1. Maintain weight in the 220's 2. Sleep 7 to 8 hours: be in bed before 11 p.m. 3. Drink 120 ounces of water daily 4. Exercise every day (two times/week with weights, five times/week cardio), always stretch, do TB12 pliability sphere daily 5. Get massage and visit chiropractor monthly 6. Eat healthy: intermittent fasting for 14 to 16 hours, good protein and veggies, eat only palm portions 7. Engage in sports: tennis, golf, and skiing (1 million vertical per year) 8. Whoop strap day strain 11+ and recovery green

Professional

1. Successfully launch Sales Community and publish Your Go-To Sales Advisor
2. Continue adding value to Revenue Acceleration clients
3. Grow Top Talent Recruiting
4. Stay on the road to achieve the goal of being Bill Campbell of Boston, RIP
5. Cultivate my go-to executive relationships
6. YPO: Inside the Boardroom, Emerson Forum, learning/leverage events, Shannon YNG
7. Boards (three), Advisory Boards (eight), Consulting (eight)
8. Leverage Trish—invoicing, expenses, forms, and burn rate tracking; delegate to leverage time

Financial

1. Track money earned and net worth
2. Invest well
3. Burn rate, charitable giving, insurance

Social

1. Make a difference in the world, help friends/family/strangers
2. Always be positive and smiling, be interested in others (ask questions), and listen well
3. Support charities: St. Sebastian's School, Boston College, Malta, Harvard and Duke Baseball, Mass Mentoring
4. Take relationships with friends deeper
5. Entertain friends and kids in the backyard
6. Help with marriages
7. Stay active in clubs: Brae Burn and Wellesley, apply to Ocean Reef and The Quin
8. Take trips and Beaver Creek

Mental

1. Read daily WSJ/Globe and magazines
2. Read books and summaries via Jeary/YPO extracts, including one fiction (improve here!)
3. Personal: budget time on calendar and see how I spend it; say NO

Longer Term Vision: be happy, laugh, be in the moment, and serve others

1. Family: great marriage, relationships, traditions, trips, improve dancing
2. Spiritual: daily devotion, service
3. Physical: healthy, lean, golf, tennis, skiing, sleep eight hours, drink water
4. Professional: keep working, mentor, serve on boards, teach, support charities, consult, nourish relationships
5. Financial: donate, build net worth
6. Social: friends

Phase Two of My Life (50-60)

1. Create sustainable businesses
2. Need $xx liquid net worth to have option to retire
3. Write a book

Phase Three of My Life (60-70)
1. Maintain more personal, family, friends time
2. Work (boards and consulting) only because I want to, not because I have to, be Bill Campbell of Boston
3. Stay relevant and help others
4. Take YPO Gold and CEO trips/events

Phase Four of My Life (70+)
1. Be fully retired(?), invest in grandkids (time, fun, and teaching), invest time with friends
2. Janet: love, fun, travel, tennis, golf, ski, and something new
3. Mentor/coach: be Bill Campbell of Boston, serve on boards, consult, help others

Last Year Review and This Year Plan Template
Short Form:
Last Year: • Sit in a quiet place and simply breathe for a few minutes first, allowing my shoulders, my jaw, and any other places of tension in my body to relax.   • Think about what stands out from last year; just breathe and let the answers take what time they need to come.   • What worked best for me last year?   • What were my top three lessons learned?   • What personal and professional qualities did I develop?   • What were my biggest wins and challenges?   • What would I love to do less of?   • What would I love to do more of?   • What activities had me jumping out of bed in the morning?   • What kind of people did I love being around?   • What conversations left me feeling most fully myself?   • What am I proudest of achieving?   • How did I surprise myself?
This Year: • What would I like this coming year to be about; what will be my theme for the year?   • What personal and professional qualities do I want to develop?   • Who do I need help from to achieve these goals?   • Next year, how will I finish this sentence? This year I'm proudest of having.....

VIP: Just like in business, you should have goals for your life.

4. Use These Performance Criteria to Ensure You Have the Best People and Teams Possible

Use these best practices to give and get feedback with your team.

To aid in the process of getting and giving feedback, you will need to be doing these things on a continual basis:

- Coaching. Be sure you're continuously improving and developing your people. I've found it best to make coaching an ongoing part of your culture, versus an annual event. There are two very effective ways to give ongoing feedback:

  1. Ask, "May I give you some feedback?" Often, as a manager, I will be on a sales call with a rep, and I will ask the individual if he/she has any feedback for me on anything I could have done differently or better. People are typically shocked that an executive would ask that question, yet I am very open to their feedback. Then, after I get the feedback from that person, I ask, "May I give you some feedback?"

     This concept is a great communication tool, whether you're giving feedback to someone who reports to you or someone you report to, or even if you're the one getting feedback. Even though the person receiving the feedback knows it could be either positive or negative, or a little of both, it breaks the ice and prepares the person to be receptive to it. By the way, this works great with family and friends, and especially great with your kids.

  2. Say, "When you _____, I feel _____, because _____." This is another great way to give feedback, especially for something the person really needs to improve on. For example, you could say, "When you said you would have the proposal out by today and you didn't, I felt disappointed that you let me down; you didn't do something you said you would do, and I fear that could hurt our sales cycle."

- Utilizing 360-degree review

- Having fun! Work is work, obviously; yet hopefully you're ultimately having fun doing it.

VIP: No matter how great a leader you are, you're only as good as your team—both your direct and indirect reports—so make sure you have a culture of giving and getting feedback.

5. Use the Stack Ranking Tool to Objectively Rank Your Team and Allow Others to Give Feedback

Here's an example:

Smith – Channel
Team Stack Ranking

	Name	FY 19 Rating	FY 20 Rating	State	Role	Dev Plan	Successor Ready	Deliver Financial Commits	Leader-ship	Selling/ Relationship Building	Product Knowledge
				VP Name: Nonie Smith, Sales Leader				Skills Assessment (1-5)			
	John	EE	EE	IL	DRC Director	Field and BU Exposure	N	4	5	5	5
	Bob	EE	EE	CO	West Region Director	Exposure/Time in Role	N	5	5	4	4
	Sally	EE	SE	MD	Federal Director	Cross-BU Communication	N	5	4	4	4
	Dick	SE	EE	FL	Southeast & Operations Director	Time in Role; Executive Exposure	N	5	4	4	4
	Susan	SE	SE	CA	Commercial Distributors Manager	Commercial Experience	N	4	4	5	4
	George	EE	SE	CT	Northeast Region Director	Field Sales Relationships	N	4	4	4	4
	Ron	AE	AE	AZ	HPU/BN Manager	Time in Role; BU Exposure	N	4	5	4	3
	Kaylee	AE	AE	OH	GBU Lead	Consistent Performance	N	4	3	3	4
	Steve	SE	EE	PA	North Central Region Director	Cross BU and Field Relationship Development	N	4	4	4	3

The more objective you can make the stack-ranking process, the easier it will be for you. Because people are our most important aspect, I would always have my direct reports prepared and discuss the stack ranking of their teams in any quarterly business review and in team meetings. Too often managers are lazy and do stack rankings based only on sales numbers; this is bad for a number of reasons. There are many ways to do the stack ranking, but here are some areas that you should consider.

- I hate seeing someone ranked number one because of a huge bluebird deal (did little to no work to earn the deal) and they have mediocre sales behavior.
- Have each person ranked top to bottom based on both present performance and potential. Be sure to consider their territory in this decision. If they have a fantastic territory but are just selling at goal, they may not be as good as someone who has a bad territory but is actually making a goal.
- Show their ratings for each of the past two years plus proposed ratings for the current year.
- List one or two key development areas.
- Indicate whether they are successor ready (yes or no).
- Determine who is at risk (who may be leaving for whatever reason).
- You should be building your bench of talent in your team in case you need to backfill. It's always a best practice to have a bench per person per position.
- Some of the skill areas to assess can include sales results, sales behaviors/skills, territories, leadership, and potential.

VIP: A stack-ranking process is a must-have for any sales leaders to know objectively the status and quality of their team.

6. Lead by Example with These Best Practices

- Treat others how you want to be treated, with fairness and respect. I think everyone can look back and see where they've had managers who have done that well and others who haven't.

  At my first management job at EMC, I was in charge of the inside sales group. The CEO was Dick Egan, and his wife Maureen was the receptionist. When people came in to interview with me for an inside sales job or to be part of our sales training program, I would get her feedback about how they treated her. It was a great way to get valuable insights (sometimes shocking) about the people I was interviewing.

- Live and breathe vision and optimism.
- Be open, fair, consistent, trustworthy, and willing to take risks.
- Have a great:
  - Work ethic
  - Attitude
  - Energy
  - Presence
- Learn by listening, and take specific action.
- What can you say you have done for your team?
- Be customer-focused. Invest time in your customers, versus internal meetings, etc., that don't increase your pipeline and sales. Your people will follow your lead.
- Winners have fun and celebrate!

VIP: By leading by example, you influence the attitude and behavior of other people.

7. Have a Fast-Start Plan for Your First Ninety Days

Whether you're taking a new job as an individual contributor or a CRO, make sure you have a written plan for your first ninety days on the job. It's always a great idea to include any objective metrics, get buy in, and share. Here are some ideas:

- First thirty: Listen, gain trust, assess, and create wins
- Next thirty: Diagnose, focus on what you can control, give open feedback
- Next thirty: Create a game plan with messages and actions, involving the right people in the right roles
- Beyond three months: Execute and exceed plan

- Also:
  - Accelerate learning
  - Match your company's strategy to your team's
  - Secure early wins
  - Negotiate success
  - Achieve alignment
  - Strengthen your team[10]

In their book, *You're in Charge—Now What?: The 8-Point Plan*, Thomas Neff and James Citrin list these ideas from their Spencer Stuart 8-Point Plan for the First Hundred Days:

1. Prepare yourself during the countdown.
2. Align expectations
3. Shape your management team
4. Craft your strategic agenda
5. Start transforming culture
6. Manage your board/boss
7. Communicate
8. Avoid common pitfalls[11]

Here is a sample fast-start plan for a manager:

The Transformation to Support Profitable Growth
30-60-90 Day Fast-Start Plan

Observations:

Things to build on
- Focus on cloud marketspace
- Extensive market share in electronic trading
- Ease of choice of offering
- Human capital loyalty
- Customer loyalty
- Recognition of the *need* to build a new market to facilitate growth

Things to work on
- Lack of new customer acquisition
- Channel execution
- Cloud messaging
- Awareness of the solution
- Leverage of tech partners

The Process:

- Operational processes
  - Evaluate processes
  - Develop best practices
  - Build management system
  - Execute
  - Repeat all of the above

- People
  - Mentorship
  - Performance evaluation (objective, not subjective beauty contest, friendship or history),
  - External recruit
  - Management layer rationalization
  - Roundtables to build and assess morale

- Portfolio
  - Unique value prop to customers
  - Unique value prop to partners
  - Customer segmentation
  - Vertical messaging

The Approach:

- Predictability
  - Stated goal revenue, orders, and date +/- 2 percent
  - Accepted goal +/- 10 percent
    - Sales orders and date, secondary revenue
    - Delivery revenue
  - FY 19 planning (set a plan that is achievable)

- Profitability
  - Sales compensation
  - Rationalize sales coverage
  - Normalize to profitable customer segments

- Growth
  - Demand generation
  - Culture of prospecting
  - Engage with channel partner sales
  - Customer mix

30-Day Plan: Learn

- Logistics setup (communications, computer, etc.)
- Complete company training/requirements
- Initial meetings with peers and functional heads
- Initial meetings with product management
- Initial meetings with directs and their directs
- Spend time on the phones shadowing inside sales resources
- Press release and communications
- Visit employees
- Visit largest partners/distributors
- Begin on-going dialogue with board
- Kick off channel program review
  - Recruitment targets
  - Channel enablement
  - Channel development
  - Reach out via phone to all existing channel partners
  - Reach out via phone to top twenty customers

60-Day Plan: Learn and Validate

- Repeat meetings with staff, and establish on-going meetings
- Establish repeating meetings for management system: CEO, board, etc.
- Meet with CEO, CFO, HR for feedback and observations
- Meet with key product partners to gain access to cloud customers
  - Microsoft
    - Use Tracey Galloway RVP central Microsoft sales for guidance
  - VMWare
    - Frank Rauch, VP North American Channel, leverage to get to the right people
  - NetApp
    - Jeff McCullough, VP NA Channels and Jean English, CMO
- Pick key leaders in tech partners as mentors/champions
- Meet with key customers in person: focus on references
- Develop on-going communications process with CEO
- Develop external vision with marketing
- Hold all hands call: focusing on state of the business, and external vision

- Try to add value in a non-disruptive way: introduce close plans
- Develop mentorship approach to key functions: sales, marketing, product management

90-Day Plan: Execute and Establish Alignment

- Review learnings and validations from the first 60 days
- Socialize process (operational process, people and portfolio) and approach (predictability, profitability, growth)
- Build and implement new sales process: cadence and forecast
- Execute vision roadshow
  - Visit ten cities to communicate and listen with cross section of team and customers
  - Consider marketing events and speaking opportunities
  - Generate article with CRN on communications
- Begin FY21 model planning and prepare for planning workshop

90 Days and Beyond Plan: Execute and Grow

- Review learnings and validations from the first 90 days
- Help any new resources personally
- Execute new sales process: cadence and forecast
- Ongoing morale and communication with the team
- Marketing/demand generation plan
- Engage key resources in various special projects
  - Channel expansion
  - Sales process improvements
  - Best practice socialization
- Visit top twenty new prospects
- Attend tech partners' key meetings and conferences
- Consider distributor value

   Ingram, Arrow, SYNNEX, Tech Data

Here is a sample fast-start plan for an individual contributor:

Account Executive
30-60-90 Day Fast-Start Plan—Selling
More and Attacking the Territory

It is important to start fast and finish strong and identify a clear roadmap that will lay the foundation to sustainable growth and consistent revenue generation. Every touchpoint with the prospect or partner is an opportunity to demonstrate the value that XYZ brings to the table, as well as learn what is important to the customer base with regard to their specific goals and objectives regarding their data and cloud initiatives.

This 30-60-90 day plan illustrates what areas I believe will allow for success in this role, and how this success can be sustainable and consistent over time.

Goals

- Achieve 110 percent of YTD quota after first six months
- Increase current pipeline to 3x of quota
- Identify top-tier accounts to maintain high levels of engagement, and identify accounts where channel can drive activity and create/maintain engagement
- Establish executive-level relationships at top tier accounts to fully understand business objectives and organizational initiatives
- Identify top channel partners utilizing XYZ and establish relationships, define engagement, and establish regular cadence calls
- Engage with ISR team and SE to understand landscape in new account patch and important contacts within accounts
- Get three customers to attend an XYZ marketing event
- Establish regular cadence calls with SE and inside sales specialists to maximize our contact and activity within accounts

30-Day Objectives

Complete Full Scale Territory Analysis

- Review all current opportunities that exist within XYZ pipeline and work to close "commit" opportunities
- Segment the territory into "A," "B" and "C" accounts based on data size and capital spending
- Discuss account segmentation with my extended team, SE, Inside Sales Specialists, to maximize coverage model
- Mine install base within accounts, determine expiring contracts and maintenance schedule, look for cross sell and up sell opportunities and wedge these strategies into these accounts
- Create a Territory Business Plan to ensure alignment of my goals, objectives, and actions

Sales Activity

- Identify path to closure on all committed opportunities for the quarter
- Review all best case and pipeline deals in the territory, determine which deals have real potential, and pursue. Omit inaccurate or unqualified opportunities

- Build pipeline: Focus on prospecting, twenty to twenty-five hours a week to start (four to five hours per day), increase up to thirty hours a week after the first two to three weeks, based on meeting activity

Channel Engagement
- Identify and meet all major channel partners in conjunction with XYZ to understand where the low hanging fruit is
- Coordinate introductions and top level meetings with top channel partners (CDW, Sirius, Ahead, SHI, etc.)
- Establish regular cadence calls with individual sales reps within each channel partner utilizing my SE, and Inside Sales Specialists

Product knowledge
- Review all appropriate internal product trainings available
- Schedule a recurring training with an SE for the first ninety days for supplemental education
- Schedule new hire sales training
- Understand the XYZ culture and become an expert in the XYZ solution to hit the ground running on day 31

60-Day Objectives
Sales Activity
- Cold call and reach out to contacts to schedule meetings with top twenty-five "A" install base accounts to understand challenges and future growth, develop executive contacts, and gain an understanding of their major business initiatives
- Utilize my SE, Inside Sales, and Channel reps for bottom "B" and "C" account engagement and activity
- Be relentless with research and understand who the top CIOs are in the territory
- Who will make my number this year?
- Grow the pipeline 2x in the first sixty days

Channel Engagement
- Hold introductory meetings with key regional partners in the territory, develop specialized sales campaign programs with each partner to increase pipeline and revenue in the territory
- Have partner enablement days with the top partners in the territory to make the pitch of the XYZ message
- Continue education around XYZ, licensing models, competitive environment, and our internal processes

90-Day Objectives

Sales Activity

- Continue to focus on pipeline growth twenty to thirty hours per week, depending on meeting activity
- Begin to schedule and hold meetings with the top half of "B" accounts to establish Commvault as a strategic vendor, while focusing on opportunity development in these top "B" accounts
- Start building detailed account plans for the top seven to ten customers/prospects
    - Rate executive sponsorships and relationships
    - Detailed organization chart
    - Top business and IT initiatives
    - IT budget review, top vendor(s) spend
    - Business partner mapping
    - Flow chart of budgetary and PO approval process
    - Account action items
    - Current and future opportunities
- Work to close all outstanding committed deals for the quarter
- Deliver twenty proposals for growth of existing accounts
- Deliver twenty proposals for new business growth
- Meet with five CIOs in "A" accounts
- Meet with five CIOs in "B" accounts
- Close five deals within the first quarter
- Exceed Q1 number
- Bring Larry Irvin on a minimum of five sales calls by the end of Q1

Develop and Implement Marketing Plan

- Focus on demand generation of XYZ and make sure to engage channel
- Work with the local marketing manager to develop targeted email blasts to customers
    - Create clear, concise, one-page documents around XYZ solutions, offerings, and benefits
    - Follow-up with phone calls to discuss proposed solution/topic in the email
    - Hold marketing event with a minimum target of twenty customers once enough interest is generated
- Constantly improve the marketing approach on a quarterly basis based on previous campaign's results

Channel Engagement
- Continue to create weekly appointments, setting meetings with my key partners
- Involve my key channel partners in all marketing activity
- Task channel partners reps to generate attendance for specific marketing events
- Create incentive programs for a small subset of partners for pipeline development, appointment setting campaigns, and other demand-generation activities
- Have a strong understanding of the XYZ solution and competitive landscape
- I anticipate that the outlined plan will take on its own shape based on other factors not addressed. I am confident that with my experience, skills, and work ethic executing this plan will provide me an excellent base-line to generate the revenue needed to hit my number my first year and beyond.
- If given the chance, I will make an impact!!!

VIP: Get a fast start to success in your new job by having a written plan for your first ninety days.

8.   Shape Your Company's Culture and Values—Quickly

Many HR people will say you can't change a company's culture and values quickly, but I would argue you can. You can do it by acknowledging, measuring, and rewarding the behaviors you want. For example, when I worked at HP, we wanted to transform the sales culture, so we put in place certain metrics and then measured and rewarded the behaviors of the team members based on those metrics. In one of my managers' meetings with over 300 people managers, I explained the behaviors I expected. I also said I understood that some managers may not have been coached in these areas, so my team and I were happy to help; but we needed them to want to make these improvements. I could see by some of their facial expressions that they didn't like what I was saying, so I kindly suggested they could speak with their manager and we would facilitate a respectful departure for them. VIP: You can quickly change your company's culture and values by acknowledging, measuring, and rewarding the behaviors you want.

9.   Use a Performance-Management Discussion Guide to Give and Get Feedback with Your Employees

Below is an example of a Performance-Management Discussion Guide I did for a client, which facilitates a discussion between managers and employees. Here are some important considerations when conducting the performance-management interactive discussions, which should be an ongoing occurrence, not just a couple of times a year:

- Drive alignment of performance with business priorities and objectives.
- Engage effectively giving and getting feedback between the employee and manager.
- Improve business results and retention with stronger employee engagement.
- Giving and getting feedback needs to be ingrained in your culture. As an example, any time I went on sales calls, I would always ask for feedback on anything I could do different or better, even though I was a senior executive. Once I would get feedback, then it was easy for me to say, "May I give you some feedback?" This helps to break the ice and make the discussion less awkward and less confrontational.
- Discuss performance expectations and career development.
- Consider what was accomplished and how it was accomplished.
- Make sure the goals are fair and relevant; adjust if needed.
- Always be honest and open about the employee's strengths and development areas.

Here are some additional considerations for using the guide:

- To develop the guide, you need to identify all the different areas you want to measure. You can categorize the metrics and topics as you like.
- I always prefer to have the employee make a first pass at their self-assessment. This saves time for the manager in helping to see if the employee has a fair view of him/herself. I usually find that top talent are more critical of themselves, and lower performers rate themselves higher than they should.
- Two important aspects that usually get left out are, "What does the manager do well?" and "What can the manager do differently or better?"
- I find the actual ratings to be less important; what's most important is to have an open discussion and a good written game plan of areas to improve and develop.
- Most "A" players thrive on and really appreciate this approach, which not only helps with their performance but also with retention.

See the guide below:

2020 SALES PERFORMANCE REVIEW DISCUSSION GUIDE		
Employee Name:	**Date:**	**Period:**
Manager:		

Employee Instructions: Please complete the self-assessment. Summarize your strengths and opportunities for development with respect to the performance competencies and give feedback on your manager.

Manager Instructions: Discuss the assessment with the employee and provide feedback and rating for the sales competencies listed below. Managers and employees also have the option to add "role-specific" categories in the blank boxes at the end of the section.:

Use this rating scale for the evaluation:
- **(4) Exceeded Expectations:** Employee significantly exceeded performance expectations and is consistently a high performer. Level of work completed by this employee to meet individual, departmental, company or team goals is consistently at the highest level. Going above and beyond in their work and deliverables is the norm. Often performs exceptional work with high quality.
- **(3) Met Expectations:** Employee consistently meets performance expectations. At times employee is a high performer who exceeds expectations, Employee is consistently doing high-quality work.
- **(2) Partially Met Expectations:** Employee only partially met performance expectations; level and quality of work is below expectations or deadlines are missed.
- **(1) Did not Meet Expectations:** Employee did not meet performance expectations.

KEY PERFORMANCE COMPETENCIES:

1. Ensures flow of communication by developing strong cross-functional relationships, formally and informally, through verbal and written means in pursuit of mutually beneficial results. Demonstrates active listening.

Measure	Self-Rating	Manager Rating
Strong cross-functional relationships		
Demonstrates active listening		
Open, honest, direct		
Escalates issues early and often		
Positive morale and attitude		
Gives and gets feedback		
Shares best practices		
Team player		
Respect and trust		
Overall Rating:		

2. Drives for results by identifying and removing obstacles, prioritizing, and following through on commitments. Plans work (workload, calendars, resources, and schedules) to ensure tasks and deliverables are met on time with minimal supervision. Demonstrates high quality work, dependability, and adaptability.

Measure	Expectations	Results	Self-Rating	Manager Rating
Identifies and removes obstacles				
Follows through on commitments				
Plans work				
Demonstrates high-quality work				
Dependability				
Adaptability				

Quota attainment:	Expectations	Results	Self-Rating	Manager Rating
• #New accounts from prospecting				
• Pipeline quantity				
• Pipeline quality				
• SFDC hygiene				
• # Proposals				
• Predictability				
• # Calls/week				
• # Demos				

Sales behaviors:	Expectations	Results	Self-Rating	Manager Rating
• Refuses to lose attitude				
• Confident and positive				
• Aggressive in a good way				
• Sense of urgency				
• Work ethic				
• Research and pre-call planning				
• Sales call agenda				
• Qualification thoroughness/accuracy				
• Prompt letters of understanding				
• Customer storytelling				
• Reference selling				
• Demo quality/your engagement				
• CFO elevator pitch				
• Why us/why now				

Measure				
• Customer relationships				
• Partner relationships				
• Presentation skills overall				
• Presentation skills—your solutions				
• Owns performance management and development plan				
Overall Rating:				

3. Demonstrates appropriate level of knowledge and technical/applicable skills specific to role. Applies knowledge to solve a range of problems. Ensures work is thorough, complete, and accurate. Meets deadlines and fulfills commitments.

Measure	Self-Rating	Manager Rating
Level of knowledge:		
• Technical skills		
• Solves problems		
• Work is thorough, complete, and accurate		
• Meets deadlines and fulfills commitments		
Overall Rating:		

4. Takes initiative, raises issues of importance and acts as an agent for change. Reaches across the organization to improve collaboration. Shows strong support for and actively works toward the organization's strategic goals and vision.

Measure	Self-Rating	Manager Rating
• Takes initiative, raises issues of importance		
• Acts as an agent for change		
• Reaches across the organization to improve collaboration		
• Shows strong support for and actively works toward the organization's strategic goals and vision		
• Has a mentor (external)		
Overall Rating:		

5. Provides strong management: Demonstrates the ability to drive the team toward accomplishing goals. Promotes efficiency and team cohesion. Exhibits organizational effectiveness and operational excellence. *(Only applicable to those who manage/lead other staff members)*

Measure	Self-Rating	Manager Rating
• Demonstrates the ability to drive the team toward accomplishing goals		
• Promotes efficiency and team cohesion		

Measure	Self-Rating	Manager Rating
• Exhibits organizational effectiveness and operational excellence		
• Removes obstacles		
• Coaching		
• Constructive criticism/gives feedback		
• Open, available, responsive		
• Team morale		
• Internal promotions		
• Recruiting bench		
• Hires the best, new hire productivity		
• Retention		
• Performance management (fast start, performance discussions, upgrading)		
• Talent development (HIPO planning, stack ranking, and action plans)		
• Is a mentor		
• Reduces non-revenue generating meetings/ activities for you and team		
• Win and loss reviews (why, what learn, and share)		
• Celebrates and recognizes		
Overall Rating:		

6. Provides strong leadership: Inspires and motivates throughout the organization. Ability to build consensus and relationships cross functionality. Develops individuals and teams in alignment with company strategy. *(Only applicable to those who manage/lead other staff members).*

Measure	Self-Rating	Manager Rating
• Inspires and motivates throughout the organization		
• Ability to build consensus and relationships cross functionally		
• Develops individuals and teams in alignment with company strategy		
Jack Welch best leadership behaviors:		
• Leaders relentlessly upgrade their team, using every encounter as an opportunity to evaluate, coach, and build self-confidence.		
• Leaders make sure people not only see the vision; they live and breathe it.		

• Leaders get into everyone's skin, exuding positive energy and optimism.		
• Leaders establish trust with candor, transparency, and credit		
• Leaders have the courage to make unpopular decisions and gut calls.		
• Leaders probe and push with a curiosity that borders on skepticism, making sure their questions are answered with action.		
• Leaders inspire risk taking and learning by setting the example.		
• Leaders celebrate.		
Overall Rating:		
Comments:		

OVERALL COMMENTS		
Summary of Strengths:		
Summary of Development Areas:		
Specific Development Areas of Focus:	**Action**	**Timeframe**
•		
•		
•		
•		

What does my manager do well? What helps me overall? What helps me to sell more?		
What can my manager do differently or better overall to help me to sell more?		

VIP: The Performance-Management Discussion Guide facilitates giving and getting feedback between employee and manager; this feedback is vital to develop, succeed, and sell more.

10. Measure and Inspect These Areas to Accelerate Growth and Exceed Your Financial Plan

These metrics are listed as a courtesy of HubSpot from its excellent blog post that features a very complete list of sales metrics. Thank you, Hub-Spot! The blog, written by Aja Frost, is called "The Ultimate Guide to Sales Metrics: What to Track, How to Track It, & Why," and is found at https://blog.hubspot.com/sales/sales-metrics. You can go to the blog and download the metrics for yourself, and get a free sales metric calculator to boot.[12]

Sales Key Performance Indicators (KPIs)

1. Total revenue
2. Revenue by product or product line
3. Market penetration
4. Percentage of revenue from new business
5. Percentage of revenue from existing customers (cross-selling, upselling, repeat orders, expanded contracts, etc.)
6. Year-over-year growth
7. Average lifetime value (LTV) of user or customer
8. Net Promoter Score (NPS)
9. Number of deals lost to competition
10. Percentage of sales reps attaining 100 percent quota
11. Revenue by territory
12. Revenue by market
13. Cost of selling as a percentage of revenue generate

Thanks to SaaStr for posting some great SaaS metrics to obsess about, that, I would add, deserve Board level review (on top of MRR/ARR):

- Obsess about *decreasing* churn
- Obsess about *increasing* deal size
- Obsess about *increasing* revenue per lead
- Obsess about *growing* qualified leads month-over-month
- Obsess about *increasing* "net negative churn"
- Obsess about the *number* of logo accounts you have
- Obsess about NPS and customer referrals and satisfaction
- Obsess about your capital efficiency and sales efficiency

Thanks to Jesse Ouellette for providing some additional great metrics shown below. These are for dashboards particular useful with SaaS businesses.

Goal is to not focus on any one metric as SaaS depends on a system of growth. This is why there are such huge multiples.

The Secret to Exponential Growth and Scale
- Improve Conversion (NOT VOLUME) by 10% and you double your growth in revenue
- Having the right marketing and enablement results are more crucial for success
- When most Sales Leaders are asked, how do they grow 2x, they say 2x leads, 2x head count etc . . .
  - Does not scale, breaks because SaaS depends on system of efficiency
- 10% Optimization Across 7 Moments is a 1.1^7 improvement.

We used the wrong math in the past. We were using Addition and we needed to be using Multiplication. The conversion is more important between moments. Customer experience depends on moments that matter. Emotional connection. We were hyper focused on too many sales metrics when you can argue fewer more important ones are better.

Definitions:
- We define a MQL (marketing qualified lead) as someone who is raising their hand and wants to talk to sales. (best to avoid quasi MQL metrics that marketing frequently overstate, they have to want to talk to sales)
- We define a SQL (sales qualified lead) as a person who we talk to that we can impact and transfer to an AE
- We define a SAL (sales accepted lead) as a person who shows up to this meeting and goes into a Sales Cycle/stage 1 opportunity
- We define a WIN, bad word, call it first order, it can't be a true win until they renew
- We define a LIVE (Fully Onboarded) when the customer gets the impact they expected
- We define a MRR (monthly recurring revenue) customer is getting impact over and over and over and will renew
- We define an LTV (long term value) as the revenue generated

We suggest these best practice conversion benchmarks:
- MQL-> SQL – 30% (sales takes 30% of MQLs to SQLs)
- SQL-> SAL-> 80% (80% of SQLs go to SALs)
- SAL-> WIN-> 1:5 Deals (1 in 5 SALs become WINS)

Weekly Sales Meetings Metrics
- Total Pipeline by Type
- Won Deals by Type
- **New Leads**
- New Pipeline Created
- Win Rate
- Avg Deal Size
- Avg Deal Cycle (Days)
- Won Deals
- Open Deals
- **Total Customers**
- Churn
- Logo Churn
- Net $ Churn

Sales Pipeline Review
- Total Pipeline (Closing This Period)
- New Pipeline Created
- New Business vs Goal
- Win Rate Trend
- Average Deal Size
- Won Deals
- Open Deals
- Must-Win Deals
- Top n deals by size
- Avg Age Open Deals by Rep
- Stalled Deals
- Open Deals w/ Past Close Dates
- Deals w/out Sales Activities (n days)

Sales & Marketing Sync Meeting
- #New Leads
- Lead Conversion
- #New Meetings
- Meeting-to-Opportunity%
- Opportunity-to-Pipeline%

Marketing Team Leads Meeting
- #New Leads
- Lead Conversion Rate
- #Unqualified / Rejected Leads
- New Pipeline Created
  - Inbound
  - Outbound
- Campaign Influence & ROI ($)
- Leads not Addressed
- Average Touches Per Lead

Outbound SDR Team Meeting
- New Accounts Activated
- Activate Accounts per Opportunity
- Avg Contacts per Active Account
- Conversion Rates
- Activated-to-Engaged%
- Engaged-to-Meeting%
- Meeting-to-Opportunity%
- Avg Touches per Meeting
- Calls per BDR

Inbound SDR Team Meeting
- New Leads
- Lead Conversion Rate
- Average Response Time
- Leads Not Addressed
- Average Per Lead
- Meetings w/o Disposition

CS (customer sat) Team Meeting
- Recently Won Sales Deals
- Upcoming Renewals
- Open Upsells
- Open Expansions
- Must-Win Deals
  - Top n renewals by size
- At-Risk Accounts

Exceptions Dashboard
- Open Opps w/Past Close Dates
- Opps w/out Primary Contact
- Other Req'd Contact Roles
- New Leads 1+ Days Old
- Opps w/No Activity in Past n Days
- Meetings w/out Dispositions
- *Other Records Missing Req'd Values

Although you can blame a rep or sales management for poor performance, you should look to see if your system is to blame and should be improved. Moral fabric of an organization gets torn apart when you blame a person when you have a bad system/process, typically marketing is to blame. As great examples, the best non sales organizations (US Military, Navy Submarines, New England Patriots, etc.) blame the process and fix it. This is because they understand human variability. People make mistakes but the systems and process give you the best long-term results!

VIP: It is always important to focus on the objective financial metrics expected and exceed them.

11. Measure and Inspect These Areas to Accelerate Growth and Recruit the Best Talent

- The best leaders always recruit, develop/coach, upgrade their teams, and retain the best talent.
- Recruiting is a must do to build the best bench.
- Every new hire must have a fast-start plan.
- Create a mentoring process; everyone should have a mentor.
- Improve employee-feedback scores and your communication.
- Leverage a high potential program (HIPO Program).
- Utilize Performance Management Scoreboard Discussion Document. Individuals own their own performance management and development plans, not the manager.
- Track and improve all productivity ratios.
- Share best practices.
- Get and give feedback.

VIP: As a leader, you are only as good as your team, so make sure you put together and coach the best team possible.

12. Measure and Inspect These Areas to
Accelerate Showing up Everywhere

- Your goal should be to assign and call on 100 percent of your TAM (target addressable market), develop account coverage map by LOB (line of business), geography, partners, verticals, segments, and rep coverage.
- Track gaps and grow share of wallet/market share, leverage partners fast and aggressively.
- Lean in where doing well and create fixit plans for underperforming areas.
- Improve marketing lead generation, attendance and ROI. Too often, marketing is not aligned to support sales with real ROI metrics.
- Leverage your partners.

VIP: Successful sales teams figure out how to sell to all of their market.

13. Measure and Inspect These Areas to
Accelerate the Best Partnering

- Partners can be ISVs, SIs, VARs, solutions provider, complementary vendors, consultants, analysts, etc.
- You can also read more about partnering in the AB Best Practice section from Dave Casillo, Frank Rauch, and Aaron Mills.
- Leverage partners to sell more everywhere.
- You can map and align partners by account, rep, geography, vertical, segment, etc.
- Make sure they make good money.
- If you agree to partner, don't change partners or go direct without very good reason.
- Help them as needed.
- Do joint sales calls.
- Grade partners as you would your own sales team.
- Listen to feedback and adjust.
- Create win-win situations.

VIP: Indirect selling through and with partners is needed to get as much reach as possible.

14. Measure and Inspect These Areas to Accelerate Sales Cultural Improvement

- Having the best work ethic helps a lot.
- Customer face time is vital—do ten-plus sales calls per week.
- Improve doing the basics (research, show up early and often, qualification, set the criteria, written agendas, prompt recap notes, etc.).
- Develop the best attitude: positive, confident, refuse to lose, go on the offensive, aggressive in a good way, always demanding excellence from the team
- Create the best relationships: CXOs, customers, partners, developers, and internal.
- SEOTT (sell everything on the truck, sell anything your company sells; this saying was first developed by Rich Napolitano at Sun Microsystems in 2006); improve attach rates for services and cross sell and upsell any other complementary solution offerings.
- If you have one, leverage your inside sales engine and your presales team. Treat them very well; they are your key partners for success.
- Have open confrontation and communication and open feedback, but have decisive execution
- Improve team account planning with the right people in the right place doing the right thing.
- Reduce internal meetings Tuesday through Thursday to focus externally on revenue-generating activities.
- Be knowledgeable about your offerings, competition, corporate strategy, and customers, in your industry.
- Use every interaction as an opportunity to coach and shape the culture.

VIP: To improve culture, measure and coach what you consider the most important objective and subjective metrics.

15. Measure and Inspect These Areas to Accelerate Efficiency and Effectiveness

- Know and lead with your company strategy.
- Be easy to do business with and fix what is broken or challenging.
- Escalate issues early and often for help.
- Provide fast responses to any questions and quotes should be fast.
- Learn by doing loss and win reviews.
- Have a good sales forecasting hygiene.

- Know where to sell and where not to sell.
- Your goal should be to delight your customers.

VIP: Use all the leverage you can to be efficient and effective.

16. Measure and Inspect These Areas to Accelerate Leadership Best Practices:

- Be customer-centric with integrity, respect, urgency, teamwork, innovation, tenacity, accountability; leading by example, executing to the strategy, focusing on the customer with the best relationships and face time, helping build the best team on the planet, owning your own development plan, inspiring, celebrating, recognizing, and rewarding.

VIP: Consider the best leader you've worked for, and try to be better.

17. Share Your Top Lessons Learned with Your Team

This is something I use when presenting to groups for sharing my top lessons learned:

- Your opportunity is yours to create, raise the bar; it's easier to succeed than you think.
- Ask for help/get a mentor.
- Relationships and marriage take work.
- Help others develop, be charitable, and give back (St. Ignatius).
- Your family history affects you (e.g., alcoholism and divorce).
- Write down your goals, share with others, and review constantly.
- Communication is vital; be direct, authentic, and straightforward.
- What do you want said at your wake?
  - What is success?
  - Ethics/integrity
- Trust your gut and be decisive; when in doubt, do the right thing.
- Treat all people as you like to be treated.
- The grass isn't always greener on the other side.
- Cash is king, watch your burn rate/spending.
- Surround yourself with people you like, know, trust, respect, and can learn from.
- Be challenged every day.
- Have a balanced sense of urgency.

- Performance is measured on exceeding goals and expectations.
- Build your brand.
- Bring humor and laugh.
- Never give up.
- When in doubt, do the right thing.
- Have fun!

VIP: Use some of my top lessons learned to create your vision for a better life for yourself.

18. Be a Great Parent

Life Lesson: Ten Tips for Dads with Daughters, by Joe Kelly (I'm not sure where I got this, but it is something I've carried around for twenty-plus years as I tried to be a good father for my daughter and support her. I've cited Kelly's book below, as that is most likely where the list originated.)

- Listen to your daughter.
- Encourage her strength and celebrate her savvy.
- Respect her uniqueness.
- Get physically active with her.
- Get involved with your daughter's school.
- Get involved in your daughter's activities.
- Help make the world better for girls.
- Take your daughter to work with you.
- Support positive media for girls.
- Talk to other fathers[13].

VIP: Nothing is more important than being a great father.

19. Share Your Top Ten Passions with Your Team

Any time you take over a new team, it's helpful to identify and share your top ten passions that will help them understand you and your DNA. Here is what I shared with my team when I started at HP:

- Exceeding goal, refusing to lose, and having fun winning.
- I work for all of you, our customers, and our partners, and I'm here to help. My number one personal goal is to make sure everyone is as successful as possible. I'm very open about giving and getting feedback.
- Maniacal focus on sales execution as a team. We are a team and part of the greater HP team, which means we win together, we give and get

feedback openly, we confront, and when we make decisions we have unified execution.

- Understanding and removing barriers to your success. Some of the early feedback has been around the clarity of our vision and strategy, aligning to our five marketing campaigns, and arming our go-to-market ecosystem with the tools necessary to grow our business.

- Operational execution and alignment through our RBU team with the worldwide GBUs, TS, software, supply chain, and the various other organizations that we are dependent on.

- Listening, taking action, responsibility, and accountability.

- Focusing on revenue-generating activities that help customers save money, make money, and gain a competitive advantage.

- Confident attitude, positive, and aggressive sense of urgency.

- Sales calls, account planning, proposals, and pipeline. I will leverage my customer and partner relationships. I love customer and partner face time in building new relationships.

- Working with partners to align our resources to beat our competition early and often as we gain market share.

- It's important to be family friendly.

VIP: It's always good to be authentic with your team and share what is important to you and what you're passionate about.

20. Create a HIPO (High-Potential Program) to Develop and Retain Your Best Performers

The program should focus on skill development, visibility, networking, and recognition. Duration should be one year, and then rotate in a new group.

HIPO Program	
The objectives of the program are to:	
Identify and groom high performers who want to improve/move up/develop	
Motivate people of possibilities of promotion	
Develop skills in all relevant areas of business	
Expand personal network and visibility with FSA and the US GEM	
Provide ongoing opportunities to interact with visiting SMI executives	
Execution	
Executive Sponsor, Randy Seidl; Owner and Driver	
One meeting every 4-8 weeks	
Executive Roundtables	
Workshops/Training	
Personal Development Conversations	
Outside Activities/Readings	
Elements	
Type of Development	**Activity Description**
Visibility/Networking	Launch of program
Skill Development	Offer workshops
Skill Development/Visibility	Offer courses taught by management
Visibility/Networking	Offer brown-bag luncheons/coffee sessions with visiting executives
Visibility/Networking	Hold focus group meetings with this HIPO group. Ask their opinions and their recommendations on key challenges or problems.
Visibility/Networking	Hold 1:1 meetings with 3-4 regional managers. Each HIPO would choose 3-4 regional managers to meet with and get on "their radar screen," Meetings would focus on the HIPO's career and next move.
Recognition	Provide extra benefits for this HIPO group. • Allocate any extra stock • Allocate extra compensation increases to this group • Consider the list of this HIPO group for any key critical open positions

VIP: Use a HIPO program to continue to develop your best people and see how you can be included in these development programs yourself.

21. Every Sales Call Should Have an Agenda

Having an agenda for every sales call is valuable because:

- It forces proper preparation beforehand.
- Everyone in the meeting sees what will be covered.
- If there is more than one person selling, it helps to get alignment between who will do what.
- It helps everyone know the names and titles of all attendees.

- It helps to stay on schedule so all items are covered, especially saving time at the end for recap in next steps, which often get squeezed.

The following items should be on a proper sales call agenda:

- Date
- Location, logistics, Zoom, etc.
- Names and titles of attendees
- Topics to be covered, who is point to lead the discussion on that topic, and time allotted

Some topics that get overlooked but are of huge value when always qualifying include having the prospect/customer give feedback in the beginning about their feelings/likes/dislikes, other alternatives being considered and why, money budgeted or needed to get, internal decision-making process, ROI/TCO drivers, timing, if a POC what is success criteria, etc.

Make sure you leave enough time at the end to cover recap and next steps, and book the next meeting then. (Too often this does not get booked and needlessly delays the sales cycle.)

VIP: Use well-prepared sales agendas to roll out the red carpet so it is easy for your clients to go through a fast and well-executed sales cycle.

22. Keep Your High-Level Executive Relationships Updated

Using high-level executive relationships to get in the door can be very effective, but make sure you keep them updated with your progress.

It is valuable to get into any account top down from the highest levels. With my Revenue Acceleration consulting business, my clients use my relationships to get introduced to the right people at the account. Typically I will connect with a CXO I know, introduce the client company, explain their value, and ask for an introduction to the right point person. Once the introductions happen and the sales cycle starts, I find it priceless to send an update note to the original CXO who helped us get into the account.

Another situation where this happens is when a board member knows a CXO at an account you want to get to. Unfortunately, too often board members are not hands-on enough to help in sales situations, so I would encourage you to push them for help either directly or through your management chain.

Here is a best practice template that can be customized as an update note that can be sent to the CXO/exec contact every month or two:

- Update since you made the first introduction (Make sure you compliment folks by name, as this will get back to them and will often give them exposure they would have never received without you, which therefore helps your sales cycle!)

- Areas where they can help provide real ROI (Think like you are in the elevator with the CFO for one minute. What would you say about helping to generate revenue/save money/get a competitive advantage— without 30+ PowerPoint slides!)
- The next steps (You will likely have no asks in the beginning; but toward the end of the sales cycle, you will probably have asks and areas the CXO may be able to help. [*This is optional, and be careful not to step on the toes of your champions.*])

VIP: Top down selling can be tricky; but if properly managed, it can help you sell more and sell faster.

23. Setting the Date for the Next Meeting

If you want to help your sales cycles go faster and free up your time so you can sell more, never end a meeting or a call without agreeing to a day and time for the next meeting.

How many times have you finished a meeting saying, "We'll figure out the date for the next meeting," then it takes two weeks to connect to set the date and it's another two or three weeks until the date of the meeting? As a result, instead of your next meeting being in one or two weeks, it actually takes place in four to five weeks. It would be much better to have "Next meeting" as an agenda item and leave time at the end of each meeting to agree on the specific day and time, and ideally the attendees. I can't tell you how many clients I have where I am the one pushing to get the meeting set instead of my client's sales team.

VIP: Before you leave your current meeting, it is always a best practice to make sure you have the next meeting date confirmed.

IV
SALE METHODOLOGIES

From the 200+ interviews with our Sales Community Advisory Board, we found these to be the sales methodologies that were mentioned:

Top Sales Methodologies

	Methodology	Definition	Value Proposition	Why Sales Reps Use It
1.	Challenger	Challenger is a sales experience focused on bringing a well-researched commercial insight, tailored to the interests of a complex buying group, then building consensus and controlling the decision-making journey	More than half of today's high performers manifest Challenger skills and behaviors. They have win rates that are 54% higher and close deals as much as 2.6 times larger, and they do so 27% faster.	Challenger is a sales approach backed up by extensive global research, aligned to classic principles of persuasion and popular as a best practice among sellers and sales leaders across industries and around the world. Most importantly, it's the sales experience customers want and are willing to reward with their loyalty.
2.	Force Management: Command of the Message®	Command of the Message® enables sales teams to be audible-ready to describe their solutions to customers' problems in a way that differentiates them from competition and enables them to charge a premium for their products and services.	The Command of the Message® methodology and framework enables sales teams to validate the value and differentiation of their offerings and execute at the buyer level, repeatedly.	Sales reps leverage Command of the Message® framework to get in front of the right decision makers and have the right conversations to progress their deals and close at a high value. In addition, reps leverage CoM framework to: • Gain access to high-level decision makers • Use effective discovery • Differentiate from the competition • Improve competitive win rates • Increase average deal size and margins • Build stronger and deeper relationships with customers and within accounts • Improve the ability to assimilate new offerings and cross-sell and up-sell solutions

Command of the Sale®	Command of the Sale® provides sales teams with a buyer-driven methodology that aligns the knowledge, activities and tools necessary to consistently qualify, progress, and close opportunities.	The Command of the Sale® framework creates the discipline necessary within sales organizations to drive revenue predictability and scale.	Sales reps leverage Command of the Sale® framework to improve deal qualification and understand what it takes to move to the next stage. In addition, reps leverage CoS framework to: • Consistently qualify deals in or out early on in the sales process • Better leverage internal resources to progress opportunities efficiently • Increase their average deal velocity • Build confidence in their forecasts
Command of the Plan®	Command of the Plan® provides a framework of activities, guidelines, and success measures to equip sales teams and leaders with the insights, processes, and tools that are critical to achieving sales predictability and maximizing results.	Implementing Command of the Plan® framework enables sales organizations to build and reinforce a planning process based on accountability. When this framework is executed consistently, sales organizations are better able to build healthy pipelines and create actionable revenue forecasts.	Sales reps leverage Command of the Plan® framework to develop territory, account, and opportunity plans to build healthy pipelines, enable accurate revenue forecasts, and define their plan to hit their number. In addition, reps leverage CoP framework to: • Consistently hit or exceed their quota • Improve cross-sell, up-sell and account penetration • Improve territory and account coverage • Consider all sources of revenue available to them, beyond net-new
Command of the Talent®	Command of the Talent® equips sales managers with the processes and tools for attracting, onboarding, and developing sales reps who are capable of succeeding within a value-based, high-accountability selling environment.	Implementing Command of the Talent® framework enables sales organizations to make their sales talent a competitive advantage in their marketplace.	Sales managers leverage Command of the Talent® framework to recruit, hire, on-board, develop, motivate, and retain sales talent in a way that creates a sustainable competitive advantage. In addition, sales teams leverage CoT framework to: • Maintain a healthy candidate network • Reduce turnover and maintain territory momentum • Boost time-to-productivity of new hires • Improve sales coaching and talent development skills • Increase sales-team bench strength • Ensure sales reps understand how to be successful in their roles • Identify and promote high performers

3.	MEDDIC	MEDDIC is an acronym that stands for Metrics, Economic Buyer, Decision Criteria, Decision Process, Identify Pain, and Champion	This method is a highly disciplined, tech-driven, and tightly controlled approach to the sales process.	Through the metrics, other relevant data, and quantitative standards, reps can search and nurture the criteria for the "champion" in the prospect.
4.	Sandler Selling System	The Sandler Selling System is based on customer buying behaviors vs. formulas and processes. When executed correctly, the buyer believes they are pursuing the deal, resulting in a less pushy, non-salesy transaction.	The initial contact is more like a conversation than a sales call. Things like budget restrictions and time poverty are exposed up front, rather than later in the sales cycle.	This methodology can be a huge time-saver for sales reps because it eliminates bad deals earlier rather than later in the cycle.
5.	Sale Leader U—Prescriptive Productivity	Sales Leader U—PP provides an order of operations for attacking a sales territory: (1) account attributes, (2) persona-problem pairs, (3) high-impact customer interactions, and (4) cadence of interactions (APPIC).	This is a methodology for building a territory. Most reps do not have enough opportunities to qualify. They need a methodology for developing a pipeline-building strategy. For the reps who don't have enough pipeline, this methodology guides them to the best investment of their time and effort.	Time management and prioritization skills are critical success factors for reps, and reps commonly cite these as skills they need to improve. This is a simple framework that helps them prioritize time and effort across a territory.
6.	Selling Through Curiosity	This methodology enables an entire customer-facing organization to systematically do flawless discovery and qualification, map their solution to specific customer needs, and improve their important sales metrics.	This method helps reps understand their customers better than their competition does, know how to ask the hard questions, build faster relationships, know the value of their solution, and learn in days/weeks rather than in months/years.	It helps reps sell more, sell better, and sell faster, so their customers want their solution—almost no matter the price.
7.	Visualize– the leading provider of the ValueSelling Framework	ValueSelling is a sales and marketing execution framework enabling teams to align to the buyer's business objectives and challenges while articulating the unique business value.	ValueSelling is a simplified, highly adoptable framework and methodology that enables all customer-facing roles to better prepare and execute a value-based conversation. ValueSelling provides more than just the "what," but also the "why" and, most importantly, the "how," leading to more wins, increased deal velocity, and larger deal size.	It's simple, repeatable, and effective. More than just a tool for qualification, ValueSelling works to improve preparation and execution without requiring undue administration, forms, or questions that salespeople detest. It's as simple as it is aligned to the buyer's journey and the buying process—and it works!

Here are some additional sales methodologies not necessarily focused on tech sales that were not mentioned by our Advisory Board but are worth noting:

Additional Top Sales Methodologies

	Methodology	Definition	Value Proposition	Why Sales Reps Use It
1.	SPIN Selling	SPIN stands for Situation, Problem, Implication, and Need-Payoff	Focuses on leading the conversation with the right questions at each of these stages	Effective because it asks thought-provoking, non-pushy questions that tell sales reps exactly what the prospect needs.
2.	Solution Selling	Focuses on problem-solving at large, not on the product itself. The solutions are usually highly customized products or services based on each customer's needs.	Conversations will largely focus on the prospect, their company, and the problem, not the spec and benefits of the product.	This usually incorporates other strategies similar to the value selling methodology that show how this solution creates an optimal outcome for the problem.
3.	Conceptual Selling	Shares many of the same characterizes as solution selling, except reps are not selling a product, per se. Rather, the "product" is an idea of the solution.	The main objective is to align the sales process with how customers buy to create a win/win/ situation with every opportunity.	This provides sales reps with an effective framework for planning and conducting customer interactions.
4.	Inbound Selling	Inbound selling allows sales teams to meet the customer wherever they are in the buying journey and delivery value and meaning throughout the conversation. Heavy emphasis on marketing and less on sales.	This method takes into account that reps are working with an informed prospect who already knows something about solutions.	Sales reps assume less of a salesperson role and more of a consulting role to customers to buy what they already want.
5.	SNAP Selling	SNAP is an acronym that encompasses four directives for sellers: Keep it **Simple**, be **Invaluable**, always **Align**, and raise **Priorities**.	With these principles in mind, reps can more effectively reach prospects with valuable knowledge and connect what they're selling with what's most important to the potential client.	Sales reps can more effectively keep deals on track; makes it easy for prospect to buy.

V
TONY'S
SALES BEST
PRACTICES

A. PREPARATION

1. Know Your Opportunity Type

Knowing the type of opportunity you have in front of you is an extremely valuable distinction. Take the time to think through it. Is it a one-time opportunity to get the action you want, or will it take two or three steps? Is it a medium or large opportunity? Is it transactional? Is it a long-term strategic opportunity? Will it introduce you to other opportunities?

If I am selling to someone and they say, "I want to start with a one-day relationship with you," I think about the potential. If they're a big organization and they fit my ADOME profile, I think, Is there potential for a long-term relationship here? Are there multiple impacts? What's the size of the opportunity? How about any future opportunities that might follow?

You can create an opportunity that is a one-time, short-term transaction, or you can rethink the bigger picture and determine a long-term, relationship-based approach. For example, you may turn a three-month sales cycle into a two-year deal, or maybe turn it into more of a transactional decision for a software license with an ongoing renewal. The longer opportunity-type sale obviously reaps enormous benefits, as it provides value over and over again for both parties. You want to be strategic and think about ways to deposit into a long-term relationship so you can provide ongoing usefulness and win repeatedly down the road.

Help your prospects win. Strategically providing extra value could include faster timing, short cuts, opening doors, or giving them tools, which all help you create a relationship that positions you and your organization. Being clear on the type of relationship you want is important; then setting systems and added value items that exceed their expectations ensures more strategic wins.

VIP: Have clarity on the type of opportunity in front of you and respond accordingly to achieve the best results.

2. Understand Your Stakeholders

Being fully aware of what everyone wants and what they can give is often not on everyone's radar screen as a strategy. We recommend developing a Stakeholders Matrix (see below) that documents every person who can ultimately influence results.

Look at your opportunity. Who has a say in the final outcome? If a board is involved in making the buying decision, the information you present may be cascaded to its members collectively or individually. It's important that you consider how the information in your sales approach could be utilized so your message gets to them in the most effective way. You need to think about how you can best arm the people you're selling to so they can present to the real decision makers.

Gather as much information about each stakeholder as possible. List what outcome is important to each individual or group (i.e., the board) and be sure when presenting your idea or proposal to them that you address each person's priorities. It could be that a person at the top has a mission; and if you're not relating to that mission, the sale could go south. This important step can give you a strategic advantage, yet it is often left out of the vetting process. Be sure to list on the matrix what they can do for you to help you accomplish your mission. Also determine each person's DISC personality profile so you can communicate with them in the right way. (See No. 23.)

VIP: Gather information about the stakeholders to ensure that you're addressing the priorities of each person.

STAKEHOLDERS MATRIX

#	Stakeholder	DISC	What They Want	What They Can Do
Owners				
Executive Management				
Member/Associates				
Strategic Partners				
Customers				
Influencers i.e. Promoters, Rainmakers, Media				

3. Recognize the Presentation Phases
(Preparation, Delivery, Follow-Up)

Often, people focus only on delivering their presentation, and they realize too late that they overlooked what I consider the more important components of a successful pitch: preparation and follow-up. The best presenters gather thorough research and have a solid follow-up approach to stop inertia from setting in.

Remember that your presentation is not just an event you do; rather it is a strategic process that should not be about you. Often, the likelihood of closing the deal increases proportionately based on the thoroughness of your preparation, which should include determining what content to present that will support your objectives and produce your desired results.

The proper follow-up after delivery can often seal the deal. We've found one single, solid best practice for follow-up that many organizations don't make as a standard, and yet they should. That is taking exceptional notes (preferably on a screen for everyone to see) during the presentation, and following up immediately by sending the notes to all participants with the agreed-upon next steps/actions highlighted. This is not only an awareness item; it is also a discipline item.

The mistake many make is thinking presentation is just a skill set they can improve. It's much more than that, and that's why I've authored twenty-six books on the topic in which I explain and validate my point. When you reach the level of Presentation Mastery™, you're being strategic at all three stages of presentation— preparation, delivery, and follow up.

VIP: Be strategic about focusing on all three stages of your presentations— preparation, delivery, and follow up— to ensure greater results.

4. Gather Intelligence Strategically

Remember, companies don't buy; individuals do. It's valuable to collect information on the company; however, it's even more powerful to collect intelligence about the decision maker(s). Find out what that person wants; then, as you're presenting, whether it's by Zoom, in person, or by email, specifically relate your messages based on the intelligence you discovered about the individual.

This truly is the age of information, and there is so much of it readily available at a moment's notice. We all live in the world of Google and social media, and with just a few clicks and a small amount of time, you can often collect names, histories, preferences, backgrounds, and even priorities—all powerful pieces of data. There are many license or subscription-based assets like Hoovers and Dun and Bradstreet where you can get information on companies and their competitors. You can also check in with LinkedIn or other social media outlets so you can leverage shared contacts who can provide information. Be sure to check for anything you may have in common, such as colleges you attended or charities you support. It is also a good idea to ask your friends and colleagues to share their general knowledge on a particular company or person. Information is power. The more you know, the more power you put into your hands and the less you leave to chance.

VIP: Gather as much information as you can about each decision maker so you can personalize your sales pitch to their wants and needs and maximize your chances of success.

5. Know Your Competition

As part of the intelligence-gathering process, knowing and understanding your competition will dramatically increase your odds of closing a deal in most cases. If you have connections who can tell you what relationships the competition may have, that will help you strategically build your case. Knowing your competition can help you intentionally ensure you're offering strengths against what you understand are their weaknesses. Take an inventory of their strengths and offerings versus your own to determine if either of you have any gaps. Also, you can often gain a competitive edge by learning from the competition's mistakes. In today's digital world, there is much information available that could help you shape the best possible pitch to get the win. Study your competition's website(s), 10-Ks, PR blasts, and any other information you can find so you know where your true strengths are and exploit them accordingly.

VIP: Know your competition so you can intentionally offer your strengths against the competition's weaknesses to gain a competitive edge.

6. Figure Out What You Really Want

Knowing what your stakeholders want is important, as stated earlier. Yet an awareness piece that is definitely overlooked by many, and one that is even more vital, is knowing what you really, really want—down to the smallest detail.

Clarity creates a pulling power that has a major influence on you and those around you. For example, some people may say, "What I want to do is sell the account" when they are preparing for an important presentation. Instead, maybe they should be saying, "What I really want is to advance the selling process to the next step, build trust, and create a champion in this organization who wants me to win." It's a given that you want the sale and the commission; yet there may be other things that are important to you, like referrals, testimonials, open doors, intelligence, relationships, insights, learning, and credibility. Take time to reflect, and then write down or type into your computer/smartphone exactly what's important to you, and include the "why." Make a habit of becoming super aware of what you want out of each presentation and out of each relationship. You're in a better position to persuade when you're really clear on what you want.

VIP: Become super aware of what you want to gain out of each presentation and relationship so you're in a better position to effectively persuade others.

7.   Be Early and Be *Presentation Ready*

I'm sure you've heard the saying, "Early is on time and on time is late." When you schedule one-on-one time, be early, be Presentation Ready, and be prepared so you can maximize time—both yours and others'. Being early could even yield the added benefit of having a chat with the receptionist on another team member you have a relationship with to get special or updated insights before your meeting.

Have you thought through your tools and messaging for both prepared and impromptu presentation opportunities? You should have all necessary tools and information organized and ready to go, and be ready to share them and take notes, even at a moment's notice.

Also, rehearse your presentation in advance—out loud! Time yourself to ensure you can get all your important points across in the time given to you. Be prepared to leave behind the appropriate information that will seal the deal and that will answer any questions they may have after you leave. When people believe you've invested a considerable amount of time learning about them and preparing for them, they can't help but enjoy, appreciate, and even be impressed with you. They will be more likely to buy your offering. Take the time to be truly Presentation Ready. And remember, a call with tough questions can come at any time—before and after a formal presentation. If you're really ready—you've planned in advance, discussed possible tough questions, and have mentally prepared to present the answers—it will show.

VIP: Carefully think through your tools and messaging for your presentations, and have all necessary tools and information organized and ready to go so you can be *Presentation Ready* at all times.

8.   Practice *Planned Spontaneity*

In 2004, I authored a best-selling book called *Life Is a Series of Presentations*, and it was endorsed a couple of years ago by Daymond John on *Shark Tank* as one of the six must-read business books. In the book I introduced a concept called *Planned Spontaneity*, which is simply being so prepared going into your presentation that you can spontaneously and quickly react to your audience in a way that keeps getting your message across. It's preparing to the extreme and being so prepared and planned on the front end that you can be spontaneous and genuine in the moment; that makes a huge difference to your audience. Having everything prepared in such detail ahead of time allows you to be so connected when you arrive that you can create a great experience with the people you're talking to.

Take the time to think about, brainstorm and, in some cases, actually list out why people may say "no," stall, or pause. Then genuinely address each one in your communication. Know your message. Know your offering or request. Then, when someone gets you off your agenda or you just want to move your agenda around, take questions, or make any other adjustments, you'll be able to stay calm and move forward with linking to your particular audience. Or when someone doesn't show up or shows up late, or they didn't read the information you sent in advance, it's no problem. You've planned so well that you can spontaneously move where you need to go and then strategically move right back on target. Planned Spontaneity is a quality that separates the master sales professionals from those who are merely good.

VIP: The more prepared you are, the more spontaneous you can be.

9. Really Qualify the Prospect

As a professional salesperson, you know the importance of qualifying a prospect. You know that before investing a significant amount of time preparing a proposed offering for a prospect, you need to take the time to make sure they fit your target market. What you may not have thought of is the value of creating your own personal avatar and vetting your prospects out to ensure you don't contract with/sell to someone you really don't want to do business with. Many times we can put too much energy into something we shouldn't, and we can get burned.

When qualifying a prospect, ask yourself strong qualifying questions, such as:

- Do they fit both my company's and my personal avatar?
- Do they want to do business with us?
- Can they afford us?
- Will the effort required provide ROI/ROE (Return on Investment/ Return on Effort)?

Let me share something with you that we've done in my firm. We got so clear with our target market that we were able to adopt a mnemonic for the type of client we want to serve: ADOME.

A – Aggressive, abundance thinker, and appreciative. We want clients who are able to make decisions as we drive their *Strategic Acceleration*; we want clients who see us as an investment rather than an expense; and we want them to appreciate how we positively impact their businesses and their lives.

D – Desire to do business with us. We want people coming into our world saying, "Yes, we get who you are and we want you to help us!"

O – Open-minded. Occasionally we have people who come to us with their arms folded, and I say, "Do I need to talk you into working with me? I've been doing this for thirty-something years. We have a unique and one of the best supercharger options in the world; and if you come in here open-minded, we can pour into you and your results will take off." We want open-minded people who are ready for that.

M – Millions to be made. We prefer to work with people online or in the RESULTS Center where there are millions being made and millions more to be gained by being more effective.

E – Equity play. We like to have the opportunity for some kind of success fee—maybe participating in part of the ownership or the growth of the company based on the results we help them achieve. We actually prefer to take the biggest part of our compensation based on results we help achieve.

VIP: Create an avatar that fits both your own and your company's target market and vet your prospects accordingly so you attract who you want to do business with.

10. Define the Situation, Needs, Value, Outcomes, Deliverables, and Terms

Having a 360-degree view of the landscape is essential to putting together a winning pitch. We use a Statement of Work (SOW) template that clearly lays out the following:

Situation: A detailed recap/overview/summary (proves you know the deal)

Needs: What the prospect/customer/client wants, wants more, or wants to avoid

Value: What we can uniquely provide and how it will help them

Outcomes: The bigger picture of what they want

Deliverables: Exactly what the prospect will receive from our offering to help them get the outcome they want (products, services, connections, etc.)

Terms: The business agreement

Perhaps this format could be helpful for you.

Understanding these critical success factors will help you put together a comprehensive presentation that is results-oriented and will provide excellent clarity for your prospect.

VIP: Address the situation, needs, value, outcomes, deliverables, and terms of an agreement so you can put together a comprehensive presentation that is results oriented and will provide excellent clarity for your prospect.

11. Leverage the 3-D Outline™

When most people prepare a presentation, they primarily look at "What" they will present and begin putting their pieces together accordingly. To get the best strategic results, almost two decades ago I developed the 3-D Outline™ process, which is a powerful outline format that includes primarily the What, Why, and How aspects of a presentation and is used for compressing the preparation process. It can also include the When and the Who. Once your objectives are established and you have reviewed all the "What's" of your presentation, the "Why" for each "What" should support the objectives. If it doesn't, consider eliminating it for this presentation. The "How" is important so you vary your presentation style throughout to keep the audience engaged and make sure you are using what will make the most impact for the situation. There are at least 36 different ways to present:

Activity	Present (talk)
Application	Prop
Audience Champion	Q&A
Audio Clip	Quiz
Cartoon	Review
Case Study	Role Play
Co-facilitate	Sample
Contest	Skit
Demo	Slides (PowerPoint)
Discussion	Smart Report
Expert/Authority	Statistic
Facilitation	Story
Flipchart	Tablet(s)
GoToMeeting/Skype	Train
Group Activity	Trivia
Guest	Video Clip
Handout	White Board
Photographs	YouTube/Web Link

By utilizing this 3-D approach, you will be able to review in a snapshot your entire presentation approach and ensure it aligns with the wants and needs of the prospective customer. Review the sample 3-D Outline™ below and see how it can be effectively used to build a strategic presentation.

Sample 3-D Outline™ Template

The 3-D Outline™

Presentation Title		Delivery Date	
Audience		Start Time	
Objectives		End Time	
Final Preparation Checklist					
#	Time	What	Why	How	Who
1.					
2.					
3.					
4.					
5.					
Total Time					

Our 3-D Outline™ process (and software) is used for shortening the planning process, and it ensures every minute of your presentation is maximized. Whether you're presenting to one person or a large group, in a meeting or from a stage, the 3-D Outline™ enables you to better clarify and see three-dimensionally in your mind what you're going to say on each of the topics, why you're presenting that topic (your objectives), and how you're going to deliver.

VIP: Incorporate the 3-D Outline™ into your preparation process to shorten the process, ensure every minute of your presentation is maximized, and gain three-dimensional clarity about what you're going to say and how you're going to deliver.

12. Prepare an Objections Matrix

Creating an Objections Matrix in advance that prepares you for pushback or difficult questions keeps you responsive versus reactive. Consider what would cause someone to stall and/or not say yes to your proposal. Then go to the next level and think through a response, or maybe a variety of responses based on your personality, on the type of customer, and on your relationship with the customer. You can then preempt them in your communication or fully prepare yourself or your team to respond.

Sample Objections Matrix:

Objections Matrix		
Objection	**Response**	**Who**

VIP: Create an Objections Matrix to prepare for pushback or difficult questions so you can preempt them in your communication and ensure you and your team are responsive versus reactive.

13. Think Through the "What Ifs"

When you are preparing for any event, ask yourself, *What could possibly happen?* When you're making a presentation or leading an important meeting with a client, what could happen?

Thinking through the "what-ifs" equips you to address any contingencies before they arrive. For example, think ahead about what you would do if someone shows up late to a meeting (virtual or in person) or if someone leaves a meeting early. Have a backup summary document, so when someone needs to leave early, you can hand or email it to them and they'll have the summary of what they're missing. Or if someone shows up a third of the way into the meeting, you can hand or email them a briefing document they can read over and catch up with everyone else. And be sure to have extra handouts available in case more people show up for an in-person meeting than you expected. You'll want to consider as well "what if" the technology doesn't work for a Zoom call and have a backup plan for that.

A smart approach is to list the possible things that could happen, along with the best action or response, and who will respond. Brainstorm with your team members or a partner about what could happen ahead, and resolve any "what-ifs" in advance so you can be ready to respond with best actions. If you happen to get asked a question during the meeting that you haven't considered, ask them to clarify the question with additional information so you can have a *breathing space* to consider the best answer.

Thinking about and taking precautions for the what-ifs in advance can be very powerful and impressive. It's a level of preparedness everyone should aspire to have.

VIP: Before each presentation, brainstorm with your team members or a partner about what could happen, and take precautions to resolve any "what-ifs" in advance so you can be ready to respond with best actions.

14. You Can't Get Where You're Going Without a Plan

Success is very seldom about pure luck. We are successful when we achieve objectives on purpose. In other words, we have thought through our vision, are clear on what we want to achieve, and then systematically go about taking the actions that will get us where we want to go. In a nutshell, this is what planning is about.

If you don't create a plan, it's almost impossible to achieve your vision. Having a mission statement (the why) and a set of goals or objectives (the targets) are important (both personal and business) in order to achieve the right results faster. Every entrepreneur needs a clean and current action plan. If you don't have one, you're simply costing yourself time and money, living your business life on autopilot. That's not a way to operate.

Your plan should be a values-based strategy for the long haul. By values-based, we mean that it's critical to establish clarity about what matters most to you first as the leader, and then create your vision, mission, and objectives from your values. Remember the great explorers Christopher Columbus and Lewis and Clark? They had a vision. They had a plan. A plan will help you navigate treacherous waters, or avoid them altogether, and help keep you focused.

As a sales leader, you'll want to include things in your plan that you may not have thought of, such as:

- What's the real avatar we're after?
- How many avatars do we want to bring in?
- When we're making a sale, what's the plan for getting the testimonial from the customer? Or what's the plan for getting an endorsement from someone we did business with inside their company three years ago?
- What's the plan for getting the referral?

VIP: Without a values-based plan or strategy, it is almost impossible to achieve your vision.

15. Initially Structure the Partnership Properly

If you feel a partnership in any venture is the right move, leave nothing to chance. Structure the partnership with all the "what-ifs" in mind. In business, you don't get what you deserve—you get what you negotiate. We've all heard and know this. Have an agreement in place and know your exit options up front—how you will get out (or how someone else will get out) from day one, if that time ever comes. Think ahead to all the possibilities.

Let's say you start a partnership with a friend. The business is successful and thrives. Twenty years later, your friend wants to retire but you don't. What happens now? Have a plan in place for all the possibilities so there's no question. Use an expert (or whole team) to put the plan in place and have all parties sign off so there are no misunderstandings down the line. Include things like divorce, lawsuits, if children want to buy in, if you need more capital, etc. Cover the most common "what-ifs."

> Something I believe in strongly is moving from a vendor mindset to a partnership mindset. It starts with what you believe in your own personal relationship methodology. I wrote a book several years ago called *Rich Relationships, Rich Life*, and Randy and I both live out the distinctions we included in that book. In each of our relationships, we look at how we can help the other person win. That's the core distinction of having a partnership mentality; and as a salesperson, those are the types of customers you want to attract. When you have a mutual goal of helping each other win, it is easy for them to say, "I want to refer someone to you because that's who I am. I have a partnership mentality."

VIP: Strategically structure a partnership with all the "what-ifs" in mind and leave nothing to chance.

16. Watch for the Warning Signs

Before any deal crashes, there are signs. A bad real-estate market doesn't just happen overnight, for instance. There are always signs; and if you can see them early, you just might be able to avoid trouble. If it's a real estate project and the lots aren't selling, ask yourself why. Detect deficiencies. Recognize early on when you are in trouble so you don't lose your decision-making ability. Cut your losses and don't feed a bad deal. Most don't get better. Ask yourself, "Is this deal headed for success?" And, "What's the best use of my time right now?" These questions will help raise your self-awareness and help you understand your motives and actions for doing what you do, and will also identify bad habits or weaknesses in your business or in yourself. Continually examine your deals and activities and watch for any signs of weakness or areas for improvement. Be willing to move on. Take time to evaluate, and pay attention to the warning signs. Then act accordingly.

VIP: Recognize deficiencies and warning signs early on so you don't lose your decision-making ability and can cut your losses early and move on if necessary.

17. Know the Rules of Negotiation

In order to understand the rules of negotiation, you have to understand what negotiation really is. It's not just talking and determining what you want and how you're going to get it. Negotiation is about making things happen by understanding what other people want. Remember, it's best if you win when they win. Yet if you think they want something other than what they really want, you may address the wrong points and miss the mark.

Have you ever met people who talk over everyone? Those people don't win, because they don't listen carefully to the other person. They're also not good negotiators, because they are only focused on themselves; and negotiation, of course, is a balance of give and take.

It all starts with other people's interest. Do your homework strategically and thoroughly, and discover everything in advance about the other party—their motivations, promotions, values, biases, and timing. Knowledge is power. Once you understand their position and priorities, you can implement your powers of persuasion to make an impact and often more easily persuade them to your thinking.

It's not about winning at all costs. Some people want to win no matter what, even at the expense of everyone else; yet inevitably, that will cost you in the long run. You don't have to be a friend to everyone in the world, either. However, you don't need to make enemies. You never know when you might need the person you're trying to negotiate with, or where your next deal will come from. It may be a friend of the person you want to say no to. It's best to leave a good impression every time. Have people leave your office happy. When you must say no, have them feel like you said yes. Look for alternatives. The true art of negotiation is when you can help make everyone win.

VIP: Recognize that negotiation is about making things happen by understanding what other people want. Remember, you really win when everyone wins.

B. DELIVERY
18. People Buy, Not Companies

Here's a big "aha" and an often-unnoticed mistake: many people sell to what a company wants versus to the decision makers who run the company. People—not companies or organizations—make final decisions. There could be several decision makers involved, and there may be a big difference in what the decision makers want, so be aware.

Your relationships are with people. So many times we in the business world get confused. We try to sell to the benefits of the company. It's much more effective to know the people and then sell to their motivations, desires, and responsibilities.

Discover and be aware of what your stakeholders really want and care about. Verbally ask people what's important to them, their organization, their company, their colleagues, and their associates. Your products and services are definitely important to the sales process.

VIP: Know the people involved and sell to the motivations, desires, and responsibilities of the stakeholders, not the company.

19. Use Different Communication Approaches (Email, Print, Phone, Web, One on One, Group)

When we are communicating with others, sometimes we limit our options. In today's world, however, there are at least six approaches we can take, either singularly or in combination. Understanding where you are most comfortable, what the other person prefers, and how to combine it all into a winning presentation is important to moving the prospect/audience member to the taking-action state. Ask what's the preferred option from these six. Or is a combination best? Then structure your approach accordingly.

Communication Approaches

ADVANTAGES	DISADVANTAGES
Email	
1. Saves time	1. Tone often misconstrued
2. No face-to-face needed	2. Requires internet service
3. Multiple contacts at once	3. Lack of articulation
Print	
1. Better clarity	1. Labor intensive to create
2. Can add branding	2. Requires in person
3. Allows for a leave-behind	3. Additional time to collate
Phone	
1. Personal connection	1. Often more time
2. Can overcome objections	2. Nothing in writing
3. Better clarity	3. Usually requires follow-up
Web	
1. Provides branding	1. Generic in nature to all
2. Detailed information	2. Requires internet
3. Has variety	3. Doesn't tie back
One-on-One	
1. Builds relationship	1. May require travel time
2. Clear communication	2. May miss key players
3.Can often get decision	3. Need to return for group
Group	
1. Utilizes multiple expertise	1. Can create distractions
2. Connects to all players	2. Not as easy to know them
3.Gets all on same page	3. Possible negative influence

[Note: The matrix details are not absolutes; they are for advancing thinking, In some cases, the opposite could apply.]

VIP: Understanding where you are most comfortable in your communication approach, what the other person prefers, and how to combine it all into a winning presentation is important to moving the prospect/audience member to the taking-action state.

20. Show People a Clear Picture

Clarity of your vision is so important, and you need to be able to communicate that to your stakeholders. Show people the clear picture using an infographic, map, vision board (what I've coined in my world as a RESULTS board) or other visuals, then verbally describe the opportunity.

A sale is rarely made or fulfilled on one individual's efforts alone. Communicate clearly your vision to get others on board and work together for a common goal. Similarly, when you are presenting, make sure there is clarity of vision and that the presentation given supports achieving that vision. Paint the picture of what could be, include details, and, of course, share how each recipient wins.

In the sales arena, one of the things we sometimes fail to do is to discover the entire buying process and link the dots so people see the steps clearly. We need to clearly delineate the exact steps from the beginning to the end of the process so the customer has complete clarity. Then what often happens is the customer may say something like, "Oh, there's one more thing I forgot to tell you. We have a budget cycle, and in June we can release a lot more opportunities to deploy." That's a piece to the puzzle you may not have received if you had not been detailing out the steps so everyone would have clarity. When you paint the clear picture at the beginning, you're on the same path, and you can uncover potential objections or roadblocks.

VIP: Show the clear picture of the vision to all stakeholders in order to get others on board and work together toward a common goal.

21. Present to People the Way They Want to Receive Information

When most people communicate, they're communicating through their own window and not thinking about the windows of the people they're talking to, and then they wonder why their message isn't being received well. When you want someone to be very receptive to the message you're sharing, you need to mentally prepare and think about how they see the world. A good general rule of thumb is to be thinking about other people and not so much yourself, and then most of the time your message will be much better received.

I have seen time and time again that using others' communication preferences will positively impact results. Using the method your audience/prospect most prefers (versus the method you prefer) will create greater buy-in. Not sure what approach to take? Just ask them! It's an overlooked skill for many. Improve your skills at determining how people prefer to be presented to.

Remember, your preferred style is not necessarily theirs. Some people want the details, others want to hear case studies, others want to see charts, and yet others just want the brief with backup information. Some want to have a handout they can study. Change it up and make it fit your recipient.

If you're presenting to a group, it is important to switch up your method of presenting and not just present slide after slide or talk constantly. You will most likely have a group of mixed personalities; presenting in multiple styles will help ensure people don't zone out. Engaged participants win. They win, you win. Don't get stuck in your style or your preferences. Do it their way. [Note: We will talk more about personality styles in No. 23 below.]

VIP: Using others' communication preferences will positively impact results. Study your audience to gain an in-depth understanding of how they wish to be presented to and respond accordingly.

22. Give People "The Why"

When you provide the reasoning behind what you are asking of others, they will take action much more quickly. This is so powerful, and yet people miss it all the time! Most people have an intrinsic desire to know how things fit together in the bigger picture, and they will generally provide greater support when they understand. Supplying the "why" will create better buy-in and faster results. To get your team members behind you, you will get more support when people understand the "why." In addition to the "why," sharing with them how their part contributes to the success of the whole can better prepare you for closing the sale.

Using "why" in preparation is important, yet be sure to use "why" when delivering as well. Make sure your prospects are clear on the reasons they would want to select you as their provider of choice no matter what others are offering. Often, the one who articulates the best "why" wins, and that is a skill you want to leverage.

Make sure to give the why by using words like "because" and "so that." It's so important to do that in every presentation—even in an email! I might say, for example, "One of the things I encourage you to do is build an outstanding arsenal *so that* you're more content-rich when you need to give a presentation."

I've been in Sydney, Australia, several times in the last few years, and I'm very fascinated with the Sydney Opera House. The architecture is very intriguing, which includes quite a few angled panels. On one of the panels there is a sign that says, "In the interest of safety do not climb on angled panels." Notice they gave the why, "in the interest of safety," before they asked for the action. Giving the people the why helps them take ownership.

VIP: Provide reasoning behind what you're asking of others to convey the "why" factor to your audience and achieve buy-in—and hence results—faster.

23. Be Flexible and Communicate in a Style That Matches Theirs

Understanding personality styles will help you excel at business, because you can communicate with people in the way they will best understand. You may be into details, and yet you're presenting to a prospective buyer who only desires a high-level, fast overview. This person doesn't want all the details. By knowing your prospective buyer's personality style in advance, you can adapt your presentation to give a high-level view.

When your objective is to win people over, leverage personality styles to achieve the outcome you desire. One of the most common models is DISC:

D **Direct**: High Level, Results-Oriented	**I** **Influential**: Enjoy a Fun Format, Social
C **Compliant**: Lots of Detail, Wants a Clear Path	**S** **Steady**: Loyal, Step by Step with a Smile

Dr. Robert Rohm and I wrote a book together some years back called *Presenting with Style*. It's a powerful book, using the DISC Model of Human Behavior. Dr. Rohm has taught me so much as he's talked about how he has raised his kids according to their personality styles and about understanding the distinctions of a person's style and presenting accordingly.

If a person has a style of a driver (D), for example, what do they want? They want to receive information fast and without too many details. If a person is more of an influencer (I), their style is happy-go-lucky and they're really into socialization. You want to make sure you communicate with them with some humor and fun. If they're more stable and steady (S) and into process, you want to strategically answer and communicate in steps. And if they're very cautious (C), communicate to them with a number of details.

Knowing and understanding different personalities will help you present in the way that is most comfortable to the people you're presenting to. Match up your presentation style with their preference and get the results you want.

Note: Talk to Jesse about the new software that's available that can take information from a person's LinkedIn and tell what their DISC personality is.

VIP: Use the DISC model to understand your prospective buyer's personality style in advance so you can adapt your presentation and communicate to the prospect as effectively as possible.

24. Show People How to Help You

If you show others how to help you, they won't be as inclined to focus on how it can't be done; instead, they will be more inclined to see how it can and to do what you ask. Don't assume that people will make the connections on their own; take ownership of the outcome by being clear and direct. Show the process/steps/actions you'd like to include in how they win, and you have a winning formula. If you're fuzzy and they're fuzzy, I promise the results you desire will be negatively impacted. It's up to you.

Here's an example: You might say to someone who has not quite reached buy-in on a project, "Before I have my call with Randy, one way you could really help me is to tell me which of these three actions you think matters the most from a priority standpoint. If you can give me that insight, I can present them to Randy in the most efficient order." You've not only enlisted their help in a clear and concise manner, you've also likely made an impact on their value of the project you're discussing with Randy—or at least invited them to take a second look.

VIP: To create a winning formula, take ownership of the outcome you want by clearly and directly showing the process/steps/actions you would like to include in how your prospect wins.

25. Leverage Testimonials

Social proof is a concept that has been around for decades and can be deployed in many ways. People want what other people have or have experienced, and testimonials are an excellent way to share positive experiences.

One of the most frequently overlooked opportunities is creating a system for capturing testimonial notes, quotes, and letters, and then making them usable on an individual and/or an organization-wide basis. Testimonials prove that others have trusted you and benefited from their interaction. For example, if I were to tell you that the president of Walmart flew his jet to Dallas to sit down with me to strategize his plan (which he did), you would think, *Wow! If Tony's good enough for the president of the largest company in the world, maybe he's good enough for me.*

Categorize your testimonials by type of business, type of results, and even by type of service. Then they will be readily available to you when you are presenting to a prospect so you may select those that would best resonate with that particular person. When other people see a testimonial from someone they respect, it adds credibility to your side.

People often fail to ask for testimonials because they don't know how. There are actually many different ways you can ask. For example, Jack Furst, my super-successful partner who offices next door to me in the RESULTS Center, said, "Tony, you're the most efficient man on the planet." I said, "Hey, may I quote you on that?" He said, "Sure," and all of a sudden I had a powerful testimonial from a guy with a ton of credibility.

Social proof is powerful. Make sure you leverage it.

VIP: Create a system for capturing testimonial notes, quotes, and letters, and then make them usable on an individual and/or an organization-wide basis. Testimonials prove that others have trusted you and benefited from their interaction.

26. Share Case Studies

Well-chosen case studies show situations similar to your prospect's and clearly demonstrate the problem, solution, and results. A simple model that is easily digestible answers three questions: What was the problem? What was the solution? What were the results?

Sample Case Study

Problem:	Gain clarity and refocus; was losing $10M a year in 2012.
Solution:	We worked together to develop a strategic plan using our *Strategic Acceleration* best practices, met quarterly with the Executive Leadership Team (ELT) in our SA Studio, and established a close Executive Coaching relationship with the CEO as well as other ELT team members for accountability.
Results:	Stock in X Y Z went up over 700% in two years, trajectory of growth and huge ESI gain in 24 months.

VIP: Chose a case study that show situations similar to your prospect's and clearly demonstrates the problem, the solution, and the results.

27. Sharpen Your Sword with Precise Communication

How many emailed articles a week do you trash or ignore? How many books would you like to read but just don't have the time? How many blogs/newspapers/articles are left unread, beyond the headlines? This glut of words has become a factor in the way you compete for business and communicate your value. Information is coming at us at lightning speed. While the digital age makes it easier to compile and share text, the competition for the time people invest in reading has increased dramatically.

When you're communicating with others, you need to be concise, so sharpen your sword! Most people use far more words to make their point—both on paper and in emails—than is really necessary. Their writing rambles on and on, talking about things that aren't essential. And that could be because many of us who are above forty were taught to write in paragraphs. That works for a novel, yet not in business communications. If you want to communicate or sell an idea, you have to frame the important things and capture the value proposition in as few words as possible. *If you're sharpening your sword, you really want to bring it down to bullets—especially in emails.*

This seems obvious. So why do people have such a hard time achieving it? It's because people often lack clarity regarding what they most need to communicate. And the key to achieving clarity here is found in the word "why." It relates to the positive perceptions people have about purpose and value. When it comes to communicating your ideas through conversation, email, or phone calls, simply ask yourself, "What are the objectives or actions I'd like to get accomplished?" This will give clarity and is the key ingredient that will make your messages powerful.

VIP: Sharpen your sword with precise communication—frame the important things and capture the value proposition in as few words as possible (preferably using bullets when appropriate).

28. Aim for the 87 Percent

There's a saying that goes, "Excellence adds value; perfection just adds time." So many people are out for perfection to such a degree that they either stop because they can never reach their desired state, or they put in significantly more time than there is value for the last few percent.

My great friend, partner, and client Peter Thomas, with whom I coauthored a book called *Business Ground Rules,* has a concept he calls the Rule of 87 Percent. You will be amazed at the results if you quit being a perfectionist and understand that as a rule, 87 percent is just fine. Do you want to be known for value? Do you want to be known for excellence? Absolutely. Excellence often comes in at 87 percent. Striving for perfection will sidetrack your results and make your customers wait. They want results, and they want them fast.

When you're negotiating a deal or engaging in any kind of business proposition, don't lose sight of what's important. Focus on production and the critical factors in the project. Focus on your highest-leveraged items and activities, and when you hit 87 percent success, celebrate! Why not 100 percent? Because in all our years of experience in coaching and living in the entrepreneurial world, we've seen that analysis paralysis and the stress of focusing on perfection cause people to lose more than they win. If you're continually focused on achieving 100 percent, you'll be continually disappointed, especially where other people are involved. Speed matters. Of course, 87 percent is not a license for being sloppy. You get my point.

High expectations are great, yet there are always other factors in any situation. In many cases, 87 percent will be just as good as 100 or better because of the worrying, stress, and negative energy that come with trying to achieve a perfect score.

VIP: Excellence often comes in speed, and that can often be at 87 percent. Striving for perfection will often sidetrack your results and make your customers wait. They want results, and they want them fast.

29. Be Known for Something

What are you known for? You don't have to be good at everything, yet you should be excellent in at least one area. Find that one thing and be the expert. Know your God-given talents. I get results. My clients and prospects know that I help them get what they want faster, and that I am a true "encourager." Something else I bring to the table is vibe. I'm able to bring a ton of energy to the people I touch.

My friend Peter Thomas is a deal maker, and he's been very successful at it. He had a vision for making Century 21 Canada a success when no one else believed in it, and he did. Then he sold the company for many millions.

Randy is another good example. His shining star is his ability to build and nourish relationships The new company he has started, Sales Community, provides networking opportunities for technology sales professionals. And we know it will lift off fast because Randy has been kindling relationships for two or three decades.

Whatever you are good at, be known for it, and consistently excel in that field. Understand what's driving that success and identify any areas that are holding you back. If you don't feel you're good at any one particular thing, ask yourself why. You may already be very successful. On the other hand, you may have struggled with achievement and may not be as successful as you would like. Whichever the case, it may be a good idea to look at the choices you have made and the principles governing those choices. Regardless of your current achievement level, you can always improve. Get clear on your strengths; know yourself well. Leverage your strengths and talents.

VIP: Understand what you are good at, be known for it, and consistently excel in that niche of sales or the whole field.

30. Brand Yourself

A successful brand (reputation) reflects who you are. Your brand is your unique promise. Build a brand based on not only who you want to be and how you want to live, but also who you actually are and the core of how you live today.

What's important to your prospective client? Chances are, it isn't just about making money. People want to do business with people they trust. People also want to do business with people they respect. They want to know you can get the job done; and they also have specific values that are important to them, such as security, follow-up communication, and relationship.

Understand what's important to people and what they value, and build your brand authentically. Be who you say you are. As an entrepreneur, what is it that makes you stand out from everyone else? Brand yourself distinctly and create a profile that people remember. Marketing your brand to your clients can be just as important as business processes, communication, technology, and sales.

No matter what your brand is, make sure you're known as someone who follows through. In all the business ventures I've entered over the years, there have always been people with integrity and people without it. The ones without integrity are the ones no one wants to do business with, and that is consistent across industries. In the Bible, Isaiah 32:8 reads, "But the noble man devises noble plans; and by noble plans he stands" (NASB). Be noble. Be the one people trust. Loyalty, trust, and nobility go a long way toward making your business grow.

Think of it this way: When you are in an important business presentation against your competitor, if you don't know your prospect and they don't know you, it all comes down to who they feel they can trust. People make gut decisions based on who they like and trust. Can they trust you? A lot of it comes down to the way you have built and communicated your brand. People want to be confident that they're not going to be misled or stabbed in the back. They need to know they're spending their money wisely and investing in good people. Build your brand on nobility— it's not just about marketing your achievements.

I've included a tool below as well as on the salescommunity.com website called "Your Personal Branding Matrix." I invite you to print it off and use it to help you sort through the things you are best known for and what you want to be known for.

PERSONAL BRANDING MATRIX™

#	Element	Description	Name:		Date:
1.	Brand Description	What is the essence of my brand positioning? (10-word phrase summarizing from the 20 items below)			
2.	Core Value Proposition	Core characteristics that are valuable to my effectiveness			
3.	Business Priorities	Parameters and priorities for how I operate on a daily basis			
4.	_____ Is	Characteristics that describe me			
5.	_____ is Not	Characteristics that do not describe me			
6.	Uniqueness	What truly makes me unique? What distinctions separate me in my niche?			
7.	Packaging	The tools, expertise, image, etc. to be leveraged to the market			
8.	Visual Image	Physical image/appearance			
9.	Mission Stmt.	What drives my decisions?			
10.	Brand Power	The "thrust" behind my reputation			
11.	Tagline	Benefit-driven, descriptive (what I say often)			
12.	Positioning	Role(s) within the market/organization			
13.	Business Motto	Statement of approach to business life			
14.	What People Think of You	My perception of how I am perceived			
15.	What People Are Missing	My beliefs on what others are misunderstanding about me			
16.	Attributes Prized in the Workplace	What attributes do I possess that the market (my organization) values?			
17.	Passions	What things am I passionate about?			
18.	Top Communication Opportunities	Top meetings/presentations where my brand is impacted			
19.	Where Is My Audience/ Prospect?	Who are those I most want to impact?			
20.	External Barriers	Real world roadblocks			
21.	Internal Barriers	Self-imposed roadblocks			

VIP: Your brand is your unique promise; build it based on not only who you want to be and how you want to live, but who you actually are and the core of how you live today. Make sure you're known as someone who follows through.

31. Develop a Memorable, Influential Persona

Are you memorable? What specifically do you want people to remember about you? It's not just your brand or your personality. Your trademark expression, style, or persona also make you memorable—or not.

Have you ever met someone you just knew was different from everyone else? Maybe they were humorous, carefree, or extremely positive when no one else around you was, and you remembered them for that. That's how you want others to remember you.

Think of the big personalities with memorable personas, such as Richard Branson or Herb Kelleher. Other leaders aren't as significant or don't stand out, even if they've achieved a lot. Yet you don't have to have the most dynamic personality to be memorable. One aspect of being memorable is how well you make an impact in someone else's life; people remember that.

Since most people's favorite subject is themselves, one way to make an immediate impact is to ask them about their life. No one likes to be ignored. Yet we live in a society where everyone is ignoring everyone else in favor of texting, emailing, and talking about themselves. You could be different and memorable by being focused on other people. Say, "Tell me more!" Be genuinely interested in their response. This is an area that you could probably improve in. Most of us can.

Ask yourself, "Am I genuinely interested in people, to the point that I am building a positive, strategic presence that significantly affects my results?" If this is an area that needs work, start asking questions and being genuinely interested in others.

VIP: What specifically do you want people to remember about you? It's not only your brand or your personality, but also your trademark expression, style, or persona that make you memorable—or not.

32. Your Body Language and Appearance Impact Your Success

Most high achievers understand that it's important to be presentable. After all, you are your business; and when prospects meet you—whether in person or on Zoom—they'll judge you, your success, and their potential to have success by the things they see. It doesn't matter if it's your car, your office, or your clothes, or even what they see behind you on a Zoom call. People will form an opinion of you by what they see.

Yet looking good isn't just about how others perceive you. Some may argue that it's not important what you look like, because it's what's inside that counts. In the past decade, there's been a big trend toward casual work environments and being sloppy, wrinkled, and comfortable, especially in the tech space. In companies that are trying to attract a younger mindset, the cultural dress code might be a radically dressed-down environment. However, keep in mind not only your perceptions and desires, but your customers' as well. What kind of business are you trying to attract? And how do you personally feel when you dress for success? It's about *strategic presence*.

I devoted a whole chapter on this in my book *Strategic Acceleration*. Your *strategic presence* has a unique impact on how people will follow your lead. Make it strong. Hopefully, your vibe (your energy) plays an important role in your presence. I believe there's extraordinary, force-multiplying power in vibe, and that it is the real differentiator in ensuring success. Your presence (which affects your vibe) could incorporate things such as your voice; the amount of energy you portray; your wardrobe; how you groom your hair, your makeup, or your beard; or even the way you stand. All those components make an impression. In today's world your presence could even include the way you present yourself on Zoom. Are you making sure you look sharp, even though you're working from home? Often, people are not as strategic as they could be about that, and they may get a little sloppy. Thinking through all that and being strategic about it can have an impact on your presence—and therefore your vibe.

What do people see when they see you? Do you smile? Or do you exude a stressful energy, always looking down at your mobile device while texting? People will often judge you based on their first thirty seconds of an encounter. That leaves no room for error. Part of building your brand is the way you look—period.

This is beyond vanity; it's about excellence. Each day you make choices: Do I want to be excellent today? Do I want to think, communicate, and convey a strong, authentic, and positive image? You will be judged on the way you look, think, and communicate. A smile makes people perceive you as approachable. A scowl, or ignoring people while you text, sends a different message.

Truth is, most people build a reputation based on who they are, what they've done, or how they look, yet they aren't intentional about it. Every day we are being pre-judged by the way we look, act, talk, and dress. Judging is the only way to assess a situation, a deal, or the players involved. Judging is simply using our eyes, ears, and senses to determine what we think or believe about someone else. Are you doing your best to convey the best impression? Be wardrobe-appropriate, use open body language, and send the message that you are successful and confident.

VIP: You are your business; and when prospects meet you—whether in person or on Zoom—they'll judge you, your success, and their potential to have success by the things they see. Convey a strong, authentic, and positive image through your wardrobe, your body language, and your vibe.

C. FOLLOW-UP

33. Debrief

Most salespeople don't think deep enough about the importance of follow-up, which is, of course, an essential part of the sales process. Really, your thinking about follow-up should be two-fold:

1. You need to be thinking about how you get back to your prospect immediately, making sure your follow-up supports your value proposition.

2. As a cousin to that, if you want to be constantly improving—as you should be —you need to be asking, *What did I just do that I could*

have done better? Identify what you did right on the call and what you may have done wrong or could have done better.

VIP: Follow-up is an essential part of the sales process; it should include both getting back to the prospect immediately to support your value proposition as well as debriefing to discover how you can improve.

34. Use a Summary Sheet

One of our best tools we've ever created for follow-up is a summary sheet, which allows for quick and easy message cascading to decision makers who might not be available to hear all or part of your message. A quick one-pager with highlights of important details gets and keeps everyone involved in the process and makes later catch-up easy. In your follow-up, you should ensure every decision maker who was not in the meeting has received a summary sheet.

The summary sheet can also serve as part of your delivery when a prospect in a group setting comes in or signs on late. You can hand (or email, if the meeting is virtual) the summary sheet to the person (who sometimes is the big decision maker) and say, "We're on point four." Or if that person has to leave early, you can simply hand the summary sheet (or tell them you will email it to them) and they will have the content of where you're going with the remaining participants. Many people don't do that. If the main decision maker has to leave early and you don't have this prepared, it could cost you the sale.

VIP: Utilize a one-pager that summarizes the highlights of your presentation to get and keep everyone involved in the process and make future catch-up easy.

D. IMPROVEMENT
(AUTOMATIC, HABITS, AND THINKING)

35. Strategically Listen to Needs

One of the magic principles shared in one of my favorite books ever written, *How to Win Friends and Influence People*, is to be a good listener.

In business, listening is a critical skill. People who don't listen often miss key indicators, clues, and components that drive the sale, as well as important opportunities. They aren't in touch with anyone's needs except their own. Listening well can make the difference between success and failure. You can't do a good business deal if you aren't armed with all the facts. And the only way to understand everything is to listen carefully. Sometimes you'll gain new information that radically changes the direction of your decision.

Listening is the key to excellent decision-making. Think about how you feel when someone appears to not be listening to you. There is no greater sign of disrespect than ignoring someone's needs, words, or wishes. If you don't listen to your spouse, the relationship disintegrates. When you don't listen to your teenager, you can miss very important clues, major life events, or issues that need attention. When you do not listen to your boss, you can miss important details on a project or misinterpret what he or she needs. When you don't listen to a prospective client, the client notices and just may want to take his/her business elsewhere.

Listening involves concentration and contribution. You must have concentration to actually hear the information and the point the person talking is conveying. It requires concentration to block out distracting thoughts and discipline to refrain from speaking when you have something to say. Contribution should only come after the person talking has adequately communicated his/her ideas. Then when it's appropriate to contribute, you can add to the conversation or ignite a spark that will offer solutions and ideas.

It is particularly important when you research a company or a business opportunity that you make sure you also understand the humans within the culture. When you talk to them or meet with them face-to-face, don't let your previous assumptions or knowledge about the company override the human factor. Listen to them talk to understand their personalities and ask questions when the time is right, with the right words, the right strategy, and the appropriate mindset. People ultimately will make the decision on whether or not to buy your product or service, or to do business with you. This is why it's essential to be a good people person. Be genuinely interested in what others have to say. Listening will help you ensure you're on track with your presentation or communication, or if you need to make a shift. Remember, it's not about you—it's about them.

BE BOTH INTERESTING AND INTERESTED.

To take listening as a concept or idea to the highest level, we have found that notetaking is the secret formula. Whether the notes are taken on a legal pad, your phone or tablet, flipchart, or live on a screen, the dynamics that happen from deploying this discipline can be magic. If you take good notes, you can then say, "Here's what I heard you say," and then paraphrase and repeat it back to the person to confirm you heard it correctly. That gives the person an opportunity to correct you if you didn't get it right, and you can adjust your notes accordingly. This practice of paraphrasing and confirming can take place whether you're "talking" by email, by text, or verbally.

As part of the listening process, be prepared to alter your message. Remember, regardless of all your good intentions, if you present information that is important to you yet is not important to your prospect, it will not likely result in a sale. Listening is the key to becoming a trusted colleague or provider, and trust is a significant component in establishing a positive relationship. Whatever you're selling is important; yet in the end, people want to be heard, and they want what they want.

VIP: Listening well is a critical skill and can make the difference between success and failure.

36. Help Others Win

My good friend and mentor, the late Zig Ziglar, famously said, "You can have everything in life you want if you will just help enough other people get what they want." In selling, people often tend to take a short-sighted view of their relationships with customers—they think about the deal on the table instead of the big picture. Helping as many people get what they want and teaching others to do the same will create a ripple effect of wins, including wins for yourself. I really believe if people will live their lives looking for ways to give others more than they expect, they would attract more, enjoy more, and become more. New opportunities will follow, time and time again.

Any time people are interacting with others, whether in a sales call, any other type of presentation, or even in a one-on-one conversation, I think they often make the mistake of looking for ways to make themselves look good versus how to make the person they're presenting or selling look good. When you're able to genuinely use words like "You're right" or "Great idea" or "Tell me more" it's a powerful stimulator for helping people feel good about themselves.

Sometimes you can help people win if you know what their goals are based on how they are being measured. For example, the people you're selling to may be measured by standards set by their board, or by a quota, or by any number of different metrics. If you know how they are being measured, you may be able to find ways that your product can help them reach their goals. In a somewhat extreme example, let's say a front-desk receptionist is measured by the number of ingoing and outgoing calls she/he can handle. If you can find a way to help that person handle calls faster, whether that's within or outside of your normal parameters, you would create a huge win for that individual.

Remember that success is often built on a series of connecting relationships. No matter what your industry is, you will be dealing with others to buy, sell, and promote. You can't do it alone, no matter how smart you are. John Donne spoke the truth when he wrote, "No man is an island." We're all a part of something larger than ourselves, and we are interconnected in a way that assures our success only when we fully accept our interconnectedness. Often people in business focus solely on the people they want to do business with and neglect the people around them. Yet they're losing out, because sometimes it's the people close to them who are the key to unlocking the next door, and we're not just talking about gatekeepers. There are seemingly innocuous people you may encounter in life or in business you would be surprised about if you knew their connections.

Build relationships by having a genuine approach and by appreciating others. Treat strangers, business associates, and others with care. Talk, listen, and nurture your relationships because they are equity. People will help make deals happen and endorse you and your business. Each time you make a new contact, ask yourself, "How can I nourish that relationship? How can I give this person something of value? How can I do more than is expected to help him or her win?" I have my team log new contacts into our database and catalog it in a way that will help us connect with the person in a meaningful way. When you help those around you win, they will, in turn, want to help you win. It's fairly simple to do, and it reaps huge benefits for all stakeholders.

We encourage you to sit down and make a list of all the key people around you. Then be more intentional about nurturing those relationships and asking for their help in reaching your goals. Make it a two-way street, and ask what you can do for them, as well. You may start moving toward your goals a lot faster!

It takes skill to appropriately dig, ask questions, and figure out what your prospect/audience really wants. Get good at it—really good—and make it not just a habit; make it a cultural norm.

VIP: Helping as many people get what they want and teaching others to do the same will create a ripple effect of wins, including wins for yourself.

37. Have a Strategic Mindset

Since the mind is the engine of action, we ultimately become and do what we think. So if the results you're getting are less than you want or expect, you need to develop a new way of thinking about what it takes to be successful. To get better results, you have to have better execution, and better execution comes from knowing the right actions to take. And the best way to know what actions to take is to have the right mindset—a *Strategic Mindset*.

The very best top achievers, those who have extraordinary results in their life, are *Intentionally Strategic* in all areas of their life. You're being *Intentionally Strategic* when you're directing deliberate and calculated thinking toward your purpose, your objectives, and/or your goals. Changing your thinking changes your results. Right thinking enables you to be *Intentionally Strategic* about everything you do, and that leads to incredible results.

Being *Intentionally Strategic* can have an extraordinary impact on your sales career. Having a *Strategic Mindset* allows you to lift up like a helicopter and look at the whole picture, which gives you an understanding about how all the pieces of the puzzle fit together. For example, thinking strategically can help you see not only the immediately benefits your product can bring to your prospect or the pains it will eliminate now; it will also help you see what it will mean strategically to that prospect a year from now or three years from now. Or perhaps even what it will mean to your prospect's career, or to his/her organization or culture.

Most people think of "strategy" as a business word, and yet many go through life not being *Intentionally Strategic* in either their business or their personal lives. The very best top achievers, those who have extraordinary results in their lives, are *Intentionally Strategic* in all areas—whether that involves seeking advice from the best coaches or strong mentors, managing their time, nourishing their relationships, living a healthy lifestyle, being a great parent, or any other area.

Being intentional is different from having clarity or focus. Intentionality comes from the root of your intention. It centers not just around thought, but action. Be intentional about who you spend time with. Hang around others who match your values. Be intentional about every action.

It all starts with clarity. When you are in tune with your values and you know the values you live by, you become intentional about every aspect of your life. In business, we say you should have set standards for what you want and what you don't want, well thought out and documented. If a big part of your success is the people around you, then replace those who aren't right for you with some who are. Be intentional about how much stress you can manage, how many projects you can take on, and why. Don't do things without thinking. Think. Be strategic, then do things fast and your energy and resources will be expended and utilized in the best way.

What we value in ourselves and what others appreciate about us often relate to our self-esteem. Take time to identify the qualities and characteristics you like about yourself—your natural talents and strengths. When you take time to think about and identify your values, you become much more intentional.

Intentionality exists when you know exactly what you want, and everything flows from that. First, you must know what you really want. Then you can be intentional about taking action.

VIP: Direct deliberate and calculated thinking toward your purpose, your objectives, and/or your goals to become *Intentionally Strategic* and achieve maximum success.

38. Clarity Pulls You to Accomplishment

What do you want out of life? Your business? Your deals? Clarity, focus, and successful execution are necessary tools for getting what you want.

Authentic vision has the power to pull you out of your circumstances and toward a better life and better results. This pulling power comes from having complete clarity about what you truly want. Clarity opens up new opportunities and connections and empowers you to better make strategic choices that will lead to superior results faster.

I say the most successful people design their own lives, and then live their lives on purpose. But the first step is clarity. The definition of clarity is: Understanding and documenting your targets clearly and determining the "why" behind reaching them. It's about developing a clear vision, outlining priorities and objectives, and tackling goals with a real sense of urgency and focus. Clarity is achieved when ideas and concepts are clearly explained and presented internally and externally; it's when we know where we are in relation to where we want to go. When clarity is lost, or never achieved in the first place, it is almost impossible to generate the kind of focus necessary to be capable of acting swiftly and deftly on a daily basis. The requirements for clarity are specific with respect to three issues:

1. Purpose—relates to the "why" of things, thought through and documented

2. Value—relates to the real benefits that can be acquired (for all stakeholders to win)

3. Objectives—relates to the premise that unless objectives are stated clearly and understood by all, the likelihood of achieving them is slim

When you have an authentic vision, things happen. If you have no vision, there is nothing to tie your objectives to and nothing to measure your progress or performance against. When you have clarity about your vision, you discover yourself being pulled toward it and all you have to do is follow the connecting opportunities that carry you along, allowing you to make connections faster. Think about a time when you've been excited and regenerated at the thought of achieving a big goal. There's nothing like the adrenaline rush of having complete clarity about what it is you want to achieve, perhaps a sales target. When you have clarity, you get that excitement that builds and fuels your energy toward your dream. The results you achieve will often come faster than you may have thought possible. Clarity and focus together form the basis of execution. So get completely clear about the things you want and then take action.

There's a great strategy in having clarity of not only your own goals as a sales person, but also of what the people you're selling to want. Once you've defined what they really want, you can take advantage of that pulling power to more easily connect with them and communicate why your product will be a win for them.

VIP: Authentic vision has the power to pull you out of your circumstances and toward a better life and better results. This pulling power comes from having complete clarity about what you truly want.

39. Focus on Your HLAs *(High Leverage Activities)* Instead of Your LLAs *(Low Leverage Activities).*

There are 168 hours in the week. You spend about 12 hours on personal maintenance and should spend 56 on sleep, which means you're left with about 100 hours. If you think in terms of that limited time block, it makes you really effective at managing time. You want 70–80 percent of your 100-plus hours directed toward your *High Leverage Activities* (HLAs). A good balance is about 35 hours on personal HLAs and about 35 hours on professional HLAs. These are the activities that can give you the most impact in accomplishing your vision, goals, and objectives.

Your *High Leverage Activities* are those activities that you should be so clear on that you can develop an improved habit of saying no to the things not on your HLA list. You want to learn to say no to what's not mission-critical (distractions) and say yes to those important activities that are focused on helping you reach your goals. Continually ask yourself, "What's the best use of my time right now?" and then prioritize accordingly. Examples of professional HLAs might include:

- Attracting strong, qualified business
- Delivering great value to your clients and colleagues
- Clarifying direction and improving operations
- Building processes, business acumen, best practices, and tools
- Nourishing and building connections, extending value, and positively communicating with them
- Nurturing your people

I think many salespeople miss the critical importance of prioritizing with HLAs what matters most, what matters a little less, and what doesn't matter much at all. That's the prioritization strategy that many fight, and yet those who are good at it do so much better in their careers. If you want to be the most successful, you have to invest your time where it matters most.

What are your HLAs? How much of your time do you invest in them? How much more could you achieve if you increased that number by 10 to 20 percent? Developing the habit of HLA living gives high achievers a strong advantage. It's a habit that successful people often form naturally over time—looking at HLAs and comparing them to other opportunities that flow into their lives. Forming the habit of doing this effectively will serve you in leading your best life.

You also need to think about things to avoid—*Low Leverage Activities* (LLAs)—to ensure you stay on track and focused.

Low Leverage Activities (LLAs) are those things that steal your time, such as wasted meeting time, doing activities that subordinates should be doing, spending time on prolonged telephone calls, and chasing down things you need because you are unorganized. They're activities that don't lead you directly to the results you want. Most people burn fifteen to twenty hours a week on things they shouldn't be doing. If you want the best results, you have to get super intentional and get rid of those LLAs.

In general, what percentage of your time do you invest in *High Leverage Activities*, and what percentage of your time do you spend in *Low Leverage Activities*? Think about how much of your time you spend doing the things that truly matter the most, and then think of all of the activities you do that waste many of your minutes each day.

Remember, nothing has a more powerful impact on results than focusing on your *High Leverage Activities*, so make sure you write down your HLAs in your phone, both personal and professional, and look at them several times a day.

VIP: Clearly defined HLAs are the secret to avoiding distractions and multiplying achievement, both personally and professionally.

40. Leverage or Force Multiply Efforts

A *force multiplier* is a factor that dramatically increases (multiplies) the effectiveness of something you're doing. In the military, it's a term that applies to a capability that significantly increases the combat potential of a military force and thus enhances the probability of a successful mission. One example would be night goggles. If a combat force goes into a particular area at night, night goggles would significantly enhance their chances of a successful mission.

A force multiplier, then, refers to any factor that dramatically increases your results in whatever you're doing. It's really about leverage. Wouldn't you like to multiply every effort you make? Remember, if you change your thinking, you'll change your results.

In my book RESULTS Faster! I devote an entire chapter to force multipliers, and I talk about three primary force-multiplier components: preparation, connections, and tool chest.

1. Preparation. Chances are there are multiple areas in your personal and professional life where you can get better results by preparing more effectively. I've found that most people prepare for major events and opportunities, and yet few people prepare as strategically and as widely as they should.

2. Connections. Connections are one of the most significant force multipliers you can leverage. The first key to leveraging relationships is to first **build them**. Once you have them, it's about nurturing them – knowing what's important to them, being a giver in the relationship, and being willing to introduce them to each other for mutual benefit.

   You can have a long list of connections, and yet if you don't nourish them, what do you think will happen when you need to call in a favor? Not much! Be a person of value in all your relationships so there is never a question of whether they will respond if you call. Today I can make phone calls or send emails all around the world, and people respond instantly. Why? Because I nourish people. You can utilize your relationships to help you multiply your efforts, gain intelligence, and get things done.

3. Tool Chest. We may all have a great electronic tool chest—in our phones, for instance, where we've downloaded certain software or applications—and yet there's so much more. There are undoubtedly tools specific to your particular situation or business that can provide leverage. For example, in the area of marketing you may have tools like videos, promotional pieces and smart giveaways. Do you have the right tools? And do you keep tools in all the different places you operate so you can easily get to them when you connect with people? Everywhere I go I'm loaded with tools (items of value I can easily share), because I know the power of their leverage.

   The best tools—whether they are the hottest technological devices out there, innovative marketing pieces, or great tools that help you plan and prepare—will help give you the leverage you need to get the extraordinary results you want. In the turbulent climate of change today, you must seize advantages where you can.

As a team, what can you be doing to dramatically increase the effectiveness of your sales approach? Maybe you want to collapse a sales cycle, or perhaps you want to compress the time between your pitch and the time when you get a yes. You may be able to force multiply that effort with a tool, a template, a software, a video, or even by sharing best practices so you can bring the best ones to the top and spread them across your organization.

VIP: Leverage *force multipliers* such as preparation, connections, and tools to dramatically increase your results.

41. Mastery Is the Goal of the Journey

We all know that good just isn't good enough anymore. What if you could strive to go beyond great? Great is a high standard, yet an even higher standard would be to become the master in your field. There's a quarterback, and then there's the best quarterback in the nation. There's a runner, and then there's the runner with the fastest time. You don't have to make it an all-out competition with everyone else, yet you might want to become the master in your vocation as a sales professional. It's about being better than you already are and achieving a level of mastery that others will notice.

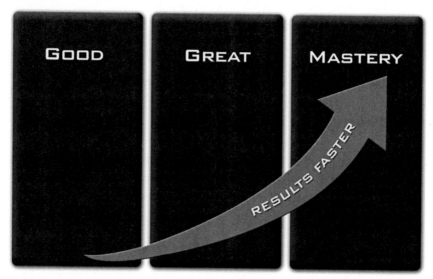

What is mastery? The simple definition means "control or superiority over" something else. It doesn't mean winning at the expense of others. It sets you apart from others who have become content with the status quo or even great. Mostly, mastery is about rising above contentment if you find you're no longer growing your thinking, yourself, or your business. Although I have no scientific data to support it, I believe less than 5 percent of people really live and work in mastery. What are the characteristics of those who do? I believe:

THE ENEMY OF MASTERY IS GREATNESS.

- They are big-picture thinkers and they think outside the box. They consistently ask themselves if there is a better or faster way to accomplish the same result.
- Once they've accomplished a goal, they ask what's next.
- They take initiative, and they're resilient.
- They are self-motivated and they believe there is a way to accomplish things that haven't been done before.
- They are results-driven and are willing to work harder and smarter than most.
- They are relationship nurturers.
- They accept nothing short of excellence, and they are focused on continuous improvement—not because of lack of contentment but because they don't want to settle for less than the best.

Moving into mastery mode is more than just polishing existing skills; it's a different way of thinking and a strategic asset that can dramatically transform results for both individuals and organizations.

A focus on constant improvement is what propels you into mastery mode, where you are consistently getting the results you want. Sharpening your existing proficiencies, as well as building new skills and continuing to learn, is really a ticket to winning more.

Examine your business and your habits. Are there any areas, concerns, or situations that are preventing you from achieving mastery? Strive for a higher level of success and make mastery your goal.

A big part of becoming the master at something is how well you execute in order to achieve results. You can say the right things, do the right things, and even look the right way. Yet if you're not achieving results for people, you're not providing value; perhaps you could seek mastery in everything you do, and value will be a natural result.

VIP: Moving into mastery mode is more than just polishing existing skills; it's a different way of thinking and a strategic asset that can dramatically transform results for both individuals and organizations.

42. Avoid Negative Thoughts

We have seen that successful people have similar habits. The same can be said of unsuccessful people and their thoughts. Often while the successful leader is thinking about how something can be done, the unsuccessful individual is thinking of why it can't be done.

Garbage can fill your home just as easily as beautiful furniture. Obviously, beautiful furniture is more valuable than the garbage we remove from our homes when it starts to smell or when the container is full. A negative thought is like a piece of garbage. Negative thoughts clutter our mind and use the same mental real estate that positive ones do, even though they do not have the same importance or power. You wouldn't keep garbage in your living spaces, so why would you keep a negative thought in your brain? Sometimes you have to do a pattern interrupt and step back and completely move the negative garbage out of your brain so you can get into the leveraging momentum of the positive.

One of my personal daily standards is to stretch, flex, and breathe with both confidence and gratitude. I want to keep my body healthy, and I want to appreciate everything I have. Gratitude makes you a better person and helps you be better mentally prepared for your future. There are many opportunities to dwell on the negative things that happen. You have to choose not to dwell on those, and decide instead to be grateful for all your blessings. That's what I focus on every day, and you should too. I prayerfully count my blessings each morning, and I balance contentment and enjoying what I have with constantly looking at my goals and aspirations and seeing where I want to go.

Aesop said, "Gratitude is the sign of noble souls." It is noble, indeed, to be thankful, as such a gesture shows humility and selflessness. When we step outside our sometimes-egocentric world to recognize that we cannot and do not control everything, we can acknowledge our day-to-day existence as a gift. Being grateful for whatever benefits we receive enables us to remember how fortunate and blessed we really are. This habit of expressing gratitude is also a fast track to a more positive outlook.

Where in your life do you need to eliminate negative thinking? How much better will you feel if you recognize negative thoughts and sweep them out like garbage?

VIP: Negative thoughts clutter your mind and use the same mental real estate that positive ones do, so take the initiative to remove the garbage from your mind. Choose to dwell on the positive and be grateful for your blessings.

43. Get a Coach

Advice Matters. I believe that so much that I coauthored a book by that name several years ago. If you want to really be ahead of the game as you strategically prepare for your future, arrange to get advice from those who have done what you want to do. Ask them to share their learnings with you so you can enhance your decision-making effectiveness.

Seeking advice from others who have achieved the kind of results you're looking for is one of the wisest and quickest ways to design, prepare for, and live a successful career/life and hit that next level of success. In fact, seeking advice is often the crucial piece of the success puzzle that catapults your results into an arena you could never have achieved alone. Wise advice can also help you avoid pitfalls that could derail your success. Ask me; I can tell you many things not to do based on my failures

If you want different and better results, you need new thinking—it's that simple! If you act alone, you can only be as successful as your own mind allows you to be. New information stimulates both your reasoning processes and your creative juices and helps you think better. Learning strategically from the wisdom and insight of others helps you be more successful *faster.* Remember, in today's market speed often is your competitive advantage and directly impacts your ability to compete and win.

Coaching isn't just for professional athletes. The concept of coaching has been in place for decades. Top leaders and CEOs—like Randy—have coaches who guide them with personal and professional advice. As top notch as Randy is in his profession, he reached out to me ten years ago and said, "I want to be coached so I can be better. I want you to pour your advice into my life." He shares his goals with me about every other year so we can evaluate where he is and where he's going. Randy has even reached out on an informal basis to his Sales Community Advisory Board members and asked them to "coach" us in putting this book together. He's asked for their advice on the best choice for the cover and the title and how to make the book even more content rich. Many sales professionals have coaches who challenge and inspire them to be their best. Do you have a powerful coach?

It's worth noting that a coach is different from a mentor: Coaches offer paid advice, while a mentor is generally free advice from someone who wants to give back. A colleague can be a trusted advisor who coaches you, yet don't confuse them with a coach. Some people say, "I have a trusted colleague, so I don't need a coach." If this is your thinking, you may want to reframe it. Coaching is an investment in yourself, your business, and your results. Everyone should have one (or more) mentor, and everyone should have a coach.

I call coaching the "secret weapon of many of the world's top achievers." Few people automatically understand what it takes to prepare for success, reach their goals, overcome their weaknesses, and grow their strengths. One-on-one coaching can advance your career, grow your leadership skills, help you build your brand, and uncover *Blind Spots*. The right coach can take you to the next level, where you see a significant increase in your income, reach your goals faster, and become stronger in all areas of your life.

I've been fortunate to have had the same coach for more than thirty years, Mark Pantak. This man serves up the best books, introduces me to special people, makes me aware of *blind spots*, councils me on my thinking, and sharpens my vision. He prays for my wisdom and success often.

When you connect with the right coach for you, it's an investment—not an expense—and it should pay short, medium, and long–term dividends. The right coach should dramatically alter the results of your life.

Successful people reach higher levels through coaches who impact their thinking. Coaches can help you reach your peak performance and operate often at higher levels—like the mastery level. Choose someone who matches your values. Find an expert who already has success in your field and has proven success in the direction you want to go. Find someone who has done what you want to do, who studies, has an arsenal, has real experience, and of course has a sincere desire to help you win.

VIP: Seek advice from those who have achieved the type of results you are looking to achieve. The right coach should dramatically alter your results by taking you to the next level where you see a significant increase in your income, reach your goals faster, and become stronger in all areas of your life.

44. Deploy the AMC™ Test

AMC™ stands for Attitude, Motivation, and Commitment. Before we hire people, we test them to assess how they would complement our culture and align with our standards. Are they cheerful? Is the glass half full or half empty? Are they results-driven and upbeat? Are they going to add positivity?

It's not necessarily skills or resumes that will determine how well people will perform. The strength of an individual or team often lies in their attitude, motivation, and commitment. If you're not sure which candidate you want to bring into your business, the AMC™ mental check is a good way to identify what people you want in your world, helping you succeed.

To confirm someone's AMC™, you can use a handmade pen-and-paper questionnaire or computer-based survey of some kind (we use and recommend the DISC assessment; see *www.tony-jeary-international.myshopify.*

com). If you create a questionnaire, we suggest you augment it by a series of interview questions tailored to your organization's specific needs. However you decide to assess candidates, you will want to uncover information about how they can be expected to:

- Operate emotionally under stress as well as during calmer times (Behavioral/situational "What would you do if . . ." questions are great here.)
- Respond to a negative customer or negative personal interaction
- Represent your brand and philosophies
- Pursue success, approach teamwork, and work to your standards
- Stick with your team based on previous work history queries
- Respect authority and support overall morale
- Be accountable, reliable, empowered, and self-sufficient
- Deploy personal values and ethics that match your own
- Use the strengths of their personality style, and overcome weaknesses/challenges

A recent study discovered that 46 percent of new hires failed within 18 months, and that 89 percent of the time it was due to attitude, not a lack of technical skills. Make sure you work with people who really add to your organization—not cause upheaval. Use the AMC™ test when it comes to hiring and partnering with people to ensure you create the best (life) team possible.

How about you, personally? Have you checked your AMC lately? Do you wake up with a great attitude every morning? Are you motivated to get up at 5:00, 6:00, or 7:00—whatever it takes—to work out, be your best, and study the clients you will be seeing that day?

Almost every time we're on the line with a coauthor, my writer, business development manager, sessions manager, and I are on the call anywhere from fifteen to thirty minutes early, double checking to make sure we're ready, preparing an agenda that covers our objectives, anticipating what the coauthor may ask, and thinking about what assets we need to have ready so we don't have to waste time digging around for them. Collectively, we have an attitude that is committed to being ready and having the right AMC. Do you, as a salesperson, have that type of commitment?

VIP: Look for more than a potential employee's skill set or resume; the strength of an individual or team often lies in their attitude, motivation, and commitment.

45. Ask Your Coaches and Mentors for
Their Recommended Read List

The smartest people we've met, advise, and work with love to learn—they thrive on new ideas, read a ton of books, study videos, and pore over articles that help change and challenge their thinking. Talk to any high achiever, and chances are they'll mention a book that influenced their life at some point and helped them achieve their dreams. (See our list of favorite books in the back.)

The same is true for my team and I. Each year, we read, study, and recap dozens of books, not only for our own learning, but also to help mentor and coach others. I recognized two decades ago that I would often only retain a very small portion of an author's content, even after investing hours of highlighting. Now for over 20 years, we have been recapping my books. I read and study between 50 and 100 books a year, highlight them, and have them typed into recaps that are available for us to go back and study over and over. We have thousands of recaps now that we provide to our special clients to help them advance their thinking and learning. And we don't just give them recaps of books we like—we give them summaries of books we think *they will like* that will help them be their best.

Ask your mentors and coaches which books and videos they've studied that helped them get where they are. Nearly every successful person we know will mention reading the book *Think and Grow Rich*. It's not a coincidence, either. High achievers get real results and avoid stagnation by seeking constant information and by valuing self-improvement.

New information can be gathered through reading trade and industry magazines, newspapers, books, and other publications, including brief recaps or abstracts that save time by condensing information. You can't attend every seminar, self-help session, or motivational meeting. Yet you can quickly download a book on your tablet or mobile device that will create new ideas, catalyze change, and help you get where you're going in life. A good coach will always have a new book, article, or video to share with you; so ask them what they're studying and be prepared to take notes.

VIP: High achievers get real results and avoid stagnation by seeking constant information and by valuing self-improvement. Ask your mentors and coaches which books and videos they've studied that helped them get where they are.

46. Avoid FUD

There are three factors that inhibit most humans from reaching their goals and achieving their potential: Fear, Uncertainty, and Doubt (FUD). When we give into FUD, we set ourselves up for failure. My friend, client, and business partner Peter Thomas shares a story in his *LifePilot* seminar that illustrates the way FUD can work, and how you can overcome it:

> FUD is fear, uncertainty, and doubt. When I was thirty-five, I started buying the rights to Century 21 in Canada. I was excited and began to share my goal to do that with a business partner. The partner said it would never work, and when I asked him to invest money, he said no. So I went to another guy. He said it was a stupid idea. I asked my lawyer; he said no. Even my wife didn't think it was a good idea! The feedback I got ranged from, "It'll never work," to "No realtor is going to wear that gold jacket to work." (Century 21 had an interesting brand in which you could identify the realtors by their gold jackets.) So at that time, I really bought into the vision and no one else around me did. I had a vision that no one else could see. I forged ahead despite the warnings and naysayers because I believed in it! And it was a success. Later, I sold it for many millions. Sometimes everyone else is blind and your vision is crystal clear.
>
> In my early selling days, I always had a 4x6 card taped hanging from the rear-view window of my car. On the card was written in capital letters: "THIS WILL BE THE BEST PRESENTATION I HAVE EVER GIVEN." It was my reminder that I would not experience any fear, uncertainty, or doubt. Sure enough, every time I put on a presentation, I made it the best presentation I had ever given.

It is so important to always give your best. Never allow yourself to give a mediocre performance, no matter what the circumstances, even if fear creeps in. Sometimes your best performances can come when it is most difficult for you to perform.

So what if you start to feel a case of the FUD coming on? The way to overcome it is to maintain clarity, stay focused on your goal, be persistent, and execute. Ask yourself: *What are twenty things I can do to be better? What are twenty things I can do to create more clients? Twenty things I can do to close more business? Twenty things I can do to shorten the sales cycle on my current pipeline?* Don't allow fear or uncertainty or doubt to rule your emotions, thoughts, or actions. If you really believe in something, keep doing it until you achieve your goal with a perfect performance.

VIP: Do not allow fear, uncertainty, and doubt (FUD) to cloud your thoughts or actions.

47. Lead a No-Excuses Culture

This simply means that each person takes responsibility for whatever the situation is. Whether you did it or didn't do it, own up to it and say, "Hey, let's get it done," with the emphasis on getting results, versus pointing fingers. In our research of organizations, we found that the higher the person's self-esteem, the more they will accept the responsibility and want to take action to get the desired result. This shows that fostering a positive mentality, appreciation, and true ownership within your organization can really matter.

Help all your people grow and see themselves in the best light possible, while being genuine. Make it known (with written performance standards) that you're not after excuses; you're after results. An example of this no-excuses culture could be that if you're going to have a discussion and bring up a roadblock or an issue, you're also required to offer a solution simultaneously. This is a great kind of system to have in place to help people move away from a defensive response, and instead move toward getting the desired result.

How about you, personally? Are you the type of person who, when you say you're going to own something, you offer no excuses and get it done? As a salesperson, you have to be involved in a culture that fosters no excuses!

VIP: Take responsibility for your actions and nourish a culture that does the same by focusing on getting results, rather than excuses.

48. Understand Positive and Negative Procrastination

Let's face it—we all procrastinate sometimes. Yet you can't produce results until you start doing something.

There are two kinds of procrastination: positive and negative. Positive procrastination can be beneficial, whereas negative procrastination just impedes production and therefore results. An example of positive procrastination is when you legitimately need some "mental percolation" time to gather your thoughts. Negative procrastination is based on a flimsy excuse to avoid doing something now. *Production Before Perfection* (PBP) is a concept I coined. It's the self-talk that says it doesn't have to be perfect to get it going—get it going and perfect it along the way. And remember, 87 percent is often good enough. (Refer back to No. 29.) *Production Before Perfection* is my solution to negative procrastination.

Again, you can't produce results until you start doing something, right? If you do nothing, that is exactly what you'll get—nothing. If you do something, the possibilities are endless. Just a warning: When you start to practice PBP, you will be doing things in a way that conflicts with the thinking of 90 percent of people on this planet, so be ready to encounter resistance. It is not the natural thing to do, and you will have to hear and overcome objections on why you should wait. Yet waiting and getting results are not compatible. If you wait, you burn time you cannot get back.

The same goes for your team and your entire organization. People who use planning to avoid action often get tangled in an unhealthy emotional cycle of evaluation and analysis paralysis. Preparation and planning are important, but excessive preparation is nothing more than procrastination; it's that simple. It is only when you start doing what you need to do that you can begin to produce results.

Sometimes the best way to manage your emotions is to ignore them and keep pushing through to achieve what it is you need to do. If you procrastinate, it means you are fearful of failure and may not be confident in your ability to succeed. This is when self-talk and what you say to yourself becomes extremely important. People who quit too easily or give up in the face of adversity generate a complex chain of emotions and events that negatively impact their mind, hence their business results. It is always easy to quit, and too many people prefer quitting to the discomfort they experience when the going gets tough. The reason is simple: Adversity is painful. When you quit in the face of adversity, it means you are deficient in the mental substance it takes to persevere and overcome. Go as far as you can see, and then you'll see farther. This concept has the power to nip procrastination in the bud before it has a chance to flower. You don't always have to understand all the details between where you are and where you want to be. You simply have to forge ahead, despite any resistance or desire to procrastinate. Your success is right around the corner.

VIP: Recognize the difference between positive and negative procrastination; do not allow perfectionism or the fear of failure or to stop you from starting.

49. Stay Competitive

High achievers have to know what's going on with their competitors. That doesn't mean you have to invest mental energy on knowing what your competition is doing day-to-day; however, as a successful professional, it's important to know how your competitors are talking to your existing clients or prospects. What are they saying about you? What are they saying about your business? Do they have an online footprint that you don't have?

Successful people keep up with changing technology to remain competitive, and that includes social media. Yet, as with everything, there's a balance. Many people are making a ton of money with face-to-face contact, and many people are losing money because they're completely focused on social media and not on face-to-face relationships. Do your due diligence and know where your *blind spots* are. Stay competitive on the ground and stay competitive in virtual spaces.

You can make a small business seem like a medium- or large-size business by harnessing the power of technology. One way is to utilize email contact databases. Successful people build a database of existing clients and customers and then they drip value and market to them year after year for repeat business. Email blasts, text marketing, and other ways of communicating virtually and not just through social media sites like LinkedIn or Facebook can help you stay in touch with your customers and communicate vital messages.

You may not need the latest advances in technology. However, one thing is for sure: You will need whatever it is that your customers want. If you're still using LinkedIn or Facebook five years from now and your customer is using a completely different method of social media to communicate with people, you could be missing out. It's no different than talking to your spouse in a way he or she does not comprehend. Leverage the power of technology in your business to strengthen relationships with clients. Set up specific systems so you have a method for automatically generating a message with new information to clients systematically. In this mobile world, technology makes it simple to foster stronger relationships; and if you're not using it, you're losing.

Let's put an interesting twist on the subject of being competitive and look at it through a different lens for just a moment. I think there's a balance to be had here, in that you can be extremely effective when you become competitive with your own track record. One of the things I taught my kids was to be competitive against the time versus being competitive against each other. You can compete with other people or you can compete against a result. Of course, I'm not saying you should avoid being competitive in the market. There's definitely a place for both viewpoints.

VIP: Know what's going on with your competitors, keep up-to-date with changing technology, and know what your customers want to maintain a competitive edge.

50. Channel Your Emotions and Control Your Ego

There are external factors to your success and there are internal factors. Living a well-managed life includes managing your emotions and all of the inner workings of your mind, which is so powerful. Things happen. Life is not perfect. Things get in the way. The market changes, the world changes, presidents change; that's just the way life works.

How well do you manage your emotions? No one knows yourself better than you, so prepare and plan for managing the myriad of emotions that will come as you face the challenging yet exciting life of a sales professional.

In life and relationships, emotions and ego are always a factor. How well you control those things will impact your ability to connect with others and persuade them to see things the way you need them to in order to achieve results. Sometimes we don't see that our own emotions are creating destructive results. It could be anger, stress, or ego that's getting in the way of bonding with colleagues, attracting new clients, or closing deals. Emotions can impact a relationship in both positive and negative ways. Similarly, people often make business decisions (or don't make them) based on emotion. Learning to separate emotion from business decisions will help you accelerate your results.

VIP: How well you control your emotions and ego will impact your ability to connect with others and persuade them to see things the way you need them to in order to achieve results.

CONCLUSION

Our connection as coauthors has come together nicely because we both have a commitment to helping others grow, be better, and win.

We have both highlighted the immense importance of the word "accelerate" by the fact that Randy used it in the name of his company (Revenue Acceleration) and Tony used it in the name of his foundational methodology (*Strategic Acceleration*). We're hoping that much of the content of this book will *accelerate* your success and the success of your team, both now and in the future. Of course, we understand that things change. However, we were careful in the way we wrote the book so it would have a long shelf life. We hope you will be referring back to the book—reading it, studying it, highlighting it, and utilizing it for years to come—and encouraging others on your team to do the same. And hopefully we've introduced you to a few ideas, models, and tools you hadn't thought about that you can now put to use.

Our intent was for the entire book to be so jam packed with *value* as you think back through it that you would want to recommend it or actually buy it as a gift for others and pass it on. In fact, we hope you will want all those who are part of your life in the technology sales space to have it so it can impact their lives as it has yours.

We said in the introduction that "Success to us looks like adding value, giving back, and exceeding expectations, so you sell more." If we have prevailed in *accelerating* your success and imparting more *value* than you expected, then we have done our job. We would love to hear from you, and we invite you to go to salescommunity.com and let us know how you put these best practices and principles to work to help you sell more.

VIPS
(VERY IMPORTANT POINTS)

Randy's Success Ideas

1. Use this tool to be the best leader you can be, with the goal of reaching a level five in each area.

2. Use these tools to make you deliberately aware of the areas of your life that are balanced (in whatever way you define success) and those you want to improve in, so you can hold yourself accountable and ultimately achieve happiness.

3. Just like in business, you should have goals for your life.

4. No matter how great a leader you are, you're only as good as your team—both your direct and indirect reports—so make sure you have a culture of giving and getting feedback.

5. A stack-ranking process is a must-have for any sales leaders to know objectively the status and quality of their team.

6. By leading by example, you influence the attitude and behavior of other people.

7. Get a fast start to success in your new job by having a written plan for your first ninety days.

8. You can quickly change your company's culture and values by acknowledging, measuring, and rewarding the behaviors you want.

9. The Performance-Management Discussion Guide facilitates giving and getting feedback between employee and manager; this feedback is vital to develop, succeed, and sell more.

10. It is always important to focus on the objective financial metrics expected and exceed them.

11. As a leader, you are only as good as your team, so make sure you put together and coach the best team possible.

12. Successful sales teams figure out how to sell to all of their market.

13. Indirect selling through and with partners is needed to get as much reach as possible.

14. To improve culture, measure and coach what you consider the most important objective and subjective metrics.

15. Use all the leverage you can to be efficient and effective.

16. Consider the best leader you've worked for, and try to be better.

17. Use some of my top lessons learned to create your vision for a better life for yourself.

18. Nothing is more important than being a great father.

19. It's always good to be authentic with your team and share what is important to you and what you're passionate about.

20. Use a HIPO program to continue to develop your best people and see how you can be included in these development programs yourself.

21. Use well-prepared sales agendas to roll out the red carpet so it is easy for your clients to go through a fast and well-executed sales cycle.

22. Top down selling can be tricky; but if properly managed, it can help you sell more and sell faster.

TONY'S BEST SALES PRACTICES VIPS

1. Have clarity on the type of opportunity in front of you and respond accordingly to achieve the best results.

2. Gather information about the stakeholders to ensure that you're addressing the priorities of each person.

3. Be strategic about focusing on all three stages of your presentations—preparation, delivery, and follow up— to ensure greater results.

4. Gather as much information as you can about each decision maker so you can personalize your sales pitch to their wants and needs and maximize your chances of success.

5. Know your competition so you can intentionally offer your strengths against the competition's weaknesses to gain a competitive edge.

6. Become super aware of what you want to gain out of each presentation and relationship so you're in a better position to effectively persuade others.

7. Carefully think through your tools and messaging for your presentations, and have all necessary tools and information organized and ready to go so you can be Presentation Ready at all times.

8. The more prepared you are, the more spontaneous you can be.

9. Create an avatar that fits both your own and your company's target market and vet your prospects accordingly so you attract who you want to do business with.

10. Address the situation, needs, value, outcomes, deliverables, and terms of an agreement so you can put together a comprehensive presentation that is results oriented and will provide excellent clarity for your prospect.

11. Incorporate the 3-D Outline™ into your preparation process to shorten the process, ensure every minute of your presentation is maximized, and gain three-dimensional clarity about what you're going to say and how you're going to deliver.

12. Create an Objections Matrix to prepare for pushback or difficult questions so you can preempt them in your communication and ensure you and your team are responsive versus reactive.

13. Before each presentation, brainstorm with your team members or a partner about what could happen, and take precautions to resolve any "what-ifs" in advance so you can be ready to respond with best actions.

14. Without a values-based plan or strategy, it is almost impossible to achieve your vision.

15. Strategically structure a partnership with all the "what-ifs" in mind and leave nothing to chance.

16. Recognize deficiencies and warning signs early on so you don't lose your decision-making ability and can cut your losses early and move on if necessary.

17. Recognize that negotiation is about making things happen by understanding what other people want. Remember, you really win when everyone wins.

18. Know the people involved and sell to the motivations, desires, and responsibilities of the stakeholders, not the company.

19. Understanding where you are most comfortable in your communication approach, what the other person prefers, and how to combine it all into a winning presentation is important to moving the prospect/audience member to the taking-action state.

20. Show the clear picture of the vision to all stakeholders in order to get others on board and work together toward a common goal.

21. Using others' communication preferences will positively impact results. Study your audience to gain an in-depth understanding of how they wish to be presented to and respond accordingly.

22. Provide reasoning behind what you're asking of others to convey the "why" factor to your audience and achieve buy-in—and hence results—faster.

23. Use the DISC model to understand your prospective buyer's personality style in advance so you can adapt your presentation and communicate to the prospect as effectively as possible.

24. To create a winning formula, take ownership of the outcome you want by clearly and directly showing the process/steps/actions you would like to include in how your prospect wins.

25. Create a system for capturing testimonial notes, quotes, and letters, and then make them usable on an individual and/or an organization-wide basis. Testimonials prove that others have trusted you and benefited from their interaction.

26. Choose a case study that shows situations similar to your prospect's and clearly demonstrates the problem, the solution, and the results.

27. Sharpen your sword with precise communication—frame the important things and capture the value proposition in as few words as possible (preferably using bullets when appropriate).

28. Excellence often comes in speed, and that can often be at 87 percent. Striving for perfection will often sidetrack your results and make your customers wait. They want results, and they want them fast.

29. Understand what you are good at, be known for it, and consistently excel in that niche of sales or the whole field.

30. Your brand is your unique promise; build it based on not only who you want to be and how you want to live, but who you actually are and the core of how you live today. Make sure you're known as someone who follows through.

31. What specifically do you want people to remember about you? It's not only your brand or your personality, but also your trademark expression, style, or persona that make you memorable—or not.

32. You are your business; and when prospects meet you—whether in person or on Zoom—they'll judge you, your success, and their potential to have success by the things they see. Convey a strong, authentic, and positive image through your wardrobe, your body language, and your vibe.

33. Follow-up is an essential part of the sales process; it should include both getting back to the prospect immediately to support your value proposition as well as debriefing to discover how you can improve.

34. Utilize a one-pager that summarizes the highlights of your presentation to get and keep everyone involved in the process and make future catch-up easy.

35. Listening well is a critical skill and can make the difference between success and failure.

36. Helping as many people get what they want and teaching others to do the same will create a ripple effect of wins, including wins for yourself.

37. Direct deliberate and calculated thinking toward your purpose, your objectives, and/or your goals to become Intentionally Strategic and achieve maximum success.

38. Authentic vision has the power to pull you out of your circumstances and toward a better life and better results. This pulling power comes from having complete clarity about what you truly want. Focus on

Your HLAs (High Leverage Activities) Instead of Your LLAs (Low Leverage Activities).

39. Clearly defined HLAs are the secret to avoiding distractions and multiplying achievement, both personally and professionally.

40. Leverage force multipliers such as preparation, connections, and tools to dramatically increase your results.

41. Moving into mastery mode is more than just polishing existing skills; it's a different way of thinking and a strategic asset that can dramatically transform results for both individuals and organizations.

42. Negative thoughts clutter your mind and use the same mental real estate that positive ones do, so take the initiative to remove the garbage from your mind. Choose to dwell on the positive and be grateful for your blessings.

43. Seek advice from those who have achieved the type of results you are looking to achieve. The right coach should dramatically alter your results by taking you to the next level where you see a significant increase in your income, reach your goals faster, and become stronger in all areas of your life.

44. Look for more than a potential employee's skill set or resume; the strength of an individual or team often lies in their attitude, motivation, and commitment.

45. High achievers get real results and avoid stagnation by seeking constant information and by valuing self-improvement. Ask your mentors and coaches which books and videos they've studied that helped them get where they are.

46. Do not allow fear, uncertainty, and doubt (FUD) to cloud your thoughts or actions.

47. Take responsibility for your actions and nourish a culture that does the same by focusing on getting results, rather than excuses.

48. Recognize the difference between positive and negative procrastination; do not allow perfectionism or the fear of failure or to stop you from starting.

49. Know what's going on with your competitors, keep up-to-date with changing technology, and know what your customers want to maintain a competitive edge.

50. How well you control your emotions and ego will impact your ability to connect with others and persuade them to see things the way you need them to in order to achieve results.

ABOUT THE AUTHORS

Randy Seidl is a global technology board director, CEO, CRO, executive recruiter, sales community leader, consultant, advisor, author, and investor. Put simply, Randy helps companies and individuals grow. He is known for his unique ability to scale emerging growth and Fortune 500 technology companies as well as individuals' careers. Uniquely, he has served in start-ups/smaller companies, and industry-leading organizations such as Hewlett-Packard, Sun Microsystems, StorageTek, and EMC Corporation. Randy currently runs the three companies he started: Sales Community, Top Talent Recruiting, and Revenue Acceleration.

Randy lives with his wife and four children in Naples, Florida, and Wellesley, Massachusetts. Besides delighting in his family, he enjoys helping others, BC sports, Harvard and Duke baseball, golf, skiing at Beaver Creek, tennis, and rugby.

Randy has extensive board experience. He is currently a director at Ondas Networks (NASDAQ: ONDS), Data Dynamics, and Cloudgenera. He was previously a director of Datawatch Corporation (NASDAQ: DWCH, acquired by Altair), chaired the board of Workgroup Solutions (acquired by Advizex), and served as director of Permabit (acquired by Red Hat). He holds the American College of Corporate Directors' Masters Professional Director Certification, is a National Association of Corporate Directors Fellow, and has attended the Stanford Law School Directors' College.

Tony Jeary is a strategist, thought leader, and prolific author of over sixty titles.

For more than two decades, Tony has advised CEOs and other high achievers on how to discover new clarity for their vision, develop focus on their direction, and create powerful execution strategies that impact achievement and results.

Tony personally coaches the most accomplished people in the world, including the presidents of: Walmart, Sam's Club, Ford, American Airlines, Firestone, Samsung, and New York Life.

He practices the business mantra his father taught him growing up, "Give value; do more than is expected."

Tony lives and works in the Dallas/Fort Worth area where his brand new think tank, the RESULTS Center, is located.

info@tonyjeary.com

WHAT RANDY SEIDL
CAN DO FOR YOU

Sales Community

Randy's COVID moment led to his October 2020 launch of Sales Community, the premier global sales network that provides sales professionals from SDRs to CROs/CEOs with the tools, resources, network, engagement, and platform to sharpen their craft and harness the power of strategic selling. With an impressive Advisory Board of over 250 of the industry's best executives, we leverage the best thought leadership in the business to help you as sales professionals accelerate your skills, lead, get peer advice, network, learn, build your brand, accelerate your career, and ultimately sell more.

Revenue Acceleration

Randy founded Revenue Acceleration in 2013 to help tech companies accelerate revenue growth by leveraging his strategic and tactical go-to-market experience along with more than 1,000 tech industry executives at ISVs, OEMs, VARs, SIs, distributors, industry analysts, and end users. He also coaches CEOs and executive teams to improve in the areas of: leadership, strategy, people management, culture, operational execution, relationships, and accelerating revenue and growth.

www.revenue-acceleration.com

Top Talent Recruiting

Due to the growing demand of vetted high-performing talent, Randy founded *Top Talent Recruiting* in 2016, a boutique recruiting business where he and his team leverage his powerful network of colleagues, friends, and thousands of professionals who have worked with him over the years. The focus is to help clients hire top talent faster, at a fair cost, with the assurance that Randy always knows the candidates first hand or that they come highly recommended by someone he knows.

www.toptalentrecruiting.com

Randy is also available for select board seats.

WHAT TONY JEARY INTERNATIONAL CAN DO FOR YOU

Results Coaching

Advice Matters, if it's the right advice. Having coached the world's top CEOs, published over fifty books, and advised over 1,000 clients, Tony has positioned himself with a unique track record to take serious high achievers to a whole new level of results.

Interactive Keynotes

Tony not only energizes, entertains, and educates, he also has his team work strategically and smartly with the event team to make his part as well as the entire experience a super win. An hour with Tony often changes people's lives forever and impacts an organization's results immediately. He delivers value, a fun factor, and best practices people can really use.

Strategic Acceleration Facilitation Planning

Tony can do in a single day what takes many others days and even weeks to accomplish. He has refined a process so powerful the world travels to his results compound to experience clarity, focus, and the ability to synergistically execute. He provides at your fingertips THREE decades of best practices, processes, and tools for accelerating dramatic, sustained results in any organization.

Collaborative Relationships

We selectively partner with organizations in an annual collaborative engagement where we pour into an entire organization and help build a super-charging, motivated, and engaged *High-Performing Team*. We align with the C-Level management's vision and become an extension of them.

The bottom line is, we help: Clarify Vision, Focus on What Matters Most—*High Leverage Activities* (HLAs)—so people Execute and get the Right Results Faster!

Tonyjeary.com

ENDNOTES

1. Wikipedia, https://en.wikipedia.org/wiki/Chaos_theory.
2. Force Management Methodology, B2B Sales Growth Strategies, Consulting & Training | Force Management, https://www.forcemanagement.com/.
3. https://www.forbes.com/sites/kenkrogue/2017/10/03/2017-sales-trend-research-inside-sales-vs-outside-sales/?sh=29fd2aab70c2
4. https://www.salesforce.com/blog/15-sales-statistics/
5. "Wooden on Leadership," https://www.gmptrainingsystems.com/images/pdfs/Wooden_pyramid.pdf.
6. https://www.merriam-webster.com/dictionary/success, accessed 11/23/20
7. https://hbr.org/2016/04/if-theres-only-one-woman-in-your-candidate-pool-theres-statistically-no-chance-shell-be-hired
8. "Drinking the Kool-Aid" is an expression used to refer to a person who believes strongly in an idea, usually because of perceived potential high rewards.
9. Kerry Hannon, "Welch Shows the 'Winning' Side of Business for All," *USA Today*, April 14, 2005 edition.
10. Information taken from Michael Watkins, *The First 90 Days* (Boston: Harvard Business School, 2013).
11. Thomas J. Neff and James M. Citrin, You're in Charge—Now What?: The 8-Point Plan (New York: Crown Business, 2005).
12. Aja Frost, "The Ultimate Guide to Sales Metrics: What to Track, How to Track It, & Why," https://blog.hubspot.com/sales/sales-metrics.
13. Joe Kelly, Dads and Daughters (New York: Broadway, 2002).

NOTES

NOTES

NOTES

NOTES

NOTES

NOTES

NOTES

NOTES

DO YOU WANT TO KNOW WHAT THE WORLD'S TOP SALES PROFESSIONALS DO AND SAY? HOW TO BUILD YOUR PIPELINE? HOW TO CLOSE MORE DEALS? HOW TO MAKE MORE MONEY? IF YOU'RE A TECHNOLOGY SALES PROFESSIONAL, THE ANSWER IS YES.

We are a community of active sales professionals from hundreds of leading technology companies. Randy Seidl started the Sales Community with the goal of providing a community and assets to help enterprise tech sales professionals (SDRs to CROs) exceed goals with ease and confidence.

Sales Community is an efficient, effective and motivating way to train yourself and have motivating content for your team. That's why we created the Sales Community, the Premiere Online Community for Tech Sales Professionals:

- An Advisory Board made up of 250+ of the best in the industry responsible for over $500 billion in annual revenue
- Our platform provides a unique opportunity to grow your skills and connect with likeminded sales professionals
- Features best-in-class content from world-class consultants, coaches and members
- Leverage best practices from Randy and other members to help you sell more and break into new accounts, and get exposure to top channel partners across the world
- Access to tools, tactics, and sales methodologies shared by Sales Community members who have been on the front lines with skill sets to close deals, build pipeline and generate revenue

Scan the code below to visit the Sales Community website: